The Complete

INSTANT POT

COOKBOOK for Beginners

2000 Days of Easy, Time-Saving, and Delicious Recipes to Satisfy your taste buds—From Breakfast, Lunch, and Dinner to Desserts and Snacks

Carl Oles

TABLE OF CONTENTS

INTRODUCTION

Welcome to the World of Instant Pot Cooking!

Imagine coming home after a long day, and within minutes, the aroma of a delicious, wholesome meal fills your kitchen. No stress, no fuss—just flavorful dishes ready in a fraction of the time it usually takes. This dream scenario is now a reality for millions of home cooks around the world, thanks to the incredible versatility and convenience of the Instant Pot.

The Instant Pot has quickly become a beloved kitchen companion, transforming how we cook and eat. Whether you're a seasoned chef, a busy parent, or someone just beginning their culinary journey, this appliance offers a world of possibilities—from creamy risottos and tender roasts to fluffy rice, hearty soups, and even decadent desserts. It's a one-stop solution for anyone looking to save time, reduce effort, and still enjoy delicious, nutritious meals.

But what exactly makes the Instant Pot so special? And how can it change the way you cook forever?

Why the Instant Pot? A Kitchen Game-Changer

At its core, the Instant Pot is a multi-functional cooker that combines the functions of a pressure cooker, slow cooker, rice cooker, steamer, sauté pan, and even a yogurt maker—all in one! This all-in-one appliance allows you to prepare meals up to 70% faster than traditional methods while preserving the natural flavors and nutrients of your ingredients.

The Instant Pot's advanced technology takes the guesswork out of cooking. With pre-programmed settings and smart features, it adjusts the temperature, pressure, and cooking time automatically, making it nearly impossible to mess up a meal. Whether you're tackling a weeknight dinner or experimenting with a new recipe, the Instant Pot offers consistency and convenience every step of the way.

Healthier Meals in Less Time

In today's fast-paced world, finding time to cook healthy meals can be challenging. Many of us rely on takeout or pre-packaged foods that are often high in sodium, unhealthy fats, and preservatives. The Instant Pot offers a different path—one where nutritious, homemade meals don't require hours of preparation.

By using high pressure and shorter cooking times, the Instant Pot helps retain more of the essential vitamins and minerals in your food compared to traditional cooking methods. Steaming vegetables, cooking beans from scratch, or making bone broth has never been easier or quicker. With the Instant Pot, you can cook whole grains, legumes, and lean proteins to perfection, all while preserving their natural goodness.

Another fantastic benefit is the ability to control every ingredient that goes into your dish. Cooking at home allows you to avoid hidden sugars, artificial ingredients, and allergens. The Instant Pot empowers you to make healthier choices for yourself and your family, without sacrificing taste or convenience.

Versatility for Every Meal and Occasion

One of the most remarkable features of the Instant Pot is its versatility. This single appliance can handle an astonishing variety of dishes—from breakfast to dinner, snacks to desserts—all with minimal cleanup. Imagine waking up to a warm bowl of steel-cut oats that cooked themselves overnight, or coming home to a perfectly braised pot roast that's been simmering all day, ready to serve by dinnertime.

Need to whip up a quick side dish? The Instant Pot has you covered with perfectly steamed vegetables, creamy mashed potatoes, or fluffy rice in minutes. Want to impress your guests with a gourmet dessert? You can make cheesecakes, puddings, or even crème brûlée with ease. The possibilities are truly endless.

This cookbook will be your guide through the vast world of Instant Pot cooking. Each recipe has been designed to maximize flavor while minimizing effort, making cooking a joy rather than a chore. From classic comfort foods to modern, health-focused dishes, there's something here for every taste and dietary preference.

Getting the Most Out of Your Instant Pot

Before diving into the recipes, it's essential to understand some key tips and tricks to make the most of your Instant Pot:

1. Understanding the Settings: The Instant Pot comes with various pre-programmed settings, such as Soup/Broth, Meat/Stew, Bean/Chili, and more. Familiarize yourself with these settings and learn how they can simplify the cooking process. Don't be afraid to experiment with the Manual/Pressure Cook mode, which allows for complete control over cooking time and pressure level.

2. Layering Ingredients Properly: For best results, always layer your ingredients correctly, starting with liquids at the bottom. This prevents burning and ensures even cooking. Use the sauté function to brown meats and sauté vegetables before adding liquids, enhancing the depth of flavor in your dishes.

3. Natural Release vs. Quick Release: Understanding the difference between Natural Release (allowing the pressure to release on its own) and Quick Release (manually releasing the pressure) is crucial. Each method has its benefits, depending on the recipe. For example, Natural Release is ideal for meats and stews, while Quick Release works well for vegetables and delicate dishes.

4. Batch Cooking and Meal Prep: The Instant Pot is perfect for batch cooking and meal prep. Cook large batches of grains, beans, soups, and stews, then portion them into individual servings for quick, healthy meals throughout the week. This approach not only saves time but also helps you maintain a balanced diet, even on the busiest days.

Join the Instant Pot Revolution!

If you're ready to experience the magic of the Instant Pot, then this cookbook is for you. We'll explore all the fantastic ways this versatile appliance can save you time in the kitchen, bring a variety of flavors to your table, and make cooking more enjoyable. From everyday meals to special occasions, you'll find that the Instant Pot is a true game-changer.

Whether you're cooking for one or feeding a crowd, this book will show you just how easy and fun Instant Pot cooking can be. With every recipe, you'll learn new techniques and discover new favorites that are sure to impress family and friends alike. You'll see how the Instant Pot can transform your kitchen routine, bringing both convenience and creativity into your daily cooking.

So, grab your Instant Pot, gather your ingredients, and let's embark on this culinary adventure together! Welcome to a world where great meals are always within reach. Let's get cooking!

Chapter 1

Breakfasts

Chapter 1 Breakfasts

Cinnamon Roll Fat Bombs

Prep time: 5 minutes | Cook time: 5 minutes | Serves 5 to 6

- 2 tablespoons coconut oil
- 2 cups raw coconut butter
- 1 cup sugar-free chocolate chips
- 1 cup heavy whipping cream
- ½ cup Swerve, or more to taste
- ½ teaspoon ground cinnamon, or more to taste
- ½ teaspoon vanilla extract

1. Set the Instant Pot to Sauté and melt the oil. 2. Add the butter, chocolate chips, whipping cream, Swerve, cinnamon, and vanilla to the Instant Pot and cook. Stir occasionally until the mixture reaches a smooth consistency. 3. Pour mixture into a silicone mini-muffin mold. 4. Freeze until firm. Serve, and enjoy!

Egg Bites with Sausage and Peppers

Prep time: 5 minutes | Cook time: 15 minutes | Serves 7

- 4 large eggs
- ¼ cup vegan cream cheese (such as Tofutti brand) or cream cheese
- ¼ teaspoon fine sea salt
- ¼ teaspoon freshly ground black pepper
- 3 ounces lean turkey sausage, cooked and crumbled, or 1 vegetarian
- sausage (such as Beyond Meat brand), cooked and diced
- ½ red bell pepper, seeded and chopped
- 2 green onions, white and green parts, minced, plus more for garnish (optional)
- ¼ cup vegan cheese shreds or shredded sharp Cheddar cheese

1. In a blender, combine the eggs, cream cheese, salt, and pepper. Blend on medium speed for about 20 seconds, just until combined. Add the sausage, bell pepper, and green onions and pulse for 1 second once or twice. You want to mix in the solid ingredients without grinding them up very much. 2. Pour 1 cup water into the Instant Pot. Generously grease a 7-cup egg-bite mold or seven 2-ounce silicone baking cups with butter or coconut oil, making sure to coat each cup well. Place the prepared mold or cups on a long-handled silicone steam rack. (If you don't have the long-handled rack, use the wire metal steam rack and a homemade sling)

3. Pour ¼ cup of the egg mixture into each prepared mold or cup. Holding the handles of the steam rack, carefully lower the egg bites into the pot. 4. Secure the lid and set the Pressure Release to Sealing. Select the Steam setting and set the cooking time for 8 minutes at low pressure. (The pot will take about 5 minutes to come up to pressure before the cooking program begins.) 5. When the cooking program ends, let the pressure release naturally for 5 minutes, then move the Pressure Release to Venting to release any remaining steam. Open the pot. The egg muffins will have puffed up quite a bit during cooking, but they will deflate and settle as they cool. Wearing heat-resistant mitts, grasp the handles of the steam rack and carefully lift the egg bites out of the pot. Sprinkle the egg bites with the cheese, then let them cool for about 5 minutes, until the cheese has fully melted and you are able to handle the mold or cups comfortably. 6. Pull the sides of the egg mold or cups away from the egg bites, running a butter knife around the edge of each bite to loosen if necessary. Transfer the egg bites to plates, garnish with more green onions (if desired), and serve warm. To store, let cool to room temperature, transfer to an airtight container, and refrigerate for up to 3 days; reheat gently in the microwave for about 1 minute before serving.

Mexican Breakfast Beef Chili

Prep time: 5 minutes | Cook time: 45 minutes | Serves 4

- 2 tablespoons coconut oil
- 1 pound (454 g) ground grass-fed beef
- 1 (14-ounce / 397-g) can sugar-free or low-sugar diced tomatoes
- ½ cup shredded full-fat Cheddar cheese (optional)
- 1 teaspoon hot sauce
- ½ teaspoon chili powder
- ½ teaspoon crushed red pepper
- ½ teaspoon ground cumin
- ½ teaspoon kosher salt
- ½ teaspoon freshly ground black pepper

1. Set the Instant Pot to Sauté and melt the oil. 2. Pour in ½ cup of filtered water, then add the beef, tomatoes, cheese, hot sauce, chili powder, red pepper, cumin, salt, and black pepper to the Instant Pot, stirring thoroughly. 3. Close the lid, set the pressure release to Sealing, and hit Cancel to stop the current program. Select Manual, set the Instant Pot to 45 minutes on High Pressure and let cook. 4. Once cooked, let the pressure naturally disperse from the Instant Pot for about 10 minutes, then carefully switch the pressure release to Venting. 5. Open the Instant Pot, serve, and enjoy!

Classic Coffee Cake

Prep time: 5 minutes | Cook time: 40 minutes | Serves 5 to 6

Base:

- 2 eggs
- 2 tablespoons salted grass-fed butter, softened
- 1 cup blanched almond flour
- 1 cup chopped pecans
- ¼ cup sour cream, at room temperature
- ¼ cup full-fat cream cheese, softened
- ½ teaspoon salt
- ½ teaspoon ground cinnamon
- ½ teaspoon ground nutmeg
- ¼ teaspoon baking soda

Topping:

- 1 cup sugar-free chocolate chips
- 1 cup chopped pecans
- ½ cup Swerve, or more to taste
- ½ cup heavy whipping cream

1. Pour 1 cup of filtered water into the inner pot of the Instant Pot, then insert the trivet. Using an electric mixer, combine the eggs, butter, flour, pecans, sour cream, cream cheese, salt, cinnamon, nutmeg, and baking soda. Mix thoroughly. Transfer this mixture into a well-greased, Instant Pot-friendly pan (or dish). 2. Using a sling if desired, place the pan onto the trivet, and cover loosely with aluminum foil. Close the lid, set the pressure release to Sealing, and select Manual. Set the Instant Pot to 40 minutes on High Pressure and let cook. 3. While cooking, in a large bowl, mix the chocolate chips, pecans, Swerve, and whipping cream thoroughly. Set aside. 4. Once cooked, let the pressure naturally disperse from the Instant Pot for about 10 minutes, then carefully switch the pressure release to Venting. 5. Open the Instant Pot and remove the pan. Evenly sprinkle the topping mixture over the cake. Let cool, serve, and enjoy!

Avocado Breakfast Sandwich

Prep time: 5 minutes | Cook time: 15 minutes | Serves 1

- 2 slices bacon
- 2 eggs
- 1 avocado

1. Press the Sauté button. Press the Adjust button to set heat to Low. Add bacon to Instant Pot and cook until crispy. Remove and set aside. 2. Crack egg over Instant Pot slowly, into bacon grease. Repeat with second egg. When edges become golden, after 2 to 3 minutes, flip. Press the Cancel button. 3. Cut avocado in half and scoop out half without seed. Place in small bowl and mash with fork. Spread on one egg. Place bacon on top and top with second egg. Let cool 5 minutes before eating.

Mini Spinach Quiche

Prep time: 5 minutes | Cook time: 15 minutes | Serves 1

- 2 eggs
- 1 tablespoon heavy cream
- 1 tablespoon diced green pepper
- 1 tablespoon diced red onion
- ¼ cup chopped fresh spinach
- ½ teaspoon salt
- ¼ teaspoon pepper
- 1 cup water

1. In medium bowl whisk together all ingredients except water. Pour into 4-inch ramekin. Generally, if the ramekin is oven-safe, it is also safe to use in pressure cooking. 2. Pour water into Instant Pot. Place steam rack into pot. Carefully place ramekin onto steam rack. Click lid closed. Press the Manual button and set time for 15 minutes. When timer beeps, quick-release the pressure. Serve warm.

Gruyère Asparagus Frittata

Prep time: 10 minutes | Cook time: 22 minutes | Serves 6

- 6 eggs
- 6 tablespoons heavy cream
- ½ teaspoon salt
- ½ teaspoon black pepper
- 1 tablespoon butter
- 2½ ounces (71 g) asparagus, chopped
- 1 clove garlic, minced
- 1¼ cup shredded Gruyère cheese, divided
- Cooking spray
- 3 ounces (85 g) halved cherry tomatoes
- ½ cup water

1. In a large bowl, stir together the eggs, cream, salt, and pepper. 2. Set the Instant Pot on the Sauté mode and melt the butter. Add the asparagus and garlic to the pot and sauté for 2 minutes, or until the garlic is fragrant. The asparagus should still be crisp. 3. Transfer the asparagus and garlic to the bowl with the egg mixture. Stir in 1 cup of the cheese. Clean the pot. 4. Spritz a baking pan with cooking spray. Spread the tomatoes in a single layer in the pan. Pour the egg mixture on top of the tomatoes and sprinkle with the remaining ¼ cup of the cheese. Cover the pan tightly with aluminum foil. 5. Pour the water in the Instant Pot and insert the trivet. Place the pan on the trivet. 6. Set the lid in place. Select the Manual mode and set the cooking time for 20 minutes on High Pressure. When the timer goes off, perform a quick pressure release. Carefully open the lid. 7. Remove the pan from the pot and remove the foil. Blot off any excess moisture with a paper towel. Let the frittata cool for 5 to 10 minutes before transferring onto a plate.

Cynthia's Yogurt

- 1 gallon low-fat milk
- ¼ cup low-fat plain yogurt with active cultures

1. Pour milk into the inner pot of the Instant Pot. 2. Lock lid, move vent to sealing, and press the yogurt button. Press Adjust till it reads "boil." 3. When boil cycle is complete (about 1 hour), check the temperature. It should be at 185°F. If it's not, use the Sauté function to warm to 185. 4. After it reaches 185°F, unplug Instant Pot, remove inner pot, and cool. You can place on cooling rack and let it slowly cool. If in a hurry, submerge the base of the pot in cool water. Cool milk to 110°F. 5. When mixture reaches 110, stir in the ¼ cup of yogurt. Lock the lid in place and move vent to sealing. 6. Press Yogurt. Use the Adjust button until the screen says 8:00. This will now incubate for 8 hours. 7. After 8 hours (when the cycle is finished), chill yogurt, or go immediately to straining in step 8. 8. After chilling, or following the 8 hours, strain the yogurt using a nut milk bag. This will give it the consistency of Greek yogurt.

Cheesy Vegetable Frittata

- 4 eggs, beaten
- 2 ounces (57 g) Pecorino cheese, grated
- 3 ounces (85 g) okra, chopped
- 2 ounces (57 g) radish, chopped
- 1 tablespoon cream cheese
- 1 teaspoon sesame oil

1. Heat up sesame oil in the instant pot on Sauté mode. 2. Add chopped okra and radish and sauté the vegetables for 4 minutes. 3. Then stir them well and add cream cheese and beaten eggs. 4. Stir the mixture well and top with cheese. 5. Close the lid and cook the frittata on Sauté mode for 6 minutes more.

Lettuce Wrapped Chicken Sandwich

- 1 tablespoon butter
- 3 ounces (85 g) scallions, chopped
- 2 cups ground chicken
- ½ teaspoon ground nutmeg
- 1 tablespoon coconut flour
- 1 teaspoon salt
- 1 cup lettuce

1. Press the Sauté button on the Instant Pot and melt the butter. Add the chopped scallions, ground chicken and ground nutmeg to the pot and sauté for 4 minutes. Add the coconut flour and salt and continue to sauté for 10 minutes. 2. Fill the lettuce with the ground chicken and transfer it on the plate. Serve immediately.

Cranberry Almond Grits

- ¾ cup stone-ground grits or polenta (not instant)
- ½ cup unsweetened dried cranberries
- Pinch kosher salt
- 1 tablespoon unsalted butter or ghee (optional)
- 1 tablespoon half-and-half
- ¼ cup sliced almonds, toasted

1. In the electric pressure cooker, stir together the grits, cranberries, salt, and 3 cups of water. 2. Close and lock the lid. Set the valve to sealing. 3. Cook on high pressure for 10 minutes. 4. When the cooking is complete, hit Cancel and quick release the pressure. 5. Once the pin drops, unlock and remove the lid. 6. Add the butter (if using) and half-and-half. Stir until the mixture is creamy, adding more half-and-half if necessary. 7. Spoon into serving bowls and sprinkle with almonds.

Chicken and Egg Sandwich

- 1 (6-ounce / 170-g) boneless, skinless chicken breast
- ¼ teaspoon salt
- ⅛ teaspoon pepper
- ¼ teaspoon garlic powder
- 2 tablespoons coconut oil, divided
- 1 egg
- 1 cup water
- ¼ avocado
- 2 tablespoons mayonnaise
- ¼ cup shredded white Cheddar
- Salt and pepper, to taste

1. Cut chicken breast in half lengthwise. Use meat tenderizer to pound chicken breast until thin. Sprinkle with salt, pepper, and garlic powder, and set aside. 2. Add 1 tablespoon coconut oil to Instant Pot. Press Sauté button, then press Adjust button and set temperature to Less. Once oil is hot, fry the egg, remove, and set aside. Press Cancel button. Press Sauté button, then press Adjust button to set temperature to Normal. Add second tablespoon of coconut oil to Instant Pot and sear chicken on each side for 3 to 4 minutes until golden. 3. Press the Manual button and set time for 8 minutes. While chicken cooks, use fork to mash avocado and then mix in mayo. When timer beeps, quick-release the pressure. Put chicken on plate and pat dry with paper towel. Use chicken pieces to form a sandwich with egg, cheese, and avocado mayo. Season lightly with salt and pepper.

Chicken, Mozzarella, and Tomato Pizza

Prep time: 5 minutes | Cook time: 20 minutes | Serves 4 to 5

Crust:

- 2 eggs
- 2 tablespoons salted grass-fed butter, softened
- 1 pound (454 g) ground chicken

Topping:

- 1 (14-ounce / 397-g) can fire roasted sugar-free or low-sugar tomatoes, drained
- 2 cups shredded full-fat Mozzarella cheese
- 1 cup chopped spinach
- 1 cup grated full-fat Parmesan cheese
- ⅓ cup blanched almond flour
- ½ teaspoon dried basil
- ½ teaspoon crushed red pepper
- ½ teaspoon dried oregano
- ½ teaspoon dried cilantro

1. Pour 1 cup of filtered water into the inner pot of the Instant Pot, then insert the trivet. In a large bowl, combine the eggs, butter, chicken, cheese, and flour. Mix thoroughly. Transfer this mixture into a greased, Instant Pot-friendly dish. Cover loosely with aluminum foil. Using a sling, place this dish on top of the trivet. 2. Close the lid, set the pressure release to Sealing, and select Manual. Set the Instant Pot to 10 minutes on High Pressure and let cook. 3. Meanwhile, in a small bowl, mix together basil, red pepper, oregano, and cilantro, and set aside. 4. Once the crust is cooked, carefully switch the pressure release to Venting. Open the Instant Pot and add the tomatoes in an even layer, followed by the Mozzarella cheese and the spinach. Sprinkle the spice and herb mixture over the top of the pizza. Loosely re-cover dish with aluminum foil. 5. Close the lid to the Instant Pot, set the pressure release to Sealing, and select Manual. Set the Instant Pot to 10 minutes on High Pressure and let cook again. 6. Once cooked, let the pressure naturally disperse from the Instant Pot for about 10 minutes, then carefully switch the pressure release to Venting. 7. Open the Instant Pot, serve, and enjoy!

Keto Cabbage Hash Browns

Prep time: 5 minutes | Cook time: 8 minutes | Serves 3

- 1 cup shredded white cabbage
- 3 eggs, beaten
- ½ teaspoon ground nutmeg
- ½ teaspoon salt
- ½ teaspoon onion powder
- ½ zucchini, grated
- 1 tablespoon coconut oil

1. In a bowl, stir together all the ingredients, except for the coconut oil. Form the cabbage mixture into medium hash browns. 2. Press the Sauté button on the Instant Pot and heat the coconut oil. 3. Place the hash browns in the hot coconut oil. Cook for 4 minutes on each side, or until lightly browned. 4. Transfer the hash browns to a plate and serve warm.

Pumpkin Mug Muffin

Prep time: 5 minutes | Cook time: 9 minutes | Serves 1

- ½ cup Swerve
- ½ cup blanched almond flour
- 2 tablespoons organic pumpkin purée
- 1 teaspoon sugar-free chocolate chips
- 1 tablespoon organic coconut flour
- 1 egg
- 1 tablespoon coconut oil
- ½ teaspoon pumpkin pie spice
- ½ teaspoon ground nutmeg
- ½ teaspoon ground cinnamon
- ⅛ teaspoon baking soda

1. Mix the Swerve, almond flour, pumpkin purée, chocolate chips, coconut flour, egg, coconut oil, pumpkin pie spice, nutmeg, cinnamon, and baking soda in a large bowl. Transfer this mixture into a well-greased, Instant Pot-friendly mug. 2. Pour 1 cup of filtered water into the inner pot of the Instant Pot, and insert the trivet. Cover the mug in foil and place on top of the trivet. 3. Close the lid, set the pressure release to Sealing, and select Manual. Set the Instant Pot to 9 minutes on High Pressure. 4. Once cooked, release the pressure immediately by switching the valve to Venting. Be sure your muffin is done by inserting a toothpick into the cake and making sure it comes out clean, as cook times may vary. 5. Remove mug and enjoy!

Hard-boiled Eggs

Prep time: 2 minutes | Cook time: 2 minutes | Serves 9

- 9 large eggs

1. Pour 1 cup of water into the electric pressure cooker and insert an egg rack. Gently stand the eggs in the rack, fat ends down. If you don't have an egg rack, place the eggs in a steamer basket or on a wire rack. 2. Close and lock the lid of the pressure cooker. Set the valve to sealing. 3. Cook on high pressure for 2 minutes. 4. When the cooking is complete, hit Cancel and allow the pressure to release naturally. 5. Once the pin drops, unlock and remove the lid. 6. Using tongs, carefully remove the eggs from the pressure cooker. Peel or refrigerate the eggs when they are cool enough to handle.

Gouda Egg Casserole with Canadian Bacon

Prep time: 12 minutes | Cook time: 20 minutes | Serves 4

- Nonstick cooking spray
- 1 slice whole grain bread, toasted
- ½ cup shredded smoked Gouda cheese
- 3 slices Canadian bacon, chopped
- 6 large eggs
- ¼ cup half-and-half
- ¼ teaspoon kosher salt
- ¼ teaspoon freshly ground black pepper
- ¼ teaspoon dry mustard

1. Spray a 6-inch cake pan with cooking spray, or if the pan is nonstick, skip this step. If you don't have a 6-inch cake pan, any bowl or pan that fits inside your pressure cooker should work. 2. Crumble the toast into the bottom of the pan. Sprinkle with the cheese and Canadian bacon. 3. In a medium bowl, whisk together the eggs, half-and-half, salt, pepper, and dry mustard. 4. Pour the egg mixture into the pan. Loosely cover the pan with aluminum foil. 5. Pour 1½ cups water into the electric pressure cooker and insert a wire rack or trivet. Place the covered pan on top of the rack. 6. Close and lock the lid of the pressure cooker. Set the valve to sealing. 7. Cook on high pressure for 20 minutes. 8. When the cooking is complete, hit Cancel and quick release the pressure. 9. Once the pin drops, unlock and remove the lid. 10. Carefully transfer the pan from the pressure cooker to a cooling rack and let it sit for 5 minutes. 11. Cut into 4 wedges and serve.

Bacon and Mushroom Quiche Lorraine

Prep time: 10 minutes | Cook time: 37 minutes | Serves 4

- 4 strips bacon, chopped
- 2 cups sliced button mushrooms
- ½ cup diced onions
- 8 large eggs
- 1½ cups shredded Swiss cheese
- 1 cup unsweetened almond milk
- ¼ cup sliced green onions
- ½ teaspoon sea salt
- ¼ teaspoon ground black pepper
- 2 tablespoons coconut flour

1. Press the Sauté button on the Instant Pot and add the bacon. Sauté for 4 minutes, or until crisp. Transfer the bacon to a plate lined with paper towel to drain, leaving the drippings in the pot. 2. Add the mushrooms and diced onions to the pot and sauté for 3 minutes, or until the onions are tender. Remove the mixture from the pot to a large bowl. Wipe the Instant Pot clean. 3. Set a trivet in the Instant Pot and pour in 1 cup water. 4. In a medium bowl, stir together the eggs, cheese, almond milk, green onions, salt and pepper. Pour the egg mixture into the bowl with the mushrooms and onions. Stir to combine. Fold in the coconut flour. Pour the mixture into a greased round casserole dish. Spread the cooked bacon on top. 5. Place the casserole dish onto the trivet in the Instant Pot. 6. Lock the lid, select the Manual mode and set the cooking time for 30 minutes on High Pressure. When the timer goes off, do a natural pressure release for 15 minutes, then release any remaining pressure. Open the lid. 7. Remove the casserole dish from the Instant Pot. 8. Let cool for 15 to 30 minutes before cutting into 4 pieces. Serve immediately.

Breakfast Farro with Berries and Walnuts

Prep time: 8 minutes | Cook time: 10 minutes | Serves 6

- 1 cup farro, rinsed and drained
- 1 cup unsweetened almond milk
- ¼ teaspoon kosher salt
- ½ teaspoon pure vanilla extract
- 1 teaspoon ground
- cinnamon
- 1 tablespoon pure maple syrup
- 1½ cups fresh blueberries, raspberries, or strawberries (or a combination)
- 6 tablespoons chopped walnuts

1. In the electric pressure cooker, combine the farro, almond milk, 1 cup of water, salt, vanilla, cinnamon, and maple syrup. 2. Close and lock the lid. Set the valve to sealing. 3. Cook on high pressure for 10 minutes. 4. When the cooking is complete, allow the pressure to release naturally for 10 minutes, then quick release any remaining pressure. Hit Cancel. 5. Once the pin drops, unlock and remove the lid. 6. Stir the farro. Spoon into bowls and top each serving with ¼ cup of berries and 1 tablespoon of walnuts.

Instant Pot Hard-Boiled Eggs

Prep time: 10 minutes | Cook time: 5 minutes | Serves 7

- 1 cup water
- 6 to 8 eggs

1. Pour the water into the inner pot. Place the eggs in a steamer basket or rack that came with pot. 2. Close the lid and secure to the locking position. Be sure the vent is turned to sealing. Set for 5 minutes on Manual at high pressure. (It takes about 5 minutes for pressure to build and then 5 minutes to cook.) 3. Let pressure naturally release for 5 minutes, then do quick pressure release. 4. Place hot eggs into cool water to halt cooking process. You can peel cooled eggs immediately or refrigerate unpeeled.

Slow-Cooked Granola with Nuts

Prep time: 5 minutes | Cook time: 2 hours 30 minutes | Serves 10

- 1 cup raw almonds
- 1 cup pumpkin seeds
- 1 cup raw walnuts
- 1 cup raw cashews
- 1 tablespoon coconut oil
- ¼ cup unsweetened coconut chips
- 1 teaspoon sea salt
- 1 teaspoon cinnamon

1. In a large bowl, stir together the almonds, pumpkin seeds, walnuts, cashews and coconut oil. Make sure all the nuts are coated with the coconut oil. Place the nut mixture in the Instant Pot and cover the pot with a paper towel. 2. Lock the lid. Select the Slow Cook mode and set the cooking time for 1 hour on More. When the timer goes off, stir the nuts. Set the timer for another hour. 3. Again, when the timer goes off, stir the nut mixture and add the coconut chips. Set the timer for another 30 minutes. The cashews should become a nice golden color. 4. When the timer goes off, transfer the nut mixture to a baking pan to cool and sprinkle with the sea salt and cinnamon. Serve.

Streusel Pumpkin Cake

Prep time: 10 minutes | Cook time: 30 minutes | Serves 8

Streusel Topping:
- ¼ cup Swerve
- ¼ cup almond flour
- 2 tablespoons coconut oil or

Cake:
- 2 large eggs, beaten
- 2 cups almond flour
- 1 cup pumpkin purée
- ¾ cup Swerve

Glaze:
- ½ cup Swerve

- unsalted butter, softened
- ½ teaspoon ground cinnamon

- 2 teaspoons pumpkin pie spice
- 2 teaspoons vanilla extract
- ½ teaspoon fine sea salt

- 3 tablespoons unsweetened almond milk

1. Set a trivet in the Instant Pot and pour in 1 cup water. Line a baking pan with parchment paper. 2. In a small bowl, whisk together all the ingredients for the streusel topping with a fork. 3. In a medium-sized bowl, stir together all the ingredients for the cake until thoroughly combined. 4. Scoop half of the batter into the prepared baking pan and sprinkle half of the streusel topping on top. Repeat with the remaining batter and topping. 5. Place the baking pan on the trivet in the Instant Pot. 6. Lock the lid, select the Manual mode and set the cooking time for 30 minutes on High Pressure. 7. Meanwhile, whisk together the Swerve and almond milk in a small bowl until it reaches a runny consistency. 8. When the timer goes off, do a natural pressure release for 10 minutes, then release any remaining pressure. Open the lid. 9. Remove the baking pan from the pot. Let cool in the pan for 10 minutes. Transfer the cake onto a plate and peel off the parchment paper. 10. Transfer the cake onto a serving platter. Spoon the glaze over the top of the cake. Serve immediately.

Cauliflower and Cheese Quiche

Prep time: 10 minutes | Cook time: 10 minutes | Serves 2

- 1 cup chopped cauliflower
- ¼ cup shredded Cheddar cheese
- 5 eggs, beaten
- 1 teaspoon butter
- 1 teaspoon dried oregano
- 1 cup water

1. Grease the instant pot baking pan with butter from inside. 2. Pour water in the instant pot. 3. Sprinkle the cauliflower with dried oregano and put it in the prepared baking pan. Flatten the vegetables gently. 4. After this, add eggs and stir the vegetables. 5. Top the quiche with shredded cheese and transfer it in the instant pot. Close and seal the lid. Cook the quiche on Manual mode (High Pressure) for 10 minutes. Make a quick pressure release.

Almond Pancakes

Prep time: 10 minutes | Cook time: 15 minutes per batch | Serves 6

- 4 eggs, beaten
- 2 cups almond flour
- ½ cup butter, melted
- 2 tablespoons granulated erythritol
- 1 tablespoon avocado oil
- 1 teaspoon baking powder
- 1 teaspoon vanilla extract
- Pinch of salt
- ¾ cup water, divided

1. In a blender, combine all the ingredients, except for the ½ cup of the water. Pulse until fully combined and smooth. Let the batter rest for 5 minutes before cooking. 2. Fill each cup with 2 tablespoons of the batter, about two-thirds of the way full. Cover the cups with aluminum foil. 3. Pour the remaining ½ cup of the water and insert the trivet in the Instant Pot. Place the cups on the trivet. 4. Set the lid in place. Select the Manual mode and set the cooking time for 15 minutes on High Pressure. When the timer goes off, do a quick pressure release. Carefully open the lid. 5. Repeat with the remaining batter, until all the batter is used. Add more water to the pot before cooking each batch, if needed. 6. Serve warm.

Southwestern Egg Casserole

Prep time: 10 minutes | Cook time: 20 minutes | Serves 12

- 1 cup water
- 2½ cups egg substitute
- ½ cup flour
- 1 teaspoon baking powder
- ⅛ teaspoon salt
- ⅛ teaspoon pepper
- 2 cups fat-free cottage cheese
- 1½ cups shredded 75%-less-fat sharp cheddar cheese
- ¼ cup no-trans-fat tub margarine, melted
- 2 (4-ounce) cans chopped green chilies

1. Place the steaming rack into the bottom of the inner pot and pour in 1 cup of water. 2. Grease a round springform pan that will fit into the inner pot of the Instant Pot. 3. Combine the egg substitute, flour, baking powder, salt and pepper in a mixing bowl. It will be lumpy. 4. Stir in the cheese, margarine, and green chilies then pour into the springform pan. 5. Place the springform pan onto the steaming rack, close the lid, and secure to the locking position. Be sure the vent is turned to sealing. Set for 20 minutes on Manual at high pressure. 6. Let the pressure release naturally. 7. Carefully remove the springform pan with the handles of the steaming rack and allow to stand 10 minutes before cutting and serving.

Baked Eggs

Prep time: 15 minutes | Cook time: 20 minutes | Serves 8

- 1 cup water
- 2 tablespoons no-trans-fat tub margarine, melted
- 1 cup reduced-fat buttermilk baking mix
- 1½ cups fat-free cottage cheese
- 2 teaspoons chopped onion
- 1 teaspoon dried parsley
- ½ cup grated reduced-fat cheddar cheese
- 1 egg, slightly beaten
- 1¼ cups egg substitute
- 1 cup fat-free milk

1. Place the steaming rack into the bottom of the inner pot and pour in 1 cup of water. 2. Grease a round springform pan that will fit into the inner pot of the Instant Pot. 3. Pour melted margarine into springform pan. 4. Mix together buttermilk baking mix, cottage cheese, onion, parsley, cheese, egg, egg substitute, and milk in large mixing bowl. 5. Pour mixture over melted margarine. Stir slightly to distribute margarine. 6. Place the springform pan onto the steaming rack, close the lid, and secure to the locking position. Be sure the vent is turned to sealing. Set for 20 minutes on Manual at high pressure. 7. Let the pressure release naturally. 8. Carefully remove the springform pan with the handles of the steaming rack and allow to stand 10 minutes before cutting and serving.

Potato-Bacon Gratin

Prep time: 20 minutes | Cook time: 40 minutes | Serves 8

- 1 tablespoon olive oil
- 6 ounces bag fresh spinach
- 1 clove garlic, minced
- 4 large potatoes, peeled or unpeeled, divided
- 6 ounces Canadian bacon slices, divided
- 5 ounces reduced-fat grated Swiss cheddar, divided
- 1 cup lower-sodium, lower-fat chicken broth

1. Set the Instant Pot to Sauté and pour in the olive oil. Cook the spinach and garlic in olive oil just until spinach is wilted (5 minutes or less). Turn off the instant pot. 2. Cut potatoes into thin slices about ¼" thick. 3. In a springform pan that will fit into the inner pot of your Instant Pot, spray it with nonstick spray then layer ⅓ the potatoes, half the bacon, ⅓ the cheese, and half the wilted spinach. 4. Repeat layers ending with potatoes. Reserve ⅓ cheese for later. 5. Pour chicken broth over all. 6. Wipe the bottom of your Instant Pot to soak up any remaining oil, then add in 2 cups of water and the steaming rack. Place the springform pan on top. 7. Close the lid and secure to the locking position. Be sure the vent is turned to sealing. Set for 35 minutes on Manual at high pressure. 8. Perform a quick release. 9. Top with the remaining cheese, then allow to stand 10 minutes before removing from the Instant Pot, cutting and serving.

Mini Chocolate Chip Muffins

Prep time: 5 minutes | Cook time: 20 minutes | Serves 7

- 1 cup blanched almond flour
- 2 eggs
- ¾ cup sugar-free chocolate chips
- 1 tablespoon vanilla extract
- ½ cup Swerve, or more to taste
- 2 tablespoons salted grass-fed butter, softened
- ½ teaspoon salt
- ¼ teaspoon baking soda

1. Pour 1 cup of filtered water into the inner pot of the Instant Pot, then insert the trivet. Using an electric mixer, combine flour, eggs, chocolate chips, vanilla, Swerve, butter, salt, and baking soda. Mix thoroughly. Transfer this mixture into a well-greased Instant Pot-friendly muffin (or egg bites) mold. 2. Using a sling if desired, place the pan onto the trivet and cover loosely with aluminum foil. Close the lid, set the pressure release to Sealing, and select Manual. Set the Instant Pot to 20 minutes on High Pressure and let cook. 3. Once cooked, let the pressure naturally disperse from the Instant Pot for about 10 minutes, then carefully switch the pressure release to Venting. 4. Open the Instant Pot and remove the pan. Let cool, serve, and enjoy!

Blueberry Oat Mini Muffins

- ½ cup rolled oats
- ¼ cup whole wheat pastry flour or white whole wheat flour
- ½ tablespoon baking powder
- ½ teaspoon ground cardamom or ground cinnamon
- ⅛ teaspoon kosher salt
- 2 large eggs
- ½ cup plain Greek yogurt
- 2 tablespoons pure maple syrup
- 2 teaspoons extra-virgin olive oil
- ½ teaspoon vanilla extract
- ½ cup frozen blueberries (preferably small wild blueberries)

1. In a large bowl, stir together the oats, flour, baking powder, cardamom, and salt. 2. In a medium bowl, whisk together the eggs, yogurt, maple syrup, oil, and vanilla. 3. Add the egg mixture to oat mixture and stir just until combined. Gently fold in the blueberries. 4. Scoop the batter into each cup of the egg bite mold. 5. Pour 1 cup of water into the electric pressure cooker. Place the egg bite mold on the wire rack and carefully lower it into the pot. 6. Close and lock the lid of the pressure cooker. Set the valve to sealing. 7. Cook on high pressure for 10 minutes. 8. When the cooking is complete, allow the pressure to release naturally for 10 minutes, then quick release any remaining pressure. Hit Cancel. 9. Lift the wire rack out of the pot and place on a cooling rack for 5 minutes. Invert the mold onto the cooling rack to release the muffins. 10. Serve the muffins warm or refrigerate or freeze.

Tropical Steel Cut Oats

- 1 cup steel cut oats
- 1 cup unsweetened almond milk
- 2 cups coconut water or water
- ¾ cup frozen chopped peaches
- ¾ cup frozen mango chunks
- 1 (2-inch) vanilla bean, scraped (seeds and pod)
- Ground cinnamon
- ¼ cup chopped unsalted macadamia nuts

1. In the electric pressure cooker, combine the oats, almond milk, coconut water, peaches, mango chunks, and vanilla bean seeds and pod. Stir well. 2. Close and lock the lid of the pressure cooker. Set the valve to sealing. 3. Cook on high pressure for 5 minutes. 4. When the cooking is complete, allow the pressure to release naturally for 10 minutes, then quick release any remaining pressure. Hit Cancel. 5. Once the pin drops, unlock and remove the lid. 6.

Discard the vanilla bean pod and stir well. 7. Spoon the oats into 4 bowls. Top each serving with a sprinkle of cinnamon and 1 tablespoon of the macadamia nuts.

Nutty "Oatmeal"

- 2 tablespoons coconut oil
- 1 cup full-fat coconut milk
- 1 cup heavy whipping cream
- ½ cup macadamia nuts
- ½ cup chopped pecans
- ⅓ cup Swerve, or more to
- taste
- ¼ cup unsweetened coconut flakes
- 2 tablespoons chopped hazelnuts
- 2 tablespoons chia seeds
- ½ teaspoon ground cinnamon

1. Before you get started, soak the chia seeds for about 5 to 10 minutes (can be up to 20, if desired) in 1 cup of filtered water. After soaking, set the Instant Pot to Sauté and add the coconut oil. Once melted, pour in the milk, whipping cream, and 1 cup of filtered water. Then add the macadamia nuts, pecans, Swerve, coconut flakes, hazelnuts, chia seeds, and cinnamon. Mix thoroughly inside the Instant Pot. 2. Close the lid, set the pressure release to Sealing, and hit Cancel to stop the current program. Select Manual, set the Instant Pot to 4 minutes on High Pressure, and let cook. 3. Once cooked, carefully switch the pressure release to Venting. 4. Open the Instant Pot, serve, and enjoy!

Pecan and Walnut Granola

- 2 cups chopped raw pecans
- 1¾ cups vanilla-flavored egg white protein powder
- 1¼ cups unsalted butter, softened
- 1 cup sunflower seeds
- ½ cup chopped raw walnuts
- ½ cup slivered almonds
- ½ cup sesame seeds
- ½ cup Swerve
- 1 teaspoon ground cinnamon
- ½ teaspoon sea salt

1. Add all the ingredients to the Instant Pot and stir to combine. 2. Lock the lid, select the Manual mode and set the cooking time for 2 minutes on High Pressure. When the timer goes off, do a natural pressure release for 10 minutes, then release any remaining pressure. Open the lid. 3. Stir well and pour the granola onto a sheet of parchment paper to cool. It will become crispy when completely cool. Serve the granola in bowls.

Blackberry Vanilla Cake

Prep time: 10 minutes | Cook time: 25 minutes | Serves 8

- 1 cup almond flour
- 2 eggs
- ½ cup erythritol
- 2 teaspoons vanilla extract
- 1 cup blackberries
- 4 tablespoons melted butter
- ¼ cup heavy cream
- ½ teaspoon baking powder
- 1 cup water

1. In large bowl, mix all ingredients except water. Pour into 7-inch round cake pan or divide into two 4-inch pans, if needed. Cover with foil. 2. Pour water into Instant Pot and place steam rack in bottom. Place pan on steam rack and click lid closed. Press the Cake button and press the Adjust button to set heat to Less. Set time for 25 minutes. 3. When timer beeps, allow a 15-minute natural release then quick-release the remaining pressure. Let cool completely.

Greek Frittata with Peppers, Kale, and Feta

Prep time: 5 minutes | Cook time: 45 minutes | Serves 6

- 8 large eggs
- ½ cup plain 2 percent Greek yogurt
- Fine sea salt
- Freshly ground black pepper
- 2 cups firmly packed finely shredded kale or baby kale leaves
- One 12-ounce jar roasted red peppers, drained and cut into ¼ by 2-inch strips
- 2 green onions, white and green parts, thinly sliced
- 1 tablespoon chopped fresh dill
- ⅓ cup crumbled feta cheese
- 6 cups loosely packed mixed baby greens
- ¾ cup cherry or grape tomatoes, halved
- 2 tablespoons extra-virgin olive oil

1. Pour 1½ cups water into the Instant Pot. Lightly butter a 7-cup round heatproof glass dish or coat with nonstick cooking spray. 2. In a bowl, whisk together the eggs, yogurt, ¼ teaspoon salt, and ¼ teaspoon pepper until well blended, then stir in the kale, roasted peppers, green onions, dill, and feta cheese. 3. Pour the egg mixture into the prepared dish and cover tightly with aluminum foil. Place the dish on a long-handled silicone steam rack, then, holding the handles of the steam rack, lower it into the Instant Pot. (If you don't have the long-handled rack, use the wire metal steam rack and a homemade sling) 4. Secure the lid and set the Pressure Release to Sealing. Select the Pressure Cook or Manual setting and set the cooking time for 30 minutes at high pressure. (The pot will take about 15 minutes to come up to pressure before the cooking program begins.) 5. When the cooking program ends, let the pressure release naturally for 10 minutes, then move the Pressure Release to Venting to release any remaining steam. Open the pot and let the frittata sit for a minute or two, until it deflates and settles into its dish. Then, wearing heat-resistant mitts, grasp the handles of the steam rack and lift it out of the pot. Uncover the dish, taking care not to get burned by the steam or to drip condensation onto the frittata. Let the frittata sit for 10 minutes, giving it time to reabsorb any liquid and set up. 6. In a medium bowl, toss together the mixed greens, tomatoes, and olive oil. Taste and adjust the seasoning with salt and pepper, if needed. 7. Cut the frittata into six wedges and serve warm, with the salad alongside.

Soft-Scrambled Eggs

Prep time: 5 minutes | Cook time: 7 minutes | Serves 4

- 6 eggs
- 2 tablespoons heavy cream
- 1 teaspoon salt
- ¼ teaspoon pepper
- 2 tablespoons butter
- 2 ounces (57 g) cream cheese, softened

1. In large bowl, whisk eggs, heavy cream, salt, and pepper. Press the Sauté button and then press the Adjust button to set heat to Less. 2. Gently push eggs around pot with rubber spatula. When they begin to firm up, add butter and softened cream cheese. Continue stirring slowly in a figure-8 pattern until eggs are fully cooked, approximately 7 minutes total.

Traditional Porridge

Prep time: 5 minutes | Cook time: 4 minutes | Serves 4

- 2 tablespoons coconut oil
- 1 cup full-fat coconut milk
- 2 tablespoons blanched almond flour
- 2 tablespoons sugar-free chocolate chips
- 1 cup heavy whipping cream
- ½ cup chopped cashews
- ½ cup chopped pecans
- ½ teaspoon ground cinnamon
- ½ teaspoon erythritol, or more to taste
- ¼ cup unsweetened coconut flakes

1. Set the Instant Pot to Sauté and melt the coconut oil. 2. Pour in the coconut milk, 1 cup of filtered water, then combine and mix the flour, chocolate chips, whipping cream, cashews, pecans, cinnamon, erythritol, and coconut flakes, inside the Instant Pot. 3. Close the lid, set the pressure release to Sealing, and hit Cancel to stop the current program. Select Manual, set the Instant Pot to 4 minutes on High Pressure, and let cook. 4. Once cooked, perform a quick release by carefully switching the pressure valve to Venting. 5. Open the Instant Pot, serve, and enjoy!

Bacon Cheddar Bites

- 2 tablespoons coconut flour
- ½ cup shredded Cheddar cheese
- 2 teaspoons coconut cream
- 2 bacon slices, cooked
- ½ teaspoon dried parsley
- 1 cup water, for cooking

1. In the mixing bowl, mix up coconut flour, Cheddar cheese, coconut cream, and dried parsley. 2. Then chop the cooked bacon and add it in the mixture. 3. Stir it well. 4. Pour water and insert the trivet in the instant pot. 5. Line the trivet with baking paper. 6. After this, make the small balls (bites) from the cheese mixture and put them on the prepared trivet. 7. Cook the meal for 3 minutes on Manual mode (High Pressure). 8. Then make a quick pressure release and cool the cooked meal well.

Coddled Huevos Rancheros

- 2 teaspoons unsalted butter
- 4 large eggs
- 1 cup drained cooked black beans, or two-thirds 15-ounce can black beans, rinsed and drained
- Two 7-inch corn or whole-wheat tortillas, warmed
- ½ cup chunky tomato salsa (such as Pace brand)
- 2 cups shredded romaine lettuce
- 1 tablespoon chopped fresh cilantro
- 2 tablespoons grated Cotija cheese

1. Pour 1 cup water into the Instant Pot and place a long-handled silicone steam rack into the pot. (If you don't have the long-handled rack, use the wire metal steam rack and a homemade sling) 2. Coat each of four 4-ounce ramekins with ½ teaspoon butter. Crack an egg into each ramekin. Place the ramekins on the steam rack in the pot. 3. Secure the lid and set the Pressure Release to Sealing. Select the Steam setting and set the cooking time for 3 minutes at low pressure. (The pot will take about 5 minutes to come up to pressure before the cooking program begins.) 4. While the eggs are cooking, in a small saucepan over low heat, warm the beans for about 5 minutes, stirring occasionally. Cover the saucepan and remove from the heat. (Alternatively, warm the beans in a covered bowl in a microwave for 1 minute. Leave the beans covered until ready to serve.) 5. When the cooking program ends, let the pressure release naturally for 5 minutes, then move the Pressure Release to Venting to release any remaining steam. Open the pot and, wearing heat-resistant mitts, grasp the handles of the steam rack and carefully lift it out of the pot. 6. Place a warmed tortilla on each plate and spoon ½ cup of the beans onto each tortilla. Run a knife around the inside edge of each ramekin to loosen the egg and unmold two eggs onto the beans on each tortilla. Spoon the salsa over the eggs and top with the lettuce, cilantro, and cheese. Serve right away.

Sausage and Cauliflower Breakfast Casserole

- 1 cup water
- ½ head cauliflower, chopped into bite-sized pieces
- 4 slices bacon
- 1 pound (454 g) breakfast sausage
- 4 tablespoons melted butter
- 10 eggs
- ⅓ cup heavy cream
- 2 teaspoons salt
- 1 teaspoon pepper
- 2 tablespoons hot sauce
- 2 stalks green onion
- 1 cup shredded sharp Cheddar cheese

1. Pour water into Instant Pot and place steamer basket in bottom. Add cauliflower. Click lid closed. 2. Press the Steam button and adjust time for 1 minute. When timer beeps, quick-release the pressure and place cauliflower to the side in medium bowl. 3. Drain water from Instant Pot, clean, and replace. Press the Sauté button. Press the Adjust button to set heat to Less. Cook bacon until crispy. Once fully cooked, set aside on paper towels. Add breakfast sausage to pot and brown (still using the Sauté function). 4. While sausage is cooking, whisk butter, eggs, heavy cream, salt, pepper, and hot sauce. 5. When sausage is fully cooked, pour egg mixture into Instant Pot. Gently stir using silicone spatula until eggs are completely cooked and fluffy. Press the Cancel button. Slice green onions. Sprinkle green onions, bacon, and cheese over mixture and let melt. Serve warm.

Baked Eggs and Ham

- 4 large eggs, beaten
- 4 slices ham, diced
- ½ cup shredded Cheddar cheese
- ½ cup heavy cream
- ½ teaspoon sea salt
- Pinch ground black pepper

1. Grease two ramekins. 2. In a large bowl, whisk together all the ingredients. Divide the egg mixture equally between the ramekins. 3. Set a trivet in the Instant Pot and pour in 1 cup water. Place the ramekins on the trivet. 4. Lock the lid. Select the Manual mode and set the cooking time for 5 minutes on High Pressure. When the timer goes off, perform a quick pressure release. Carefully open the lid. 5. Remove the ramekins from the Instant Pot. 6. Serve immediately.

Chapter *2*

Beef, Pork, and Lamb

Chapter 2 Beef, Pork, and Lamb

Beef and Mozzarella Bake

Prep time: 15 minutes | Cook time: 25 minutes | Serves 3

- 12 ounces (340 g) ground beef
- 1 tablespoon chopped chives
- 1 tablespoon chopped fresh parsley
- ½ teaspoon salt
- 1 egg, beaten
- 1 cup shredded Mozzarella cheese
- 1 cup water

1. In the mixing bowl, mix up ground beef, chives, parsley, salt, and egg. 2. When the mixture is homogenous, transfer it in the big baking ramekin. 3. Top the surface of the meat with Mozzarella and wrap in the foil. 4. Pour water and insert the steamer rack in the instant pot. 5. Place the ramekin with the beef bake on the rack. Close and seal the lid. 6. Cook the meal on Manual mode (High Pressure) for 25 minutes. 7. Then allow the natural pressure release for 10 minutes.

Italian Beef Meatloaf

Prep time: 10 minutes | Cook time: 25 minutes | Serves 6

- 1 pound (454 g) ground beef
- 1 cup crushed pork rinds
- 1 egg
- ¼ cup grated Parmesan cheese
- ¼ cup Italian dressing
- 2 teaspoons Italian
- seasoning
- ½ cup water
- ½ cup sugar-free tomato sauce
- 1 tablespoon chopped fresh herbs (such as parsley or basil)
- 1 clove garlic, minced

1. In large bowl, combine the beef, pork rinds, egg, cheese, dressing, and Italian seasoning. Use a wooden spoon to incorporate everything into the meat, but do not overwork the meat or it will turn out tough. 2. Turn the meat mixture out onto a piece of aluminum foil. Use your hands to shape into a loaf. Wrap the foil up around the meat like a packet, but do not cover the top. Place the trivet in the pot and add the water. Place the meatloaf on top of the trivet. 3. Close the lid and seal the vent. Cook on High Pressure

20 minutes. Quick release the steam. 4. While the meat is cooking, whisk together the tomato sauce, herbs, and garlic in a small bowl. Heat the broiler. 5. Remove the meat and foil packet from the pot. Place on a baking sheet and spread the tomato sauce mixture on top. Broil until the glaze becomes sticky, about 5 minutes. Slice into six equal pieces.

Spicy Beef Stew with Butternut Squash

Prep time: 15 minutes | Cook time: 30 minutes | Serves 8

- 1½ tablespoons smoked paprika
- 2 teaspoons ground cinnamon
- 1½ teaspoons kosher salt
- 1 teaspoon ground ginger
- 1 teaspoon red pepper flakes
- ½ teaspoon freshly ground black pepper
- 2 pounds beef shoulder roast, cut into 1-inch cubes
- 2 tablespoons avocado oil, divided
- 1 cup low-sodium beef or vegetable broth
- 1 medium red onion, cut into wedges
- 8 garlic cloves, minced
- 1 (28-ounce) carton or can no-salt-added diced tomatoes
- 2 pounds butternut squash, peeled and cut into 1-inch pieces
- Chopped fresh cilantro or parsley, for serving

1. In a zip-top bag or medium bowl, combine the paprika, cinnamon, salt, ginger, red pepper, and black pepper. Add the beef and toss to coat. 2. Set the electric pressure cooker to the Sauté setting. When the pot is hot, pour in 1 tablespoon of avocado oil. 3. Add half of the beef to the pot and cook, stirring occasionally, for 3 to 5 minutes or until the beef is no longer pink. Transfer it to a plate, then add the remaining 1 tablespoon of avocado oil and brown the remaining beef. Transfer to the plate. Hit Cancel. 4. Stir in the broth and scrape up any brown bits from the bottom of the pot. Return the beef to the pot and add the onion, garlic, tomatoes and their juices, and squash. Stir well. 5. Close and lock lid of pressure cooker. Set the valve to sealing. 6. Cook on high pressure for 30 minutes. 7. When cooking is complete, hit Cancel. Allow the pressure to release naturally for 10 minutes, then quick release any remaining pressure. 8. Unlock and remove lid. 9. Spoon into serving bowls, sprinkle with cilantro or parsley, and serve.

Bone Broth Brisket with Tomatoes

Prep time: 5 minutes | Cook time: 75 minutes | Serves 4 to 5

- 2 tablespoons coconut oil
- ½ teaspoon garlic salt
- ½ teaspoon crushed red pepper
- ½ teaspoon dried basil
- ½ teaspoon kosher salt
- ½ teaspoon freshly ground black pepper
- 1 (14-ounce / 397-g) can sugar-free or low-sugar diced tomatoes
- 1 cup grass-fed bone broth
- 1 pound (454 g) beef brisket, chopped

1. Set the Instant Pot to Sauté and melt the oil. Mix the garlic salt, red pepper, basil, kosher salt, black pepper, and tomatoes in a medium bowl. 2. Pour bone broth into the Instant Pot, then add the brisket, and top with the premixed sauce. Close the lid, set the pressure release to Sealing, and hit Cancel to stop the current program. Select Manual, set the Instant Pot to 75 minutes on High Pressure, and let cook. 3. Once cooked, carefully switch the pressure release to Venting. Open the Instant Pot, and serve. You can pour remaining sauce over brisket, if desired.

Lamb Sirloin Masala

Prep time: 10 minutes | Cook time: 25 minutes | Serves 3

- 12 ounces (340 g) lamb sirloin, sliced
- 1 tablespoon garam masala
- 1 tablespoon lemon juice
- 1 tablespoon olive oil
- ¼ cup coconut cream

1. Sprinkle the sliced lamb sirloin with garam masala, lemon juice, olive oil, and coconut cream in a large bowl. Toss to mix well. 2. Transfer the mixture in the Instant Pot. Cook on Sauté mode for 25 minutes. Flip the lamb for every 5 minutes. 3. When cooking is complete, allow to cool for 10 minutes, then serve warm.

Herbed Lamb Shank

Prep time: 15 minutes | Cook time: 35 minutes | Serves 2

- 2 lamb shanks
- 1 rosemary spring
- 1 teaspoon coconut flour
- ¼ teaspoon onion powder
- ¼ teaspoon chili powder
- ¾ teaspoon ground ginger
- ½ cup beef broth
- ½ teaspoon avocado oil

1. Put all ingredients in the Instant Pot. Stir to mix well. 2. Close the lid. Select Manual mode and set cooking time for 35 minutes on High Pressure. 3. When timer beeps, use a natural pressure release for 15 minutes, then release any remaining pressure. Open the lid. 4. Discard the rosemary sprig and serve warm.

Paprika Pork Ribs

Prep time: 10 minutes | Cook time: 30 minutes | Serves 4

- 1 pound (454 g) pork ribs
- 1 tablespoon ground paprika
- 1 teaspoon ground turmeric
- 3 tablespoons avocado oil
- 1 teaspoon salt
- ½ cup beef broth

1. Rub the pork ribs with ground paprika, turmeric, salt, and avocado oil. 2. Then pour the beef broth in the instant pot. 3. Arrange the pork ribs in the instant pot. Close and seal the lid. 4. Cook the pork ribs for 30 minutes on Manual mode (High Pressure). 5. When the time is finished, make a quick pressure release and chop the ribs into servings.

Albóndigas Sinaloenses

Prep time: 15 minutes | Cook time: 10 minutes | Serves 6

- 1 pound (454 g) ground pork
- ½ pound (227 g) Italian sausage, crumbled
- 2 tablespoons yellow onion, finely chopped
- ½ teaspoon dried oregano
- 1 sprig fresh mint, finely minced
- ½ teaspoon ground cumin
- 2 garlic cloves, finely minced
- ¼ teaspoon fresh ginger, grated
- Seasoned salt and ground black pepper, to taste
- 1 tablespoon olive oil
- ½ cup yellow onions, finely chopped
- 2 chipotle chilies in adobo
- 2 tomatoes, puréed
- 2 tablespoons tomato passata
- 1 cup chicken broth

1. In a mixing bowl, combine the pork, sausage, 2 tablespoons of yellow onion, oregano, mint, cumin, garlic, ginger, salt, and black pepper. 2. Roll the mixture into meatballs and reserve. 3. Press the Sauté button to heat up the Instant Pot. Heat the olive oil and cook the meatballs for 4 minutes, stirring continuously. 4. Stir in ½ cup of yellow onions, chilies in adobo, tomatoes passata, and broth. Add reserved meatballs. 5. Secure the lid. Choose the Manual mode and set cooking time for 6 minutes at High pressure. 6. Once cooking is complete, use a quick pressure release. Carefully remove the lid. 7. Serve immediately.

Lamb Koobideh

Prep time: 15 minutes | Cook time: 30 minutes | Serves 4

- 1 pound (454 g) ground lamb
- 1 egg, beaten
- 1 tablespoon lemon juice
- 1 teaspoon ground turmeric
- ½ teaspoon garlic powder
- 1 teaspoon chives, chopped
- ½ teaspoon ground black pepper
- 1 cup water

1. In a mixing bowl, combine all the ingredients except for water. 2. Shape the mixture into meatballs and press into ellipse shape. 3. Pour the water and insert the trivet in the Instant Pot. 4. Put the prepared ellipse meatballs in a baking pan and transfer on the trivet. 5. Close the lid and select Manual mode. Set cooking time for 30 minutes on High Pressure. 6. When timer beeps, make a quick pressure release. Open the lid. 7. Serve immediately

Beef Cheeseburger Pie

Prep time: 15 minutes | Cook time: 30 minutes | Serves 6

- 1 tablespoon olive oil
- 1 pound (454 g) ground beef
- 3 eggs (1 beaten)
- ½ cup unsweetened tomato purée
- 2 tablespoons golden flaxseed meal
- 1 garlic clove, minced
- ½ teaspoon Italian seasoning blend
- ½ teaspoon sea salt
- ½ teaspoon smoked paprika
- ½ teaspoon onion powder
- 2 tablespoons heavy cream
- ½ teaspoon ground mustard
- ¼ teaspoon ground black pepper
- 2 cups water
- ½ cup grated Cheddar cheese

1. Coat a round cake pan with the olive oil. 2. Select Sauté mode. Once the pot is hot, add the ground beef and sauté for 5 minutes or until the beef is browned. 3. Transfer the beef to a large bowl. 4. Add the 1 beaten egg, tomato purée, flaxseed meal, garlic, Italian seasoning, sea salt, smoked paprika, and onion powder to the bowl. Mix until well combined. 5. Transfer the meat mixture to the prepared cake pan and use a knife to spread the mixture into an even layer. Set aside. 6. In a separate medium bowl, combine the 2 remaining eggs, heavy cream, ground mustard, and black pepper. Whisk until combined. 7. Pour the egg mixture over the meat mixture. Tightly cover the pan with a sheet of aluminum foil. 8. Place the trivet in the Instant Pot and add the water to the bottom of the pot. Place the pan on the trivet. 9. Lock the lid. Select Manual mode and set cooking time for 20 minutes on High Pressure. 10. When cooking is complete, allow the pressure to release naturally for 10 minutes and then release the remaining pressure. Allow the pie to rest in the pot for 5 minutes. 11. Preheat the oven broiler to 450°F (235°C). 12. Open the lid, remove the pan from the pot. Remove the foil and sprinkle the Cheddar over top of the pie. 13. Place the pie in the oven and broil for 2 minutes or until the cheese is melted and the top becomes golden brown. Slice into six equal-sized wedges. Serve hot.

BBQ Ribs and Broccoli Slaw

Prep time: 10 minutes | Cook time: 50 minutes | Serves 6

BBQ Ribs
- 4 pounds baby back ribs
- 1 teaspoon fine sea salt
- 1 teaspoon freshly ground black pepper

Broccoli Slaw
- ½ cup plain 2 percent Greek yogurt
- 1 tablespoon olive oil
- 1 tablespoon fresh lemon juice
- ½ teaspoon fine sea salt
- ¼ teaspoon freshly ground black pepper
- 1 pound broccoli florets (or florets from 2 large crowns), chopped
- 10 radishes, halved and thinly sliced
- 1 red bell pepper, seeded and cut lengthwise into narrow strips
- 1 large apple (such as Fuji, Jonagold, or Gala), thinly sliced
- ½ red onion, thinly sliced
- ¾ cup low-sugar or unsweetened barbecue sauce

1. To make the ribs: Pat the ribs dry with paper towels, then cut the racks into six sections (three to five ribs per section, depending on how big the racks are). Season the ribs all over with the salt and pepper. 2. Pour 1 cup water into the Instant Pot and place the wire metal steam rack into the pot. Place the ribs on top of the wire rack (it's fine to stack them up). 3. Secure the lid and set the Pressure Release to Sealing. Select the Pressure Cook or Manual setting and set the cooking time for 20 minutes at high pressure. (The pot will take about 15 minutes to come up to pressure before the cooking program begins.) 4. To make the broccoli slaw: While the ribs are cooking, in a small bowl, stir together the yogurt, oil, lemon juice, salt, and pepper, mixing well. In a large bowl, combine the broccoli, radishes, bell pepper, apple, and onion. Drizzle with the yogurt mixture and toss until evenly coated. 5. When the ribs have about 10 minutes left in their cooking time, preheat the oven to 400°F. Line a sheet pan with aluminum foil. 6. When the cooking program ends, perform a quick pressure release by moving the Pressure Release to Venting. Open the pot and, using tongs, transfer the ribs in a single layer to the prepared sheet pan. Brush the barbecue sauce onto both sides of the ribs, using 2 tablespoons of sauce per section of ribs. Bake, meaty-side up, for 15 to 20 minutes, until lightly browned. 7. Serve the ribs warm, with the slaw on the side.

Stuffed Meatballs with Mozzarella

Prep time: 10 minutes | Cook time: 20 minutes | Serves 6

- 1 pound (454 g) ground pork
- 1 teaspoon chili flakes
- ½ teaspoon salt
- ⅓ cup shredded Mozzarella
- cheese
- 1 tablespoon butter
- ¼ cup chicken broth
- ½ teaspoon garlic powder

1. Mix up ground pork, chili flakes, salt, and garlic powder. 2. Then make the meatballs with the help of the fingertips. 3. Make the mini balls from the cheese. 4. Fill the meatballs with the mini cheese balls. 5. Toss the butter in the instant pot. 6. Heat it up on Sauté mode and add the prepared meatballs. 7. Cook the on Sauté mode for 3 minutes from each side. 8. Then add chicken broth and close the lid. 9. Cook the meal on Meat/Stew mode for 10 minutes.

Moroccan Lamb Stew

Prep time: 5 minutes | Cook time: 50 minutes | Serves 3

- ½ cup coconut milk
- 1 teaspoon butter
- ½ teaspoon dried rosemary
- ¼ teaspoon salt
- ½ teaspoon ground
- coriander
- 13 ounces (369 g) lamb shoulder, chopped
- 1 teaspoon ground anise
- ¾ cup water

1. Slice the mushrooms and place them in the instant pot bowl. 2. Add all remaining ingredients. Close and seal the lid. 3. Set Manual mode for 45 minutes. 4. When the time is over, make natural pressure release for 10 minutes.

Beery Boston-Style Butt

Prep time: 10 minutes | Cook time: 1 hour 1 minutes | Serves 4

- 1 tablespoon butter
- 1 pound (454 g) Boston-style butt
- ½ cup leeks, chopped
- ¼ cup beer
- ½ cup chicken stock
- Pinch of grated nutmeg
- Sea salt, to taste
- ¼ teaspoon ground black pepper
- ¼ cup water

1. Press the Sauté button to heat up the Instant Pot. Once hot, melt the butter. 2. Cook the Boston-style butt for 3 minutes on each side. Remove from the pot and reserve. 3. Sauté the leeks for 5 minutes

or until fragrant. Add the remaining ingredients and stir to combine. 4. Secure the lid. Choose the Manual mode and set cooking time for 50 minutes on High pressure. 5. Once cooking is complete, use a natural pressure release for 20 minutes, then release any remaining pressure. Carefully remove the lid. 6. Serve immediately.

Egg Meatloaf

Prep time: 20 minutes | Cook time: 25 minutes | Serves 6

- 1 tablespoon avocado oil
- 1½ cup ground pork
- 1 teaspoon chives
- 1 teaspoon salt
- ½ teaspoon ground black pepper
- 2 tablespoons coconut flour
- 3 eggs, hard-boiled, peeled
- 1 cup water

1. Brush a loaf pan with avocado oil. 2. In the mixing bowl, mix the ground pork, chives, salt, ground black pepper, and coconut flour. 3. Transfer the mixture in the loaf pan and flatten with a spatula. 4. Fill the meatloaf with hard-boiled eggs. 5. Pour water and insert the trivet in the Instant Pot. 6. Lower the loaf pan over the trivet in the Instant Pot. Close the lid. 7. Select Manual mode and set cooking time for 25 minutes on High Pressure. 8. When timer beeps, use a natural pressure release for 10 minutes, then release any remaining pressure. Open the lid. 9. Serve immediately.

Beef Chili with Kale

Prep time: 10 minutes | Cook time: 10 minutes | Serves 6

- 2 tablespoons olive oil
- 1½ pounds (680 g) ground chuck
- 1 green bell pepper, chopped
- 1 red bell pepper, chopped
- 2 red chilies, minced
- 1 red onion
- 2 garlic cloves, smashed
- 1 teaspoon cumin
- 1 teaspoon Mexican oregano
- 1 teaspoon cayenne pepper
- 1 teaspoon smoked paprika
- Salt and freshly ground black pepper, to taste
- 1½ cups puréed tomatoes
- 4 cups fresh kale

1. Press the Sauté button to heat up the Instant Pot. Then, heat the oil; once hot, cook the ground chuck for 2 minutes, crumbling it with a fork or a wide spatula. 2. Add the pepper, onions, and garlic; cook an additional 2 minutes or until fragrant. Stir in the remaining ingredients, minus kale leaves. 3. Choose the Manual setting and cook for 6 minutes at High Pressure. Once cooking is complete, use a natural pressure release; carefully remove the lid. 4. Add kale, cover with the lid and allow the kale leaves to wilt completely. Bon appétit!

Korean Short Rib Lettuce Wraps

- ¼ cup coconut aminos, or 1 tablespoon wheat-free tamari
- 2 tablespoons coconut vinegar
- 2 tablespoons sesame oil
- 3 green onions, thinly sliced, plus more for garnish
- 2 teaspoons peeled and

grated fresh ginger
- 2 teaspoons minced garlic
- ½ teaspoon fine sea salt
- ½ teaspoon red pepper flakes, plus more for garnish
- 1 pound (454 g) boneless beef short ribs, sliced ½ inch thick

For Serving:

- 1 head radicchio, thinly sliced
- Butter lettuce leaves

1. Place the coconut aminos, vinegar, sesame oil, green onions, ginger, garlic, salt, and red pepper flakes in the Instant Pot and stir to combine. Add the short ribs and toss to coat well. 2. Seal the lid, press Manual, and set the timer for 20 minutes. Once finished, let the pressure release naturally. 3. Remove the ribs from the Instant Pot and set aside on a warm plate, leaving the sauce in the pot. 4. Press Sauté and cook the sauce, whisking often, until thickened to your liking, about 5 minutes. 5. Put the sliced radicchio on a serving platter, then lay the short ribs on top. Pour the thickened sauce over the ribs. Garnish with more sliced green onions and red pepper flakes. Serve wrapped in lettuce leaves.

Beef Clod Vindaloo

- ½ Serrano pepper, chopped
- ¼ teaspoon cumin seeds
- ¼ teaspoon minced ginger
- ¼ teaspoon cayenne pepper
- ¼ teaspoon salt
- ¼ teaspoon ground paprika
- 1 cup water
- 9 ounces (255 g) beef clod, chopped

1. Put Serrano pepper, cumin seeds, minced ginger, cayenne pepper, salt, ground paprika, and water in a food processor. Blend the mixture until smooth. 2. Transfer the mixture in a bowl and add the chopped beef clod. Toss to coat well. 3. Transfer the beef clod and the mixture in the Instant Pot and close the lid. 4. Select Manual mode and set cooking time for 15 minutes on High Pressure. 5. When timer beeps, use a natural pressure release for 10 minutes, then release any remaining pressure. Open the lid. 6. Serve immediately.

Braised Pork Belly

- 1 pound (454 g) pork belly
- 1 tablespoon olive oil
- Salt and ground black pepper to taste
- 1 clove garlic, minced
- 1 cup dry white wine
- Rosemary sprig

1. Select the Sauté mode on the Instant Pot and heat the oil. 2. Add the pork belly and sauté for 2 minutes per side, until starting to brown. 3. Season the meat with salt and pepper, add the garlic. 4. Pour in the wine and add the rosemary sprig. Bring to a boil. 5. Select the Manual mode and set the cooking time for 35 minutes at High pressure. 6. Once cooking is complete, use a natural pressure release for 10 minutes, then release any remaining pressure. Open the lid. 7. Slice the meat and serve.

Braised Tri-Tip Steak

- 2 pounds (907 g) tri-tip steak, patted dry
- 2 teaspoons coarse sea salt
- 3 tablespoons avocado oil
- ½ medium onion, diced
- 2 cloves garlic, smashed
- 1 tablespoon unsweetened tomato purée
- 1½ cups dry red wine
- ½ tablespoon dried thyme
- 2 bay leaves
- 1 Roma (plum) tomato, diced
- 1 stalk celery, including leaves, chopped
- 1 small turnip, chopped
- ½ cup water

1. Season the tri-tip with the coarse salt. Set the Instant Pot to Sauté mode and heat the avocado oil until shimmering. 2. Cook the steak in the pot for 2 minutes per side or until well browned. Remove the steak from the pot and place it in a shallow bowl. Set aside. 3. Add the onion to the pot and sauté for 3 minutes. Add the garlic and sauté for 1 minute. Add the unsweetened tomato purée and cook for 1 minute, stirring constantly. 4. Pour in the red wine. Stir in the thyme and bay leaves. 5. Return the tri-tip steak to the pot. Scatter the tomato, celery, and turnip around the steak. Pour in the water. 6. Secure the lid. Press the Manual button and set cooking time for 35 minutes on High Pressure. 7. When timer beeps, allow the pressure to release naturally for 20 minutes, then release any remaining pressure. Open the lid. Discard the bay leaves. 8. Remove the steak and place in a dish. Press the Sauté button and bring the braising liquid to a boil. Cook for 10 minutes or until the liquid is reduced by about half. 9. Slice the steak thinly and serve with braising liquid over.

Classic Pork and Cauliflower Keema

Prep time: 15 minutes | Cook time: 8 minutes | Serves 6

- 1 tablespoon sesame oil
- ½ cup yellow onion, chopped
- 1 garlic cloves, minced
- 1 (1-inch) piece fresh ginger, minced
- 1½ pounds (680 g) ground pork
- 1 cup cauliflower, chopped into small florets
- 1 ripe tomatoes, puréed
- 1 jalapeño pepper, seeded
- and minced
- 4 cloves, whole
- 1 teaspoon garam masala
- ½ teaspoon ground cumin
- ¼ teaspoon turmeric powder
- 1 teaspoon brown mustard seeds
- ½ teaspoon hot paprika
- Sea salt and ground black pepper, to taste
- 1 cup wate

1. Press the Sauté button to heat up the Instant Pot. Heat the sesame oil. Once hot, sauté yellow onion for 3 minutes or until softened. 2. Stir in garlic and ginger; cook for an additional minute. Add the remaining ingredients. 3. Secure the lid. Choose the Manual mode and set cooking time for 5 minutes on High pressure. 4. Once cooking is complete, use a quick pressure release. Carefully remove the lid. 5. Serve immediately.

Lamb Chops with Shaved Zucchini Salad

Prep time: 20 minutes | Cook time: 40 minutes | Serves 4

- 4 (8- to 12-ounce/ 227- to 340-g) lamb shoulder chops (blade or round bone), about ¾ inch thick, trimmed
- ¾ teaspoon table salt, divided
- ¾ teaspoon pepper, divided
- 2 tablespoons extra-virgin olive oil, divided
- 1 onion, chopped
- 5 garlic cloves, minced
- ½ cup chicken broth
- 1 bay leaf
- 4 zucchini (6 ounces / 170 g each), sliced lengthwise into ribbons
- 1 teaspoon grated lemon zest plus 1 tablespoon juice
- 2 ounces (57 g) goat cheese, crumbled (½ cup)
- ¼ cup chopped fresh mint
- 2 tablespoons raisins

1. Pat lamb chops dry with paper towels and sprinkle with ½ teaspoon salt and ½ teaspoon pepper. Using highest sauté function, heat 1½ teaspoons oil in Instant Pot for 5 minutes (or until just smoking). Brown half of chops on both sides, 6 to 8 minutes; transfer to plate. Repeat with 1½ teaspoons oil and remaining chops; transfer to plate. 2. Add onion to fat left in pot and cook, using highest sauté function, until softened, about 5 minutes. Stir in

garlic and cook until fragrant, about 30 seconds. Stir in broth and bay leaf, scraping up any browned bits. Return chops to pot along with any accumulated juices (chops will overlap). Lock lid in place and close pressure release valve. Select high pressure cook function and cook for 20 minutes. 3. Turn off Instant Pot and let pressure release naturally for 15 minutes. Quick-release any remaining pressure, then carefully remove lid, allowing steam to escape away from you. Transfer chops to serving dish. Gently toss zucchini with lemon zest and juice, remaining 1 tablespoon oil, remaining ¼ teaspoon salt, and remaining ¼ teaspoon pepper in bowl. Arrange zucchini on serving dish with lamb,

Bacon-Wrapped Pork Bites

Prep time: 15 minutes | Cook time: 20 minutes | Serves 4

- 3 tablespoons butter
- 10 ounces (283 g) pork tenderloin, cubed
- 6 ounces (170 g) bacon,
- sliced
- ½ teaspoon white pepper
- ¾ cup chicken stock

1. Melt the butter on Sauté mode in the Instant Pot. 2. Meanwhile, wrap the pork tenderloin cubes in the sliced bacon and sprinkle with white pepper. Secure with toothpicks, if necessary. 3. Put the wrapped pork tenderloin in the melted butter and cook for 3 minutes on each side. 4. Add the chicken stock and close the lid. 5. Select Manual mode and set cooking time for 14 minutes on High Pressure. 6. When timer beeps, use a natural pressure release for 5 minutes, then release any remaining pressure. Open the lid. 7. Discard the toothpicks and serve immediately.

Beef and Broccoli with Cheddar

Prep time: 5 minutes | Cook time: 10 minutes | Serves 4

- 1 pound (454 g) 85% lean ground beef
- 1 teaspoon salt
- ½ teaspoon garlic powder
- ½ teaspoon dried parsley
- ¼ teaspoon dried oregano
- 2 tablespoons butter
- ¾ cup beef broth
- 2 cups broccoli florets
- ¼ cup heavy cream
- 1 cup shredded mild Cheddar cheese

1. Press the Sauté button and brown ground beef in Instant Pot until there's no more pink. Press the Cancel button. Sprinkle seasonings over meat and add butter, broth, and broccoli. Click lid closed. 2. Press the Manual button and set time for 2 minutes. When timer beeps, press the Cancel button. Stir in heavy cream and Cheddar until completely melted.

Ground Beef Cabbage Casserole

Prep time: 5 minutes | Cook time: 4 minutes | Serves 4

- 1 pound (454 g) 85% lean ground beef
- 2 cups shredded white cabbage
- 1 cup salsa
- 1 teaspoon salt
- 1 tablespoon chili powder
- ½ teaspoon cumin
- ½ cup water
- 1 cup shredded Cheddar cheese

1. Press the Sauté button and brown ground beef. Once fully cooked, add remaining ingredients except for cheese. 2. Click lid closed. Press the Manual button and adjust timer for 4 minutes. When timer beeps, quick-release the pressure and stir in Cheddar.

Fajita Pork Shoulder

Prep time: 5 minutes | Cook time: 45 minutes | Serves 2

- 11 ounces (312 g) pork shoulder, boneless, sliced
- 1 teaspoon fajita seasoning
- 2 tablespoons butter
- ½ cup water

1. Sprinkle the meat with fajita seasoning and put in the instant pot. 2. Add butter and cook it on Sauté mode for 5 minutes. 3. Then stir the pork strips and add water. 4. Seal the instant pot lid and set the Manual mode (High Pressure). 5. Set timer for 40 minutes. 6. When the time is running out, make the natural pressure release for 10 minutes.

Buttery Beef and Spinach

Prep time: 2 minutes | Cook time: 10 minutes | Serves 4

- 1 pound (454 g) 85% lean ground beef
- 1 cup water
- 4 cups fresh spinach
- ¾ teaspoon salt
- ¼ cup butter
- ¼ teaspoon pepper
- ¼ teaspoon garlic powder

1. Press the Sauté button and add ground beef to Instant Pot. Brown beef until fully cooked and spoon into 7-cup glass bowl. Drain grease and replace pot. 2. Pour water into pot and place steam rack in bottom. Place baking dish on steam rack and add fresh spinach, salt, butter, pepper, and garlic powder to ground beef. Cover with aluminum foil. Click lid closed. 3. Press the Manual button and adjust time for 2 minutes. When timer beeps, quick-release the pressure. Remove aluminum foil and stir.

Beef Back Ribs with Barbecue Glaze

Prep time: 10 minutes | Cook time: 35 minutes | Serves 4

- ½ cup water
- 1 (3-pound / 1.4-kg) rack beef back ribs, prepared with rub of choice
- ¼ cup unsweetened tomato purée
- ¼ teaspoon Worcestershire sauce
- ¼ teaspoon garlic powder
- 2 teaspoons apple cider vinegar
- ¼ teaspoon liquid smoke
- ¼ teaspoon smoked paprika
- 3 tablespoons Swerve
- Dash of cayenne pepper

1. Pour the water in the pot and place the trivet inside. 2. Arrange the ribs on top of the trivet. 3. Close the lid. Select Manual mode and set cooking time for 25 minutes on High Pressure. 4. Meanwhile, prepare the glaze by whisking together the tomato purée, Worcestershire sauce, garlic powder, vinegar, liquid smoke, paprika, Swerve, and cayenne in a medium bowl. Heat the broiler. 5. When timer beeps, quick release the pressure. Open the lid. Remove the ribs and place on a baking sheet. 6. Brush a layer of glaze on the ribs. Put under the broiler for 5 minutes. 7. Remove from the broiler and brush with glaze again. Put back under the broiler for 5 more minutes, or until the tops are sticky. 8. Serve immediately.

Pot Roast with Gravy and Vegetables

Prep time: 30 minutes | Cook time: 1 hour 15 minutes | Serves 6

- 1 tablespoon olive oil
- 3–4 pound bottom round, rump, or arm roast, trimmed of fat
- ¼ teaspoon salt
- 2–3 teaspoons pepper
- 2 tablespoons flour
- 1 cup cold water
- 1 teaspoon Kitchen
- Bouquet, or gravy browning seasoning sauce
- 1 garlic clove, minced
- 2 medium onions, cut in wedges
- 4 medium potatoes, cubed, unpeeled
- 2 carrots, quartered
- 1 green bell pepper, sliced

1. Press the Sauté button on the Instant Pot and pour the oil inside, letting it heat up. Sprinkle each side of the roast with salt and pepper, then brown it for 5 minutes on each side inside the pot. 2. Mix together the flour, water and Kitchen Bouquet and spread over roast. 3. Add garlic, onions, potatoes, carrots, and green pepper. 4. Secure the lid and make sure the vent is set to sealing. Press Manual and set the Instant Pot for 1 hour and 15 minutes. 5. When cook time is up, let the pressure release naturally.

Coconut Pork Muffins

Prep time: 5 minutes | Cook time: 9 minutes | Serves 2

- 1 egg, beaten
- 2 tablespoons coconut flour
- 1 teaspoon parsley
- ¼ teaspoon salt
- 1 tablespoon coconut cream
- 4 ounces (113 g) ground pork, fried
- 1 cup water

1. Whisk together the egg, coconut flour, parsley, salt, and coconut cream. Add the fried ground pork. Mix the the mixture until homogenous. 2. Pour the mixture into a muffin pan. 3. Pour the water in the Instant Pot and place in the trivet. 4. Lower the muffin pan on the trivet and close the Instant Pot lid. 5. Set the Manual mode and set cooking time for 4 minutes on High Pressure. 6. When timer beeps, perform a natural pressure release for 5 minutes, then release any remaining pressure. Open the lid. 7. Serve warm.

Herbed Pork Roast with Asparagus

Prep time: 25 minutes | Cook time: 17 minutes | Serves 6

- 1 teaspoon dried thyme
- ½ teaspoon garlic powder
- ½ teaspoon onion powder
- ½ teaspoon dried oregano
- 1½ teaspoons smoked paprika
- ½ teaspoon ground black pepper
- 1 teaspoon sea salt
- 2 tablespoons olive oil, divided
- 2 pounds (907 g) boneless pork loin roast
- ½ medium white onion, chopped
- 2 garlic cloves, minced
- ⅔ cup chicken broth
- 2 tablespoons Worcestershire sauce
- 1 cup water
- 20 fresh asparagus spears, cut in half and woody ends removed

1. In a small bowl, combine the thyme, garlic powder, onion powder, oregano, smoked paprika, black pepper, and sea salt. Mix until well combined and then add 1½ tablespoons olive oil. Stir until blended. 2. Brush all sides of the pork roast with the oil and spice mixture. Place the roast in a covered dish and transfer to the refrigerator to marinate for 30 minutes. 3. Select Sauté mode and brush the Instant Pot with remaining olive oil. Once the oil is hot, add the pork roast and sear for 5 minutes per side or until browned. Remove the roast from the pot and set aside. 4. Add the onions and garlic to the pot and Sauté for 2 minutes, or until the onions soften and garlic becomes fragrant. 5. Add the chicken broth and Worcestershire sauce. 6. Lock the lid. Select Manual mode and set cooking time for 15 minutes on High pressure. 7. When cooking is complete, allow the pressure release naturally for 10 minutes and then release the remaining pressure. 8. Open the lid. Transfer the roast to a cutting board, cover with aluminum foil, and set aside to rest. Transfer the broth to a measuring cup. Set aside. 9. Place the trivet in the Instant Pot and add the water to the bottom of the pot. 10. Place the asparagus in an ovenproof bowl that will fit in the Instant Pot and place the bowl on top of the trivet. 11. Lock the lid. Select Steam mode and set cooking time for 2 minutes. Once the cook time is complete, quick release the pressure. 12. Open the lid and transfer the asparagus to a large serving platter. Thinly slice the roast and transfer to the serving platter with the asparagus. Drizzle the reserved broth over top. Serve warm.

Almond Butter Beef Stew

Prep time: 10 minutes | Cook time: 60 minutes | Serves 3

- 10 ounces (283 g) beef chuck roast, chopped
- ½ cup almond butter
- ½ teaspoon cayenne pepper
- ½ teaspoon salt
- 1 teaspoon dried basil
- 1 cup water

1. Place the almond butter in the instant pot and start to preheat it on the Sauté mode. 2. Meanwhile, mix up together the cayenne pepper, salt, and dried basil. 3. Sprinkle the beef with the spices and transfer the meat in the melted almond butter. 4. Close the instant pot lid and lock it. 5. Set the Manual mode and put a timer on 60 minutes (Low Pressure).

Blue Pork

Prep time: 5 minutes | Cook time: 20 minutes | Serves 2

- 1 teaspoon coconut oil
- 2 pork chops
- 2 ounces (57 g) blue cheese,
- crumbled
- 1 teaspoon lemon juice
- ¼ cup heavy cream

1. Heat the coconut oil in the Instant Pot on Sauté mode. 2. Put the pork chops in the Instant Pot and cook on Sauté mode for 5 minutes on each side. 3. Add the lemon juice and crumbled cheese. Stir to mix well. 4. Add heavy cream and close the lid. 5. Select Manual mode and set cooking time for 10 minutes on High Pressure. 6. When timer beeps, perform a natural pressure release for 5 minutes, then release any remaining pressure. Open the lid. 7. Serve immediately.

and sprinkle with goat cheese, mint, and raisins. Serve.

Blade Pork with Sauerkraut

Prep time: 15 minutes | Cook time: 37 minutes | Serves 6

- 2 pounds (907 g) blade pork steaks
- Sea salt and ground black pepper, to taste
- ½ teaspoon cayenne pepper
- ½ teaspoon dried parsley flakes
- 1 tablespoon butter
- 1½ cups water
- 2 cloves garlic, thinly sliced
- 2 pork sausages, casing removed and sliced
- 4 cups sauerkraut

1. Season the blade pork steaks with salt, black pepper, cayenne pepper, and dried parsley. 2. Press the Sauté button to heat up the Instant Pot. Melt the butter and sear blade pork steaks for 5 minutes or until browned on all sides. 3. Clean the Instant Pot. Add water and trivet to the bottom of the Instant Pot. 4. Place the blade pork steaks on the trivet. Make small slits over entire pork with a knife. Insert garlic pieces into each slit. 5. Secure the lid. Choose the Meat/Stew mode and set cooking time for 30 minutes on High pressure. 6. Once cooking is complete, use a natural pressure release for 15 minutes, then release any remaining pressure. Carefully remove the lid. 7. Add the sausage and sauerkraut. Press the Sauté button and cook for 2 minutes more or until heated through. 8. Serve immediately

Italian Sausage Stuffed Bell Peppers

Prep time: 15 minutes | Cook time: 17 minutes | Serves 4

- 4 medium bell peppers, tops and seeds removed
- 1 pound (454 g) ground pork sausage
- 1 large egg
- 3 tablespoons unsweetened tomato purée
- 2 garlic cloves, minced
- ½ tablespoon Italian
- seasoning blend
- ½ teaspoon sea salt
- ¼ teaspoon ground black pepper
- ½ teaspoon onion powder
- ⅓ cup tomato, puréed
- 1 cup water
- 4 slices Mozzarella cheese

1. Using a fork, pierce small holes into the bottoms of the peppers. Set aside. 2. In a large mixing bowl, combine the sausage, egg, tomato purée, garlic, Italian seasoning, sea salt, black pepper, and onion powder. Mix to combine. 3. Stuff each bell pepper with the meat mixture. 4. Place the trivet in the Instant Pot and add the water. 5. Place the stuffed peppers on the trivet. Pour the puréed tomato over. 6. Lock the lid. Select Manual mode and set cooking time for 15 minutes on High Pressure. 7. When cooking is complete, allow the pressure to release naturally for 5 minutes and then release the remaining pressure. 8. Open the lid and top each pepper with 1 slice of the Mozzarella. Secure the lid, select Keep Warm / Cancel, and set cooking time for 2 minutes to melt the cheese. 9. Open the lid and use tongs to carefully transfer the peppers to a large serving platter. Serve warm.

Braised Lamb Shanks with Bell Pepper and Harissa

Prep time: 10 minutes | Cook time: 1 hour 20 minutes | Serves 4

- 4 (10- to 12-ounce/ 283- to 340-g) lamb shanks, trimmed
- ¾ teaspoon salt, divided
- 1 tablespoon extra-virgin olive oil
- 1 onion, chopped
- 1 red bell pepper, stemmed, seeded, and cut into 1-inch
- pieces
- ¼ cup harissa, divided
- 4 garlic cloves, minced
- 1 tablespoon tomato paste
- ½ cup chicken broth
- 1 bay leaf
- 2 tablespoons chopped fresh mint

1. Pat lamb shanks dry with paper towels and sprinkle with ½ teaspoon salt. Using highest sauté function, heat oil in Instant Pot for 5 minutes (or until just smoking). Brown 2 shanks on all sides, 8 to 10 minutes; transfer to plate. Repeat with remaining shanks; transfer to plate. 2. Add onion, bell pepper, and remaining ¼ teaspoon salt to fat left in pot and cook, using highest sauté function, until vegetables are softened, about 5 minutes. Stir in 2 tablespoons harissa, garlic, and tomato paste and cook until fragrant, about 30 seconds. Stir in broth and bay leaf, scraping up any browned bits. Nestle shanks into pot and add any accumulated juices. Lock lid in place and close pressure release valve. Select high pressure cook function and cook for 60 minutes. 3. Turn off Instant Pot and let pressure release naturally for 15 minutes. Quick-release any remaining pressure, then carefully remove lid, allowing steam to escape away from you. Transfer shanks to serving dish, tent with aluminum foil, and let rest while finishing sauce. 4. Strain braising liquid through fine-mesh strainer into fat separator. Discard bay leaf and transfer solids to blender. Let braising liquid settle for 5 minutes, then pour ¾ cup defatted liquid into blender with solids; discard remaining liquid. Add remaining 2 tablespoons harissa and process until smooth, about 1 minute. Season with salt and pepper to taste. Pour portion of sauce over shanks and sprinkle with mint. Serve, passing remaining sauce separately.

Salisbury Steaks with Seared Cauliflower

Salisbury Steaks

- 1 pound 95 percent lean ground beef
- ⅓ cup almond flour
- 1 large egg
- ½ teaspoon fine sea salt
- ¼ teaspoon freshly ground black pepper
- 2 tablespoons cold-pressed avocado oil
- 1 small yellow onion, sliced

- 1 garlic clove, chopped
- 8 ounces cremini or button mushrooms, sliced
- ½ teaspoon fine sea salt
- 2 tablespoons tomato paste
- 1½ teaspoons yellow mustard
- 1 cup low-sodium roasted beef bone broth

Seared Cauliflower

- 1 tablespoon olive oil
- 1 head cauliflower, cut into bite-size florets
- 2 tablespoons chopped fresh flat-leaf parsley

- ¼ teaspoon fine sea salt
- 2 teaspoons cornstarch
- 2 teaspoons water

1. To make the steaks: In a bowl, combine the beef, almond flour, egg, salt, and pepper and mix with your hands until all of the ingredients are evenly distributed. Divide the mixture into four equal portions, then shape each portion into an oval patty about ½ inch thick. 2. Select the Sauté setting on the Instant Pot and heat the oil for 2 minutes. Swirl the oil to coat the bottom of the pot, then add the patties and sear for 3 minutes, until browned on one side. Using a thin, flexible spatula, flip the patties and sear the second side for 2 to 3 minutes, until browned. Transfer the patties to a plate. 3. Add the onion, garlic, mushrooms, and salt to the pot and sauté for 4 minutes, until the onion is translucent and the mushrooms have begun to give up their liquid. Add the tomato paste, mustard, and broth and stir with a wooden spoon, using it to nudge any browned bits from the bottom of the pot. Return the patties to the pot in a single layer and spoon a bit of the sauce over each one. 4. Secure the lid and set the Pressure Release to Sealing. Press the Cancel button to reset the cooking program, then select the Pressure Cook or Manual setting and set the cooking time for 10 minutes at high pressure. (The pot will take about 5 minutes to come up to pressure before the cooking program begins.) 5. When the cooking program ends, let the pressure release naturally for at least 10 minutes, then move the Pressure Release to Venting to release any remaining steam. 6. To make the cauliflower: While the pressure is releasing, in a large skillet over medium heat, warm the oil. Add the cauliflower and stir or toss to coat with the oil, then cook, stirring every minute or two, until lightly browned, about 8 minutes. Turn off the heat, sprinkle in the parsley and salt, and stir to combine. Leave in the skillet, uncovered, to keep warm. 7. Open the pot and, using a slotted spatula, transfer the patties to a serving plate. In a small bowl, stir together the cornstarch and water. Press the Cancel button to reset the cooking program, then select the Sauté setting. When the sauce comes to a simmer, stir in the cornstarch mixture and let the sauce boil for about 1 minute, until thickened. Press the Cancel button to turn off the Instant Pot. 8. Spoon the sauce over the patties. Serve right away, with the cauliflower.

Loaded Burger Bowls

- 1 pound (454 g) 85% lean ground beef
- ½ teaspoon salt
- ¼ teaspoon pepper
- ½ medium onion, sliced

- 2 cups shredded lettuce
- 1 cup shredded Cheddar cheese
- 4 pickle spears
- 1 avocado, sliced

1. Press the Sauté button and add ground beef to Instant Pot. When meat is browned completely, drain if needed. 2. Add salt, pepper, and onion. Continue cooking until onion is soft and translucent. Press the Cancel button. 3. Divide lettuce into four sections. Top each section with a quarter of the ground beef. Add a quarter of the Cheddar, one pickle spear, and sliced avocado. Top with favorite sauce or dressing.

Beef Meatball Stroganoff

- 1 pound (454 g) ground beef
- 1 egg
- 4 tablespoons heavy cream, divided
- 3 cloves garlic, minced
- 1 tablespoon chopped fresh parsley, plus more for garnish
- ½ teaspoon salt

- Pinch of black pepper
- 1 cup beef broth
- 8 ounces (227 g) sliced baby bella mushrooms
- ¼ cup sour cream
- 1 teaspoon xanthan gum

1. In a large bowl, combine the beef, egg, 2 tablespoons of the heavy cream, garlic, parsley, salt, and pepper. Use a spoon to work everything evenly into the beef. 2. Use a cookie scoop to divide out 24 meatballs, about 1 ounce (28 g) each. Roll them between your hands to round them out. 3. Add the broth and mushrooms to the pot. Place the meatballs on top of the mushrooms. 4. Close the lid and seal the vent. Cook on High Pressure for 12 minutes. Quick release the steam. Press Cancel. 5. Use a slotted spoon to transfer the meatballs from the pot to a bowl or platter. 6. Turn the pot to Sauté mode. Whisk in the sour cream and the remaining 2 tablespoons heavy cream. Once the broth begins to lightly boil, whisk in the xanthan gum. Continue whisking until a thin gravy consistency is reached, about 2 minutes. Pour the gravy on top of the meatballs. Garnish with fresh parsley.

Beef Steak with Cheese Mushroom Sauce

- 1 tablespoon olive oil
- 1½ pounds (680 g) beef blade steak
- 1 cup stock
- 2 garlic cloves, minced

Sauce:

- 1 tablespoon butter, softened
- 2 cups sliced Porcini mushrooms
- ½ cup thinly sliced onions

- Sea salt and ground black pepper, to taste
- ½ teaspoon cayenne pepper
- 1 tablespoon coconut aminos

- ½ cup sour cream
- 4 ounces (113 g) goat cheese, crumbled

1. Press the Sauté button to heat up the Instant Pot. Then, heat the olive oil until sizzling. Once hot, cook the blade steak approximately 3 minutes or until delicately browned. 2. Add the stock, garlic, salt, black pepper, cayenne pepper, and coconut aminos. 3. Secure the lid. Choose Manual mode and High Pressure; cook for 20 minutes. Once cooking is complete, use a quick pressure release; carefully remove the lid. 4. Take the meat out of the Instant Pot. Allow it to cool slightly and then, slice it into strips. 5. Press the Sauté button again and add the butter, mushrooms and onions to the Instant Pot. Let it cook for 5 minutes longer or until the mushrooms are fragrant and the onions are softened. 6. Add sour cream and goat cheese; continue to simmer for a couple of minutes more or until everything is thoroughly heated. 7. Return the meat to the Instant Pot and serve. Bon appétit!

Chapter 3

Poultry

Chapter 3 Poultry

Barbecue Shredded Chicken

Prep time: 5 minutes | Cook time: 25 minutes | Serves 4

- 1 (5-pound / 2.2-kg) whole chicken
- 3 teaspoons salt
- 1 teaspoon pepper
- 1 teaspoon dried parsley
- 1 teaspoon garlic powder
- ½ medium onion, cut into 3 to 4 large pieces
- 1 cup water
- ½ cup sugar-free barbecue sauce, divided

1. Scatter the chicken with salt, pepper, parsley, and garlic powder. Put the onion pieces inside the chicken cavity. 2. Pour the water into the Instant Pot and insert the trivet. Place seasoned chicken on the trivet. Brush with half of the barbecue sauce. 3. Lock the lid. Select the Manual mode and set the cooking time for 25 minutes at High Pressure. 4. When the timer beeps, perform a natural pressure release for 10 minutes, then release any remaining pressure. Carefully remove the lid. 5. Using a clean brush, add the remaining half of the sauce to chicken. For crispy skin or thicker sauce, you can broil in the oven for 5 minutes until lightly browned. 6. Slice or shred the chicken and serve warm.

Thai Coconut Chicken

Prep time: 10 minutes | Cook time: 15 minutes | Serves 4

- 1 tablespoon coconut oil
- 1 pound (454 g) chicken, cubed
- 2 cloves garlic, minced
- 1 shallot, peeled and chopped
- 1 teaspoon Thai chili, minced
- 1 teaspoon fresh ginger root, julienned
- ⅓ teaspoon cumin powder
- 1 tomato, peeled and chopped
- 1 cup vegetable broth
- ⅓ cup unsweetened coconut milk
- 2 tablespoons coconut aminos
- 1 teaspoon Thai curry paste
- Salt and freshly ground black pepper, to taste

1. Set your Instant Pot to Sauté and heat the coconut oil. 2. Brown the chicken cubes for 2 to 3 minutes, stirring frequently. Reserve the chicken in a bowl. 3. Add the garlic and shallot and sauté for 2 minutes until tender. Add a splash of vegetable broth to the pot, if needed. 4. Stir in the Thai chili, ginger, and cumin powder and cook for another 1 minute or until fragrant. 5. Add the cooked chicken, tomato, vegetable broth, milk, coconut aminos, and curry paste to the Instant Pot and stir well. 6. Lock the lid. Select the Manual mode and set the cooking time for 10 minutes at High Pressure. 7. When the timer beeps, perform a quick pressure release. Carefully remove the lid. Season with salt and pepper to taste and serve.

Chicken Tagine

Prep time: 15 minutes | Cook time: 11 minutes | Serves 4

- 2 (15-ounce / 425-g) cans chickpeas, rinsed, divided
- 1 tablespoon extra-virgin olive oil
- 5 garlic cloves, minced
- 1½ teaspoons paprika
- ½ teaspoon ground turmeric
- ½ teaspoon ground cumin
- ¼ teaspoon ground ginger
- ¼ teaspoon cayenne pepper
- 1 fennel bulb, 1 tablespoon fronds minced, stalks discarded, bulb halved and cut lengthwise into ½-inch-thick wedges
- 1 cup chicken broth
- 3 (2-inch) strips lemon zest, plus lemon wedges for serving
- 4 (5- to 7-ounce / 142- to 198-g) bone-in chicken thighs, skin removed, trimmed
- ½ teaspoon table salt
- ½ cup pitted large brine-cured green or black olives, halved
- ⅓ cup raisins
- 2 tablespoons chopped fresh parsley

1. Using potato masher, mash ½ cup chickpeas in bowl to paste. Using highest sauté function, cook oil, garlic, paprika, turmeric, cumin, ginger, and cayenne in Instant Pot until fragrant, about 1 minute. Turn off Instant Pot, then stir in remaining whole chickpeas, mashed chickpeas, fennel wedges, broth, and zest. 2. Sprinkle chicken with salt. Nestle chicken skinned side up into pot and spoon some of cooking liquid over top. Lock lid in place and close pressure release valve. Select high pressure cook function and cook for 10 minutes. 3. Turn off Instant Pot and quick-release pressure. Carefully remove lid, allowing steam to escape away from you. Discard lemon zest. Stir in olives, raisins, parsley, and fennel fronds. Season with salt and pepper to taste. Serve with lemon wedges.

Bruschetta and Cheese Stuffed Chicken

Prep time: 10 minutes | Cook time: 10 minutes | Serves 4

- 6 ounces (170 g) diced Roma tomatoes
- 2 tablespoons avocado oil
- 1 tablespoon thinly sliced fresh basil, plus more for garnish
- 1½ teaspoons balsamic vinegar
- Pinch of salt
- Pinch of black pepper
- 4 boneless, skinless chicken breasts (about 2 pounds / 907 g)
- 12 ounces (340 g) goat cheese, divided
- 2 teaspoons Italian seasoning, divided
- 1 cup water

1. Prepare the bruschetta by mixing the tomatoes, avocado oil, basil, vinegar, salt, and pepper in a small bowl. Let it marinate until the chicken is done. 2. Pat the chicken dry with a paper towel. Butterfly the breast open but do not cut all the way through. Stuff each breast with 3 ounces (85 g) of the goat cheese. Use toothpicks to close the edges. 3. Sprinkle ½ teaspoon of the Italian seasoning on top of each breast. 4. Pour the water into the pot. Place the trivet inside. Lay a piece of aluminum foil on top of the trivet and place the chicken breasts on top. It is okay if they overlap. 5. Close the lid and seal the vent. Cook on High Pressure for 10 minutes. Quick release the steam. 6. Remove the toothpicks and top each breast with one-fourth of the bruschetta.

Chicken Fajitas with Bell Peppers

Prep time: 10 minutes | Cook time: 5 minutes | Serves 4

- 1½ pounds (680 g) boneless, skinless chicken breasts
- ¼ cup avocado oil
- 2 tablespoons water
- 1 tablespoon Mexican hot sauce
- 2 cloves garlic, minced
- 1 teaspoon lime juice
- 1 teaspoon ground cumin
- 1 teaspoon salt
- 1 teaspoon erythritol
- ¼ teaspoon chili powder
- ¼ teaspoon smoked paprika
- 5 ounces (142 g) sliced yellow bell pepper strips
- 5 ounces (142 g) sliced red bell pepper strips
- 5 ounces (142 g) sliced green bell pepper strips

1. Slice the chicken into very thin strips lengthwise. Cut each strip in half again. Imagine the thickness of restaurant fajitas when cutting. 2. In a measuring cup, whisk together the avocado oil, water, hot sauce, garlic, lime juice, cumin, salt, erythritol, chili powder, and paprika to form a marinade. Add to the pot, along with the chicken and peppers. 3. Close the lid and seal the vent. Cook on High Pressure for 5 minutes. Quick release the steam.

Braised Chicken with Mushrooms and Tomatoes

Prep time: 20 minutes | Cook time: 25 minutes | Serves 4

- 1 tablespoon extra-virgin olive oil
- 1 pound (454 g) portobello mushroom caps, gills removed, caps halved and sliced ½ inch thick
- 1 onion, chopped fine
- ¾ teaspoon salt, divided
- 4 garlic cloves, minced
- 1 tablespoon tomato paste
- 1 tablespoon all-purpose flour
- 2 teaspoons minced fresh sage
- ½ cup dry red wine
- 1 (14½ ounces / 411 g) can diced tomatoes, drained
- 4 (5 to 7 ounces / 142 to 198 g) bone-in chicken thighs, skin removed, trimmed
- ¼ teaspoon pepper
- 2 tablespoons chopped fresh parsley
- Shaved Parmesan cheese

1. Using highest sauté function, heat oil in Instant Pot until shimmering. Add mushrooms, onion, and ¼ teaspoon salt. Partially cover and cook until mushrooms are softened and have released their liquid, about 5 minutes. Stir in garlic, tomato paste, flour, and sage and cook until fragrant, about 1 minute. Stir in wine, scraping up any browned bits, then stir in tomatoes. 2. Sprinkle chicken with remaining ½ teaspoon salt and pepper. Nestle chicken skinned side up into pot and spoon some of sauce on top. Lock lid in place and close pressure release valve. Select high pressure cook function and cook for 15 minutes. 3. Turn off Instant Pot and quick-release pressure. Carefully remove lid, allowing steam to escape away from you. Transfer chicken to serving dish, tent with aluminum foil, and let rest while finishing sauce. 4. Using highest sauté function, bring sauce to simmer and cook until thickened slightly, about 5 minutes. Season sauce with salt and pepper to taste. Spoon sauce over chicken and sprinkle with parsley and Parmesan. Serve.

Poblano Chicken

Prep time: 10 minutes | Cook time: 29 minutes | Serves 4

- 2 Poblano peppers, sliced
- 16 ounces (454 g) chicken fillet
- ½ teaspoon salt
- ½ cup coconut cream
- 1 tablespoon butter
- ½ teaspoon chili powder

1. Heat up the butter on Sauté mode for 3 minutes. 2. Add Poblano and cook them for 3 minutes. 3. Meanwhile, cut the chicken fillet into the strips and sprinkle with salt and chili powder. 4. Add the chicken strips to the instant pot. 5. Then add coconut cream and close the lid. Cook the meal on Sauté mode for 20 minutes.

Chicken and Spiced Freekeh with Cilantro and Preserved Lemon

Prep time: 20 minutes | Cook time: 11 minutes | Serves 4

- 2 tablespoons extra-virgin olive oil, plus extra for drizzling
- 1 onion, chopped fine
- 4 garlic cloves, minced
- 1½ teaspoons smoked paprika
- ¼ teaspoon ground cardamom
- ¼ teaspoon red pepper flakes
- 2¼ cups chicken broth
- 1½ cups cracked freekeh, rinsed
- 2 (12-ounce / 340-g) bone-in split chicken breasts, halved crosswise and trimmed
- ½ teaspoon table salt
- ¼ teaspoon pepper
- ¼ cup chopped fresh cilantro
- 2 tablespoons sesame seeds, toasted
- ½ preserved lemon, pulp and white pith removed, rind rinsed and minced (2 tablespoons)

1. Using highest sauté function, heat oil in Instant Pot until shimmering. Add onion and cook until softened, about 5 minutes. Stir in garlic, paprika, cardamom, and pepper flakes and cook until fragrant, about 30 seconds. Stir in broth and freekeh. Sprinkle chicken with salt and pepper. Nestle skin side up into freekeh mixture. Lock lid in place and close pressure release valve. Select high pressure cook function and cook for 5 minutes. 2. Turn off Instant Pot and quick-release pressure. Carefully remove lid, allowing steam to escape away from you. Transfer chicken to serving dish and discard skin, if desired. Tent with aluminum foil and let rest while finishing freekeh. 3. Gently fluff freekeh with fork. Lay clean dish towel over pot, replace lid, and let sit for 5 minutes. Season with salt and pepper to taste. Transfer freekeh to serving dish with chicken and sprinkle with cilantro, sesame seeds, and preserved lemon. Drizzle with extra oil and serve.

Turmeric Chicken Nuggets

Prep time: 10 minutes | Cook time: 9 minutes | Serves 5

- 8 ounces (227 g) chicken fillet
- 1 teaspoon ground turmeric
- ½ teaspoon ground
- coriander
- ½ cup almond flour
- 2 eggs, beaten
- ½ cup butter

1. Chop the chicken fillet roughly into the medium size pieces. 2. In the mixing bowl, mix up ground turmeric, ground coriander, and almond flour. 3. Then dip the chicken pieces in the beaten egg and coat in the almond flour mixture. 4. Toss the butter in the instant pot and melt it on Sauté mode for 4 minutes. 5. Then put the coated chicken in the hot butter and cook for 5 minutes or until the nuggets are golden brown.

Pulled BBQ Chicken and Texas-Style Cabbage Slaw

Prep time: 5 minutes | Cook time: 20 minutes | Serves 6

- Chicken
- 1 cup water
- ¼ teaspoon fine sea salt
- 3 garlic cloves, peeled
- 2 bay leaves
- 2 pounds boneless, skinless chicken thighs (see Note)
- Cabbage Slaw
- ½ head red or green cabbage, thinly sliced
- 1 red bell pepper, seeded and thinly sliced
- 2 jalapeño chiles, seeded and cut into narrow strips
- 2 carrots, julienned
- 1 large Fuji or Gala apple, julienned
- ½ cup chopped fresh cilantro
- 3 tablespoons fresh lime juice
- 3 tablespoons extra-virgin olive oil
- ½ teaspoon ground cumin
- ¼ teaspoon fine sea salt
- ¾ cup low-sugar or unsweetened barbecue sauce
- Cornbread, for serving

1. To make the chicken: Combine the water, salt, garlic, bay leaves, and chicken thighs in the Instant Pot, arranging the chicken in a single layer. 2. Secure the lid and set the Pressure Release to Sealing. Select the Poultry, Pressure Cook, or Manual setting and set the cooking time for 10 minutes at high pressure. (The pot will take about 10 minutes to come up to pressure before the cooking program begins.) 3. To make the slaw: While the chicken is cooking, in a large bowl, combine the cabbage, bell pepper, jalapeños, carrots, apple, cilantro, lime juice, oil, cumin, and salt and toss together until the vegetables and apples are evenly coated. 4. When the cooking program ends, perform a quick pressure release by moving the Pressure Release to Venting, or let the pressure release naturally. Open the pot and, using tongs, transfer the chicken to a cutting board. Using two forks, shred the chicken into bite-size pieces. Wearing heat-resistant mitts, lift out the inner pot and discard the cooking liquid. Return the inner pot to the housing. 5. Return the chicken to the pot and stir in the barbecue sauce. You can serve it right away or heat it for a minute or two on the Sauté setting, then return the pot to its Keep Warm setting until ready to serve. 6. Divide the chicken and slaw evenly among six plates. Serve with wedges of cornbread on the side.

Greek Chicken

Prep time: 25 minutes | Cook time: 20 minutes | Serves 6

- 4 potatoes, unpeeled, quartered
- 2 pounds chicken pieces, trimmed of skin and fat
- 2 large onions, quartered
- 1 whole bulb garlic, cloves minced
- 3 teaspoons dried oregano
- ¾ teaspoons salt
- ½ teaspoons pepper
- 1 tablespoon olive oil
- 1 cup water

1. Place potatoes, chicken, onions, and garlic into the inner pot of the Instant Pot, then sprinkle with seasonings. Top with oil and water. 2. Secure the lid and make sure vent is set to sealing. Cook on Manual mode for 20 minutes. 3. When cook time is over, let the pressure release naturally for 5 minutes, then release the rest manually.

Baked Cheesy Mushroom Chicken

Prep time: 5 minutes | Cook time: 15 minutes | Serves 4

- 1 tablespoon butter
- 2 cloves garlic, smashed
- ½ cup chopped yellow onion
- 1 pound (454 g) chicken breasts, cubed
- 10 ounces (283 g) button mushrooms, thinly sliced
- 1 cup chicken broth
- ½ teaspoon shallot powder
- ½ teaspoon turmeric powder
- ½ teaspoon dried basil
- ½ teaspoon dried sage
- ½ teaspoon cayenne pepper
- ⅓ teaspoon ground black pepper
- Kosher salt, to taste
- ½ cup heavy cream
- 1 cup shredded Colby cheese

1. Set your Instant Pot to Sauté and melt the butter. 2. Add the garlic, onion, chicken, and mushrooms and sauté for about 4 minutes, or until the vegetables are softened. 3. Add the remaining ingredients except the heavy cream and cheese to the Instant Pot and stir to incorporate. 4. Lock the lid. Select the Meat/Stew mode and set the cooking time for 6 minutes at High Pressure. 5. When the timer beeps, perform a natural pressure release for 10 minutes, then release any remaining pressure. Carefully remove the lid. 6. Stir in the heavy cream until heated through. Pour the mixture into a baking dish and scatter the cheese on top. 7. Bake in the preheated oven at 400°F (205°C) until the cheese bubbles. 8. Allow to cool for 5 minutes and serve.

Tomato Chicken Legs

Prep time: 10 minutes | Cook time: 35 minutes | Serves 2

- 2 chicken legs
- 2 tomatoes, chopped
- 1 cup chicken stock
- 1 teaspoon peppercorns

1. Put all ingredients in the instant pot. 2. Close and seal the lid. Set Manual mode (High Pressure). 3. Cook the chicken legs for 35 minutes. 4. Make a quick pressure release. 5. Transfer the cooked chicken legs in the serving bowls and add 1 ladle of the chicken stock.

Orange Chicken Thighs with Bell Peppers

Prep time: 15 to 20 minutes | Cook time: 7 minutes | Serves 4 to 6

- 6 boneless skinless chicken thighs, cut into bite-sized pieces
- 2 packets crystallized True Orange flavoring
- ½ teaspoon True Orange Orange Ginger seasoning
- ½ teaspoon coconut aminos
- ¼ teaspoon Worcestershire sauce
- Olive oil or cooking spray
- 2 cups bell pepper strips, any color combination (I used red)
- 1 onion, chopped
- 1 tablespoon green onion, chopped fine
- 3 cloves garlic, minced or chopped
- ½ teaspoon pink salt
- ½ teaspoon black pepper
- 1 teaspoon garlic powder
- 1 teaspoon ground ginger
- ¼ to ½ teaspoon red pepper flakes
- 2 tablespoons tomato paste
- ½ cup chicken bone broth or water
- 1 tablespoon brown sugar substitute (I use Sukrin Gold)
- ½ cup Seville orange spread (I use Crofter's brand)

1. Combine the chicken with the 2 packets of crystallized orange flavor, the orange ginger seasoning, the coconut aminos, and the Worcestershire sauce. Set aside. 2. Turn the Instant Pot to Sauté and add a touch of olive oil or cooking spray to the inner pot. Add in the orange ginger marinated chicken thighs. 3. Sauté until lightly browned. Add in the peppers, onion, green onion, garlic, and seasonings. Mix well. 4. Add the remaining ingredients; mix to combine. 5. Lock the lid, set the vent to sealing, set to 7 minutes. 6. Let the pressure release naturally for 2 minutes, then manually release the rest when cook time is up.

Chicken in Wine

- ♦ 2 pounds chicken breasts, trimmed of skin and fat
- ♦ 10¾-ounce can 98% fat-free, reduced-sodium cream of mushroom soup
- ♦ 10¾-ounce can French onion soup
- ♦ 1 cup dry white wine or chicken broth

1. Place the chicken into the Instant Pot. 2. Combine soups and wine. Pour over chicken. 3. Secure the lid and make sure vent is set to sealing. Cook on Manual mode for 12 minutes. 4. When cook time is up, let the pressure release naturally for 5 minutes and then release the rest manually.

Chicken Reuben Bake

- ♦ 4 boneless, skinless chicken-breast halves
- ♦ ¼ cup water
- ♦ 1-pound bag sauerkraut, drained and rinsed
- ♦ 4 to 5 (1 ounce each) slices Swiss cheese
- ♦ ¾ cup fat-free Thousand Island salad dressing
- ♦ 2 tablespoons chopped fresh parsley

1. Place chicken and water in inner pot of the Instant Pot along with ¼ cup water. Layer sauerkraut over chicken. Add cheese. Top with salad dressing. Sprinkle with parsley. 2. Secure the lid and cook on the Slow Cook setting on low 6 to 8 hours.

Chicken Tacos with Fried Cheese Shells

Chicken:

- ♦ 4 (6-ounce / 170-g) boneless, skinless chicken breasts
- ♦ 1 cup chicken broth
- ♦ 1 teaspoon salt
- ♦ ¼ teaspoon pepper
- ♦ 1 tablespoon chili powder
- ♦ 2 teaspoons garlic powder
- ♦ 2 teaspoons cumin

Cheese Shells:

- ♦ 1½ cups shredded whole-milk Mozzarella cheese

1. Combine all ingredients for the chicken in the Instant Pot. 2. Secure the lid. Select the Manual mode and set the cooking time for 20 minutes at High Pressure. 3. Once cooking is complete, do a quick pressure release. Carefully open the lid. 4. Shred the chicken and serve in bowls or cheese shells. 5. Make the cheese shells: Heat a nonstick skillet over medium heat. 6. Sprinkle ¼ cup of Mozzarella cheese in the skillet and fry until golden. Flip and turn off the heat. Allow the cheese to get brown. Fill with chicken and fold. The cheese will harden as it cools. Repeat with the remaining cheese and filling. 7. Serve warm.

Cider Chicken with Pecans

- ♦ 6 ounces (170 g) chicken fillet, cubed
- ♦ 2 pecans, chopped
- ♦ 1 teaspoon coconut aminos
- ♦ ½ bell pepper, chopped
- ♦ 1 tablespoon coconut oil
- ♦ ¼ cup apple cider vinegar
- ♦ ¼ cup chicken broth

1. Melt coconut oil on Sauté mode and add chicken cubes. 2. Add bell pepper, and pecans. 3. Sauté the ingredients for 10 minutes and add apple cider vinegar, chicken broth, and coconut aminos. 4. Sauté the chicken for 5 minutes more.

Chicken Meatballs with Green Cabbage

- ♦ 1 pound (454 g) ground chicken
- ♦ ¼ cup heavy (whipping) cream
- ♦ 2 teaspoons salt, divided
- ♦ ½ teaspoon ground caraway seeds
- ♦ 1½ teaspoons freshly ground
- black pepper, divided
- ♦ ¼ teaspoon ground allspice
- ♦ 4 to 6 cups thickly chopped green cabbage
- ♦ ½ cup coconut milk
- ♦ 2 tablespoons unsalted butter

1. To make the meatballs, put the chicken in a bowl. Add the cream, 1 teaspoon of salt, the caraway, ½ teaspoon of pepper, and the allspice. Mix thoroughly. Refrigerate the mixture for 30 minutes. Once the mixture has cooled, it is easier to form the meatballs. 2. Using a small scoop, form the chicken mixture into small-to medium-size meatballs. Place half the meatballs in the inner cooking pot of your Instant Pot and cover them with half the cabbage. Place the remaining meatballs on top of the cabbage, then cover them with the rest of the cabbage. 3. Pour in the milk, place pats of the butter here and there, and sprinkle with the remaining 1 teaspoon of salt and 1 teaspoon of pepper. 4. Lock the lid into place. Select Manual and adjust the pressure to High. Cook for 4 minutes. When the cooking is complete, quick-release the pressure. Unlock the lid. Serve the meatballs on top of the cabbage.

Shredded Buffalo Chicken

- 2 tablespoons avocado oil
- ½ cup finely chopped onion
- 1 celery stalk, finely chopped
- 1 large carrot, chopped
- ⅓ cup mild hot sauce (such

- as Frank's RedHot)
- ½ tablespoon apple cider vinegar
- ¼ teaspoon garlic powder
- 2 bone-in, skin-on chicken breasts (about 2 pounds)

1. Set the electric pressure cooker to the Sauté setting. When the pot is hot, pour in the avocado oil. 2. Sauté the onion, celery, and carrot for 3 to 5 minutes or until the onion begins to soften. Hit Cancel. 3. Stir in the hot sauce, vinegar, and garlic powder. Place the chicken breasts in the sauce, meat-side down. 4. Close and lock the lid of the pressure cooker. Set the valve to sealing. 5. Cook on high pressure for 20 minutes. 6. When cooking is complete, hit Cancel and quick release the pressure. Once the pin drops, unlock and remove the lid. 7. Using tongs, transfer the chicken breasts to a cutting board. When the chicken is cool enough to handle, remove the skin, shred the chicken and return it to the pot. Let the chicken soak in the sauce for at least 5 minutes. 8. Serve immediately.

Simple Chicken Masala

- 12 ounces (340 g) chicken fillet
- 1 tablespoon masala spices

- 1 tablespoon avocado oil
- 3 tablespoons organic almond milk

1. Heat up avocado oil in the instant pot on Sauté mode for 2 minutes. 2. Meanwhile, chop the chicken fillet roughly and mix it up with masala spices. 3. Add almond milk and transfer the chicken in the instant pot. 4. Cook the chicken bites on Sauté mode for 15 minutes. Stir the meal occasionally.

Rubbed Whole Chicken

- 1½ pound (680 g) whole chicken
- 1 tablespoon poultry

- seasoning
- 2 tablespoons avocado oil
- 2 cups water

1. Pour water in the instant pot. 2. Then rub the chicken with poultry seasoning and avocado oil. 3. Put the chicken in the instant pot. Close and seal the lid. 4. Cook the meal in Manual mode for 25 minutes. When the time is finished, allow the natural pressure release for 10 minutes.

Mexican Chicken with Red Salsa

- 2 pounds (907 g) boneless, skinless chicken thighs, cut into bite-size pieces
- 1½ tablespoons ground cumin
- 1½ tablespoons chili powder
- 1 tablespoon salt
- 2 tablespoons vegetable oil
- 1 (14½ ounces / 411 g) can

- diced tomatoes, undrained
- 1 (5 ounces / 142 g) can sugar-free tomato paste
- 1 small onion, chopped
- 3 garlic cloves, minced
- 2 ounces (57 g) pickled jalapeños from a can, with juice
- ½ cup sour cream

1. Preheat the Instant Pot by selecting Sauté and adjusting to high heat. 2. In a medium bowl, coat the chicken with the cumin, chili powder, and salt. 3. Put the oil in the inner cooking pot. When it is shimmering, add the coated chicken pieces. (This step lets the spices bloom a bit to get their full flavor.) Cook the chicken for 4 to 5 minutes. 4. Add the tomatoes, tomato paste, onion, garlic, and jalapeños. 5. Lock the lid into place. Select Manual and adjust the pressure to High. Cook for 15 minutes. When the cooking is complete, let the pressure release naturally for 10 minutes, then quick-release any remaining pressure. Unlock and remove the lid. 6. Use two forks to shred the chicken. Serve topped with the sour cream. This dish is good with mashed cauliflower, steamed vegetables, or a salad.

Chicken Curry with Eggplant

- 1 eggplant, chopped
- ¼ cup chopped fresh cilantro
- 1 teaspoon curry powder

- 1 cup coconut cream
- 1 teaspoon coconut oil
- 1 pound (454 g) chicken breast, skinless, boneless, cubed

1. Put the coconut oil and chicken breast in the instant pot. 2. Sauté the ingredients on Sauté mode for 5 minutes. 3. Then stir well and add cilantro, eggplant, coconut cream, and curry powder. 4. Close and seal the lid. 5. Cook the meal on Manual mode (High Pressure) for 7 minutes. 6. Make a quick pressure release and transfer the cooked chicken in the serving bowls.

Chicken with Spiced Sesame Sauce

Prep time: 20 minutes | Cook time: 8 minutes | Serves 5

- 2 tablespoons tahini (sesame sauce)
- ¼ cup water
- 1 tablespoon low-sodium soy sauce
- ¼ cup chopped onion
- 1 teaspoon red wine vinegar
- 2 teaspoons minced garlic
- 1 teaspoon shredded ginger root (Microplane works best)
- 2 pounds chicken breast, chopped into 8 portions

1. Place first seven ingredients in bottom of the inner pot of the Instant Pot. 2. Add coarsely chopped chicken on top. 3. Secure the lid and make sure vent is at sealing. Set for 8 minutes using Manual setting. When cook time is up, let the pressure release naturally for 10 minutes, then perform a quick release. 4. Remove ingredients and shred chicken with fork. Combine with other ingredients in pot for a tasty sandwich filling or sauce.

Lemony Chicken with Fingerling Potatoes and Olives

Prep time: 20 minutes | Cook time: 21 minutes | Serves 4

- 4 (5- to 7-ounce / 142- to 198-g) bone-in chicken thighs, trimmed
- ½ teaspoon table salt
- ¼ teaspoon pepper
- 2 teaspoons extra-virgin olive oil, plus extra for drizzling
- 4 garlic cloves, peeled and smashed
- ½ cup chicken broth
- 1 small lemon, sliced thin
- 1½ pounds (680 g) fingerling potatoes, unpeeled
- ¼ cup pitted brine-cured green or black olives, halved
- 2 tablespoons coarsely chopped fresh parsley

1. Pat chicken dry with paper towels and sprinkle with salt and pepper. Using highest sauté function, heat oil in Instant Pot for 5 minutes (or until just smoking). Place chicken skin side down in pot and cook until well browned on first side, about 5 minutes; transfer to plate. 2. Add garlic to fat left in pot and cook, using highest sauté function, until golden and fragrant, about 2 minutes. Stir in broth and lemon, scraping up any browned bits. Return chicken skin side up to pot and add any accumulated juices. Arrange potatoes on top. Lock lid in place and close pressure release valve. Select high pressure cook function and cook for 9 minutes. 3. Turn off Instant Pot and quick-release pressure. Carefully remove lid, allowing steam to escape away from you. Transfer chicken to serving dish and discard skin, if desired. Stir olives and parsley into potatoes and season with salt and pepper to taste. Serve chicken with potatoes.

Indian Chicken Breast

Prep time: 5 minutes | Cook time: 4 minutes | Serves 2

- ¼ teaspoon cumin seeds
- ½ teaspoon turmeric
- 1 teaspoon ground paprika
- ¾ teaspoon chili paste
- ½ teaspoon ground
- coriander
- ½ cup coconut milk
- 14 ounces (397 g) chicken breast, skinless, boneless
- 1 tablespoon coconut oil

1. Blend together the cumin seeds, turmeric, ground paprika, chili paste, coriander, coconut milk, and coconut oil. 2. When the mixture is smooth, pour it in the instant pot bowl. 3. Chop the chicken breast roughly and transfer it in the spice mixture. Stir gently with the help of the spatula. 4. Lock the lid and seal it. 5. Set the Manual mode for 4 minutes (High Pressure). 6. After this, make quick-release pressure. Enjoy!

Chicken with Tomatoes and Spinach

Prep time: 5 minutes | Cook time: 18 minutes | Serves 4

- 4 boneless, skinless chicken breasts (about 2 pounds / 907 g)
- 2½ ounces (71 g) sun-dried tomatoes, coarsely chopped (about 2 tablespoons)
- ¼ cup chicken broth
- 2 tablespoons creamy, no-sugar-added balsamic vinegar dressing
- 1 tablespoon whole-grain mustard
- 2 cloves garlic, minced
- 1 teaspoon salt
- 8 ounces (227 g) fresh spinach
- ¼ cup sour cream
- 1 ounce (28 g) cream cheese, softened

1. Place the chicken breasts in the Instant Pot. Add the tomatoes, broth, and dressing. 2. Close the lid and seal the vent. Cook on High Pressure for 10 minutes. Quick release the steam. Press Cancel. 3. Remove the chicken from the pot and place on a plate. Cover with aluminum foil to keep warm while you make the sauce. 4. Turn the pot to Sauté mode. Whisk in the mustard, garlic, and salt and then add the spinach. Stir the spinach continuously until it is completely cooked down, 2 to 3 minutes. The spinach will absorb the sauce but will release it again as it continues to cook down. 5. Once the spinach is completely wilted, add the sour cream and cream cheese. Whisk until completed incorporated. 6. Let the sauce simmer to thicken and reduce by about one-third, about 5 minutes. Stir occasionally to prevent burning. Press Cancel. 7. Pour the sauce over the chicken. Serve.

Chicken and Kale Sandwiches

Prep time: 10 minutes | Cook time: 10 minutes | Serves 2

- 4 ounces (113 g) kale leaves
- 8 ounces (227 g) chicken fillet
- 1 tablespoon butter
- 1 ounce (28 g) lemon
- ¼ cup water

1. Dice the chicken fillet. 2. Squeeze the lemon juice over the poultry. 3. Transfer the poultry into the instant pot; add water and butter. 4. Close the lid and cook the chicken on the Poultry mode for 10 minutes. 5. When the chicken is cooked, place it on the kale leaves to make the medium sandwiches.

Unstuffed Peppers with Ground Turkey and Quinoa

Prep time: 0 minutes | Cook time: 35 minutes | Serves 8

- 2 tablespoons extra-virgin olive oil
- 1 yellow onion, diced
- 2 celery stalks, diced
- 2 garlic cloves, chopped
- 2 pounds 93 percent lean ground turkey
- 2 teaspoons Cajun seasoning blend (plus 1 teaspoon fine sea salt if using a salt-free blend)
- ½ teaspoon freshly ground black pepper
- ¼ teaspoon cayenne pepper
- 1 cup quinoa, rinsed
- 1 cup low-sodium chicken broth
- One 14½-ounce can fire-roasted diced tomatoes and their liquid
- 3 red, orange, and/or yellow bell peppers, seeded and cut into 1-inch squares
- 1 green onion, white and green parts, thinly sliced
- 1½ tablespoons chopped fresh flat-leaf parsley
- Hot sauce (such as Crystal or Frank's RedHot) for serving

1. Select the Sauté setting on the Instant Pot and heat the oil for 2 minutes. Add the onion, celery, and garlic and sauté for about 4 minutes, until the onion begins to soften. Add the turkey, Cajun seasoning, black pepper, and cayenne and sauté, using a wooden spoon or spatula to break up the meat as it cooks, for about 6 minutes, until cooked through and no streaks of pink remain. 2. Sprinkle the quinoa over the turkey in an even layer. Pour the broth and the diced tomatoes and their liquid over the quinoa, spreading the tomatoes on top. Sprinkle the bell peppers over the top in an even layer. 3. Secure the lid and set the Pressure Release to Sealing. Press the Cancel button to reset the cooking program, then select the Pressure Cook or Manual setting and set the cooking time for 8 minutes at high pressure. (The pot will take about 15 minutes to come up to pressure before the cooking program begins.) 4. When the cooking program ends, let the pressure release naturally for at least 15 minutes, then move the Pressure Release to Venting to release any remaining steam. Open the pot and sprinkle the green onion and parsley over the top in an even layer. 5. Spoon the unstuffed peppers into bowls, making sure to dig down to the bottom of the pot so each person gets an equal amount of peppers, quinoa, and meat. Serve hot, with hot sauce on the side.

Pecorino Chicken

Prep time: 10 minutes | Cook time: 15 minutes | Serves 3

- 2 ounces (57 g) Pecorino cheese, grated
- 10 ounces (283 g) chicken breast, skinless, boneless
- 1 tablespoon butter
- ¾ cup heavy cream
- ½ teaspoon salt
- ½ teaspoon red hot pepper

1. Chop the chicken breast into the cubes. 2. Toss butter in the instant pot and preheat it on the Sauté mode. 3. Add the chicken cubes. 4. Sprinkle the poultry with the salt and red hot pepper. 5. Add cream and mix up together all the ingredients. 6. Close the lid of the instant pot and seal it. 7. Set Poultry mode and put a timer on 15 minutes. 8. When the time is over, let the chicken rest for 5 minutes more. 9. Transfer the meal on the plates and sprinkle with the grated cheese. The cheese shouldn't melt immediately.

Lemony Chicken Thighs

Prep time: 15 minutes | Cook time: 15 minutes | Serves 3 to 5

- 1 cup low-sodium chicken bone broth
- 5 frozen bone-in chicken thighs
- 1 small onion, diced
- 5 to 6 cloves garlic, diced
- Juice of 1 lemon
- 2 tablespoons margarine,
- melted
- ½ teaspoon salt
- ¼ teaspoon black pepper
- 1 teaspoon True Lemon Lemon Pepper seasoning
- 1 teaspoon parsley flakes
- ¼ teaspoon oregano
- Rind of 1 lemon

1. Add the chicken bone broth into the inner pot of the Instant Pot. 2. Add the chicken thighs. 3. Add the onion and garlic. 4. Pour the fresh lemon juice in with the melted margarine. 5. Add the seasonings. 6. Lock the lid, make sure the vent is at sealing, then press the Poultry button. Set to 15 minutes. 7. When cook time is up, let the pressure naturally release for 3 to 5 minutes, then manually release the rest. 8. You can place these under the broiler for 2 to 3 minutes to brown. 9. Plate up and pour some of the sauce over top with fresh grated lemon rind.

Spicy Chicken with Bacon and Peppers

Prep time: 5 minutes | Cook time: 13 minutes | Serves 6

- 2 slices bacon, chopped
- 1½ pounds (680 g) ground chicken
- 2 garlic cloves, minced
- ½ cup green onions, chopped
- 1 green bell pepper, seeded and chopped
- 1 red bell pepper, seeded and chopped
- 1 serrano pepper, chopped
- 1 tomato, chopped
- 1 cup water
- ⅓ cup chicken broth
- 1 teaspoon paprika
- 1 teaspoon onion powder
- ¼ teaspoon ground allspice
- 2 bay leaves
- Sea salt and ground black pepper, to taste

1. Press the Sauté button to heat your Instant Pot. 2. Add the bacon and cook for about 3 minutes until crisp. Reserve the bacon in a bowl. 3. Add the ground chicken to the bacon grease of the pot and brown for 2 to 3 minutes, crumbling it with a spatula. Reserve it in the bowl of bacon. 4. Add the garlic, green onions, and peppers and sauté for 3 minutes until tender. Add the remaining ingredients to the Instant Pot, along with the cooked bacon and chicken. Stir to mix well. 5. Lock the lid. Select the Poultry mode and set the cooking time for 5 minutes at High Pressure. 6. When the timer beeps, perform a natural pressure release for 10 minutes, then release any remaining pressure. Carefully remove the lid. Serve warm.

Stuffed Chicken with Spinach and Feta

Prep time: 10 minutes | Cook time: 25 minutes | Serves 4

- ½ cup frozen spinach
- ⅓ cup crumbled feta cheese
- 1¼ teaspoons salt, divided
- 4 (6-ounce / 170-g) boneless, skinless chicken breasts, butterflied
- ¼ teaspoon pepper
- ¼ teaspoon dried oregano
- ¼ teaspoon dried parsley
- ¼ teaspoon garlic powder
- 2 tablespoons coconut oil
- 1 cup water

1. Combine the spinach, feta cheese, and ¼ teaspoon of salt in a medium bowl. Divide the mixture evenly and spoon onto the chicken breasts. 2. Close the chicken breasts and secure with toothpicks or butcher's string. Sprinkle the chicken with the remaining 1 teaspoon of salt, pepper, oregano, parsley, and garlic powder. 3. Set your Instant Pot to Sauté and heat the coconut oil. 4. Sear each chicken breast until golden brown, about 4 to 5 minutes per side. 5. Remove the chicken breasts and set aside. 6. Pour the water into the Instant Pot and scrape the bottom to remove any chicken or seasoning that is stuck on. Add the trivet to the Instant Pot and place the chicken on the trivet. 7. Secure the lid. Select the Manual mode and set the cooking time for 15 minutes at High Pressure. 8. Once cooking is complete, do a natural pressure release for 15 minutes, then release any remaining pressure. Carefully open the lid. Serve warm.

Herb and Lemon Whole Chicken

Prep time: 5 minutes | Cook time: 30 to 32 minutes | Serves 4

- 3 teaspoons garlic powder
- 3 teaspoons salt
- 2 teaspoons dried parsley
- 2 teaspoons dried rosemary
- 1 teaspoon pepper
- 1 (4-pound / 1.8-kg) whole chicken
- 2 tablespoons coconut oil
- 1 cup chicken broth
- 1 lemon, zested and quartered

1. Combine the garlic powder, salt, parsley, rosemary, and pepper in a small bowl. Rub this herb mix over the whole chicken. 2. Set your Instant Pot to Sauté and heat the coconut oil. 3. Add the chicken and brown for 5 to 7 minutes. Using tongs, transfer the chicken to a plate. 4. Pour the broth into the Instant Pot and scrape the bottom with a rubber spatula or wooden spoon until no seasoning is stuck to pot, then insert the trivet. 5. Scatter the lemon zest over chicken. Put the lemon quarters inside the chicken. Place the chicken on the trivet. 6. Secure the lid. Select the Meat/Stew mode and set the cooking time for 25 minutes at High Pressure. 7. Once cooking is complete, do a natural pressure release for 10 minutes, then release any remaining pressure. Carefully open the lid. 8. Shred the chicken and serve warm.

Kung Pao Chicken

Prep time: 5 minutes | Cook time: 17 minutes | Serves 5

- 2 tablespoons coconut oil
- 1 pound (454 g) boneless, skinless chicken breasts, cubed
- 1 cup cashews, chopped
- 6 tablespoons hot sauce
- ½ teaspoon chili powder
- ½ teaspoon finely grated ginger
- ½ teaspoon kosher salt
- ½ teaspoon freshly ground black pepper

1. Set the Instant Pot to Sauté and melt the coconut oil. 2. Add the remaining ingredients to the Instant Pot and mix well. 3. Secure the lid. Select the Manual mode and set the cooking time for 17 minutes at High Pressure. 4. Once cooking is complete, do a quick pressure release. Carefully open the lid. 5. Serve warm.

Chicken Carnitas

Prep time: 5 minutes | Cook time: 15 minutes | Serves 8

- 3 pounds (1.4 kg) whole chicken, cut into pieces
- ⅓ cup vegetable broth
- 3 cloves garlic, pressed
- 1 tablespoon avocado oil
- 1 guajillo chili, minced
- Sea salt, to taste
- ½ teaspoon paprika
- ⅓ teaspoon cayenne pepper
- ½ teaspoon ground bay leaf
- ⅓ teaspoon black pepper
- 2 tablespoons chopped fresh coriander, for garnish
- 1 cup crème fraiche, for serving

1. Combine all the ingredients except the coriander and crème fraiche in the Instant Pot. 2. Lock the lid. Select the Poultry mode and set the cooking time for 15 minutes at High Pressure. 3. When the timer beeps, perform a quick pressure release. Carefully remove the lid. 4. Shred the chicken with two forks and discard the bones. Garnish with the coriander and serve with a dollop of crème fraiche.

Thai Yellow Curry with Chicken Meatballs

Prep time: 5 minutes | Cook time: 30 minutes | Serves 4

- 1 pound 95 percent lean ground chicken
- ⅓ cup gluten-free panko (Japanese bread crumbs)
- 1 egg white
- 1 tablespoon coconut oil
- 1 yellow onion, cut into 1-inch pieces
- One 14-ounce can light coconut milk
- 3 tablespoons yellow curry paste
- ¾ cup water
- 8 ounces carrots, halved lengthwise, then cut crosswise into 1-inch
- lengths (or quartered if very large)
- 8 ounces zucchini, quartered lengthwise, then cut crosswise into 1-inch lengths (or cut into halves, then thirds if large)
- 8 ounces cremini mushrooms, quartered
- Fresh Thai basil leaves for serving (optional)
- Fresno or jalapeño chile, thinly sliced, for serving (optional)
- 1 lime, cut into wedges
- Cooked cauliflower "rice" for serving

1. In a medium bowl, combine the chicken, panko, and egg white and mix until evenly combined. Set aside. 2. Select the Sauté setting on the Instant Pot and heat the oil for 2 minutes. Add the onion and sauté for 5 minutes, until it begins to soften and brown. Add ½ cup of the coconut milk and the curry paste and sauté for 1 minute more, until bubbling and fragrant. Press the Cancel button to turn off the pot, then stir in the water. 3. Using a 1½-tablespoon cookie scoop, shape and drop meatballs into the pot in a single layer. 4.

Secure the lid and set the Pressure Release to Sealing. Select the Pressure Cook or Manual setting and set the cooking time for 5 minutes at high pressure. (The pot will take about 5 minutes to come up to pressure before the cooking program begins.) 5. When the cooking program ends, perform a quick pressure release by moving the Pressure Release to Venting, or let the pressure release naturally. Open the pot and stir in the carrots, zucchini, mushrooms, and remaining 1¼ cups coconut milk. 6. Press the Cancel button to reset the cooking program, then select the Sauté setting. Bring the curry to a simmer (this will take about 2 minutes), then let cook, uncovered, for about 8 minutes, until the carrots are fork-tender. Press the Cancel button to turn off the pot. 7. Ladle the curry into bowls. Serve piping hot, topped with basil leaves and chile slices, if desired, and the lime wedges and cauliflower "rice" on the side.

Paprika Chicken Wings

Prep time: 10 minutes | Cook time: 13 minutes | Serves 4

- 1 pound (454 g) boneless chicken wings
- 1 teaspoon ground paprika
- 1 teaspoon avocado oil
- ¼ teaspoon minced garlic
- ¾ cup beef broth

1. Pour the avocado oil in the instant pot. 2. Rub the chicken wings with ground paprika and minced garlic and put them in the instant pot. 3. Cook the chicken on Sauté mode for 4 minutes from each side. 4. Then add beef broth and close the lid. 5. Sauté the meal for 5 minutes more.

Creamy Nutmeg Chicken

Prep time: 20 minutes | Cook time: 10 minutes | Serves 6

- 1 tablespoon canola oil
- 6 boneless chicken breast halves, skin and visible fat removed
- ¼ cup chopped onion
- ¼ cup minced parsley
- 2 (10¾-ounce) cans 98% fat-free, reduced-sodium cream of mushroom soup
- ½ cup fat-free sour cream
- ½ cup fat-free milk
- 1 tablespoon ground nutmeg
- ¼ teaspoon sage
- ¼ teaspoon dried thyme
- ¼ teaspoon crushed rosemary

1. Press the Sauté button on the Instant Pot and then add the canola oil. Place the chicken in the oil and brown chicken on both sides. Remove the chicken to a plate. 2. Sauté the onion and parsley in the remaining oil in the Instant Pot until the onions are tender. Press Cancel on the Instant Pot, then place the chicken back inside. 3. Mix together the remaining ingredients in a bowl then pour over the chicken. 4. Secure the lid and set the vent to sealing. Set on Manual mode for 10 minutes. 5. When cooking time is up, let the pressure release naturally.

Chapter *4*

Fish and Seafood

Chapter 4 Fish and Seafood

Steamed Halibut with Lemon

Prep time: 10 minutes | Cook time: 9 minutes | Serves 3

- 3 halibut fillet
- ½ lemon, sliced
- ½ teaspoon white pepper
- ½ teaspoon ground coriander
- 1 tablespoon avocado oil
- 1 cup water, for cooking

1. Pour water and insert the steamer rack in the instant pot. 2. Rub the fish fillets with white pepper, ground coriander, and avocado oil. 3. Place the fillets in the steamer rack. 4. Then top the halibut with sliced lemon. Close and seal the lid. 5. Cook the meal on High Pressure for 9 minutes. Make a quick pressure release.

Cod with Warm Beet and Arugula Salad

Prep time: 15 minutes | Cook time: 8 minutes | Serves 4

- ¼ cup extra-virgin olive oil, divided, plus extra for drizzling
- 1 shallot, sliced thin
- 2 garlic cloves, minced
- 1½ pounds (680 g) small beets, scrubbed, trimmed, and cut into ½-inch wedges
- ½ cup chicken or vegetable broth
- 1 tablespoon dukkah, plus extra for sprinkling
- ¼ teaspoon table salt
- 4 (6-ounce / 170-g) skinless cod fillets, 1½ inches thick
- 1 tablespoon lemon juice
- 2 ounces (57 g) baby arugula

1. Using highest sauté function, heat 1 tablespoon oil in Instant Pot until shimmering. Add shallot and cook until softened, about 2 minutes. Stir in garlic and cook until fragrant, about 30 seconds. Stir in beets and broth. Lock lid in place and close pressure release valve. Select high pressure cook function and cook for 3 minutes. Turn off Instant Pot and quick-release pressure. Carefully remove lid, allowing steam to escape away from you. 2. Fold sheet of aluminum foil into 16 by 6-inch sling. Combine 2 tablespoons oil, dukkah, and salt in bowl, then brush cod with oil mixture. Arrange cod skinned side down in center of sling. Using sling, lower cod into Instant Pot; allow narrow edges of sling to rest along sides of insert. Lock lid in place and close pressure release valve. Select high pressure cook function and cook for 2 minutes. 3. Turn off

Instant Pot and quick-release pressure. Carefully remove lid, allowing steam to escape away from you. Using sling, transfer cod to large plate. Tent with foil and let rest while finishing beet salad. 4. Combine lemon juice and remaining 1 tablespoon oil in large bowl. Using slotted spoon, transfer beets to bowl with oil mixture. Add arugula and gently toss to combine. Season with salt and pepper to taste. 5 Serve cod with salad, sprinkling individual portions with extra dukkah and drizzling with extra oil.

Chili and Turmeric Haddock

Prep time: 10 minutes | Cook time: 5 minutes | Serves 4

- 1 chili pepper, minced
- 1 pound (454 g) haddock, chopped
- ½ teaspoon ground turmeric
- ½ cup fish stock
- 1 cup water

1. In the mixing bowl mix up chili pepper, ground turmeric, and fish stock. 2. Then add chopped haddock and transfer the mixture in the baking mold. 3. Pour water in the instant pot and insert the trivet. 4. Place the baking mold with fish on the trivet and close the lid. 5. Cook the meal on Manual (High Pressure) for 5 minutes. Make a quick pressure release.

Tilapia Fillets with Arugula

Prep time: 5 minutes | Cook time: 4 minutes | Serves 4

- 1 lemon, juiced
- 1 cup water
- 1 pound (454 g) tilapia fillets
- ½ teaspoon cayenne pepper, or more to taste
- 2 teaspoons butter, melted
- Sea salt and ground black pepper, to taste
- ½ teaspoon dried basil
- 2 cups arugula

1. Pour the fresh lemon juice and water into your Instant Pot and insert a steamer basket. 2. Brush the fish fillets with the melted butter. 3. Sprinkle with the cayenne pepper, salt, and black pepper. Place the tilapia fillets in the basket. Sprinkle the dried basil on top. 4. Lock the lid. Select the Manual mode and set the cooking time for 4 minutes at Low Pressure. 5. When the timer beeps, perform a quick pressure release. Carefully remove the lid. 6. Serve with the fresh arugula.

Coconut Shrimp Curry

Prep time: 10 minutes | Cook time: 4 minutes | Serves 5

- 15 ounces (425 g) shrimp, peeled
- 1 teaspoon chili powder
- 1 teaspoon garam masala
- 1 cup coconut milk
- 1 teaspoon olive oil
- ½ teaspoon minced garlic

1. Heat up the instant pot on Sauté mode for 2 minutes. 2. Then add olive oil. Cook the ingredients for 1 minute. 3. Add shrimp and sprinkle them with chili powder, garam masala, minced garlic, and coconut milk. 4. Carefully stir the ingredients and close the lid. 5. Cook the shrimp curry on Manual mode for 1 minute. Make a quick pressure release.

Chunky Fish Soup with Tomatoes

Prep time: 10 minutes | Cook time: 8 minutes | Serves 4

- 2 teaspoons olive oil
- 1 yellow onion, chopped
- 1 bell pepper, sliced
- 1 celery, diced
- 2 garlic cloves, minced
- 3 cups fish stock
- 2 ripe tomatoes, crushed
- ¾ pound (340 g) haddock fillets
- 1 cup shrimp
- 1 tablespoon sweet Hungarian paprika
- 1 teaspoon hot Hungarian paprika
- ½ teaspoon caraway seeds

1. Set the Instant Pot to Sauté. Add and heat the oil. Once hot, add the onions and sauté until soft and fragrant. 2. Add the pepper, celery, and garlic and continue to sauté until soft. 3. Stir in the remaining ingredients. 4. Lock the lid. Select the Manual mode and set the cooking time for 5 minutes at High Pressure. 5. When the timer beeps, perform a quick pressure release. Carefully remove the lid. 6. Divide into serving bowls and serve hot.

Almond Milk Curried Fish

Prep time: 10 minutes | Cook time: 3 minutes | Serves 2

- 8 ounces (227 g) cod fillet, chopped
- 1 teaspoon curry paste
- 1 cup organic almond milk

1. Mix up curry paste and almond milk and pour the liquid in the instant pot. 2. Add chopped cod fillet and close the lid. 3. Cook the fish curry on Manual mode (High Pressure) for 3 minutes. 4. Then make the quick pressure release for 5 minutes.

Garam Masala Fish

Prep time: 10 minutes | Cook time: 10 minutes | Serves 4

- 2 tablespoons sesame oil
- ½ teaspoon cumin seeds
- ½ cup chopped leeks
- 1 teaspoon ginger-garlic paste
- 1 pound (454 g) cod fillets, boneless and sliced
- 2 ripe tomatoes, chopped
- 1½ tablespoons fresh lemon juice
- ½ teaspoon garam masala
- ½ teaspoon turmeric powder
- 1 tablespoon chopped fresh dill leaves
- 1 tablespoon chopped fresh curry leaves
- 1 tablespoon chopped fresh parsley leaves
- Coarse sea salt, to taste
- ½ teaspoon smoked cayenne pepper
- ¼ teaspoon ground black pepper, or more to taste

1. Set the Instant Pot to Sauté. Add and heat the sesame oil until hot. Sauté the cumin seeds for 30 seconds. 2. Add the leeks and cook for another 2 minutes until translucent. Add the ginger-garlic paste and cook for an additional 40 seconds. 3. Stir in the remaining ingredients. 4. Lock the lid. Select the Manual mode and set the cooking time for 6 minutes at Low Pressure. 5. When the timer beeps, perform a quick pressure release. Carefully remove the lid. 6. Serve immediately.

Ahi Tuna and Cherry Tomato Salad

Prep time: 5 minutes | Cook time: 4 minutes | Serves 4

- 1 cup water
- 2 sprigs thyme
- 2 sprigs rosemary
- 2 sprigs parsley
- 1 lemon, sliced
- 1 pound (454 g) ahi tuna
- ⅓ teaspoon ground black pepper
- 1 head lettuce
- 1 cup cherry tomatoes, halved
- 1 red bell pepper, julienned
- 2 tablespoons extra-virgin olive oil
- 1 teaspoon Dijon mustard
- Sea salt, to taste

1. Pour the water into your Instant Pot. Add the thyme, rosemary, parsley, and lemon and insert a trivet. 2. Lay the fish on the trivet and season with the ground black pepper. 3. Lock the lid. Select the Manual mode and set the cooking time for 4 minutes at High Pressure. 4. When the timer beeps, perform a quick pressure release. Carefully remove the lid. 5. In a salad bowl, place the remaining ingredients and toss well. Add the flaked tuna and toss again. 6. Serve chilled.

Italian Salmon

Prep time: 10 minutes | Cook time: 4 minutes | Serves 2

- 10 ounces (283 g) salmon fillet
- 1 teaspoon Italian seasoning
- 1 cup water

1. Pour water and insert the trivet in the instant pot. 2. Then rub the salmon fillet with Italian seasoning and wrap in the foil. 3. Place the wrapped fish on the trivet and close the lid. 4. Cook the meal on Manual mode (High Pressure) for 4 minutes. 5. Make a quick pressure release and remove the fish from the foil. 6. Cut it into servings.

Lemon Shrimp Skewers

Prep time: 10 minutes | Cook time: 2 minutes | Serves 4

- 1 tablespoon lemon juice
- 1 teaspoon coconut aminos
- 12 ounces (340 g) shrimp, peeled
- 1 teaspoon olive oil
- 1 cup water

1. Put the shrimp in the mixing bowl. 2. Add lemon juice, coconut aminos, and olive oil. 3. Then string the shrimp on the skewers. 4. Pour water in the instant pot. 5. Then insert the trivet. 6. Put the shrimp skewers on the trivet. 7. Close the lid and cook the seafood on Manual mode (High Pressure) for 2 minutes. 8. When the time is finished, make a quick pressure release.

Greek Shrimp with Tomatoes and Feta

Prep time: 10 minutes | Cook time: 2 minutes | Serves 6

- 3 tablespoons unsalted butter
- 1 tablespoon garlic
- ½ teaspoon red pepper flakes, or more as needed
- 1½ cups chopped onion
- 1 (14½-ounce / 411-g) can diced tomatoes, undrained
- 1 teaspoon dried oregano
- 1 teaspoon salt
- 1 pound (454 g) frozen shrimp, peeled
- 1 cup crumbled feta cheese
- ½ cup sliced black olives
- ¼ cup chopped parsley

1. Preheat the Instant Pot by selecting Sauté and adjusting to high heat. When the inner cooking pot is hot, add the butter and heat until it foams. Add the garlic and red pepper flakes, and cook just until fragrant, about 1 minute. 2. Add the onion, tomatoes, oregano, and salt, and stir to combine. 3. Add the frozen shrimp. 4. Lock the lid into place. Select Manual and adjust the pressure to Low. Cook for 1 minute. When the cooking is complete, quick-release the pressure. Unlock the lid. 5. Mix the shrimp in with the lovely tomato broth. 6. Allow the mixture to cool slightly. Right before serving, sprinkle with the feta cheese, olives, and parsley. This dish makes a soupy broth, so it's great over mashed cauliflower.

Ginger Cod

Prep time: 10 minutes | Cook time: 20 minutes | Serves 2

- 1 teaspoon ginger paste
- 8 ounces (227 g) cod fillet, chopped
- 1 tablespoon coconut oil
- ¼ cup coconut milk

1. Melt the coconut oil in the instant pot on Sauté mode. 2. Then add ginger paste and coconut milk and bring the mixture to boil. 3. Add chopped cod and sauté the meal for 12 minutes. Stir the fish cubes with the help of the spatula from time to time.

Mascarpone Tilapia with Nutmeg

Prep time: 10 minutes | Cook time: 20 minutes | Serves 2

- 10 ounces (283 g) tilapia
- ½ cup mascarpone
- 1 garlic clove, diced
- 1 teaspoon ground nutmeg
- 1 tablespoon olive oil
- ½ teaspoon salt

1. Pour olive oil in the instant pot. 2. Add diced garlic and sauté it for 4 minutes. 3. Add tilapia and sprinkle it with ground nutmeg. Sauté the fish for 3 minutes per side. 4. Add mascarpone and close the lid. 5. Sauté tilapia for 10 minutes.

Cayenne Cod

Prep time: 10 minutes | Cook time: 10 minutes | Serves 2

- 2 cod fillets
- ¼ teaspoon chili powder
- ½ teaspoon cayenne pepper
- ½ teaspoon dried oregano
- 1 tablespoon lime juice
- 2 tablespoons avocado oil

1. Rub the cod fillets with chili powder, cayenne pepper, dried oregano, and sprinkle with lime juice. 2. Then pour the avocado oil in the instant pot and heat it up on Sauté mode for 2 minutes. 3. Put the cod fillets in the hot oil and cook for 5 minutes. 4. Then flip the fish on another side and cook for 5 minutes more.

Coconut Milk-Braised Squid

Prep time: 10 minutes | Cook time: 20 minutes | Serves 3

- 1 pound (454 g) squid, sliced
- 1 teaspoon sugar-free tomato paste
- 1 cup coconut milk
- 1 teaspoon cayenne pepper
- ½ teaspoon salt

1. Put all ingredients from the list above in the instant pot. 2. Close and seal the lid and cook the squid on Manual (High Pressure) for 20 minutes. 3. When the cooking time is finished, do the quick pressure release. 4. Serve the squid with coconut milk gravy.

Cod with Warm Tabbouleh Salad

Prep time: 10 minutes | Cook time: 6 minutes | Serves 4

- 1 cup medium-grind bulgur, rinsed
- 1 teaspoon table salt, divided
- 1 lemon, sliced ¼ inch thick, plus 2 tablespoons juice
- 4 (6-ounce / 170-g) skinless cod fillets, 1½ inches thick
- 3 tablespoons extra-virgin olive oil, divided, plus extra for drizzling
- ¼ teaspoon pepper
- 1 small shallot, minced
- 10 ounces (283 g) cherry tomatoes, halved
- 1 cup chopped fresh parsley
- ½ cup chopped fresh mint

1. Arrange trivet included with Instant Pot in base of insert and add ½ cup water. Fold sheet of aluminum foil into 16 by 6-inch sling, then rest 1½-quart round soufflé dish in center of sling. Combine 1 cup water, bulgur, and ½ teaspoon salt in dish. Using sling, lower soufflé dish into pot and onto trivet; allow narrow edges of sling to rest along sides of insert. 2. Lock lid in place and close pressure release valve. Select high pressure cook function and cook for 3 minutes. Turn off Instant Pot and quick-release pressure. Carefully remove lid, allowing steam to escape away from you. Using sling, transfer soufflé dish to wire rack; set aside to cool. Remove trivet; do not discard sling or water in pot. 3. Arrange lemon slices widthwise in 2 rows across center of sling. Brush cod with 1 tablespoon oil and sprinkle with remaining ½ teaspoon salt and pepper. Arrange cod skinned side down in even layer on top of lemon slices. Using sling, lower cod into Instant Pot; allow narrow edges of sling to rest along sides of insert. Lock lid in place and close pressure release valve. Select high pressure cook function and cook for 3 minutes. 4. Meanwhile, whisk remaining 2 tablespoons oil, lemon juice, and shallot together in large bowl. Add bulgur, tomatoes, parsley, and mint, and gently toss to combine. Season with salt and pepper to taste. 5. Turn off Instant Pot and quick-

release pressure. Carefully remove lid, allowing steam to escape away from you. Using sling, transfer cod to large plate. Gently lift and tilt fillets with spatula to remove lemon slices. Serve cod with salad, drizzling individual portions with extra oil.

Mediterranean Salmon with Whole-Wheat Couscous

Prep time: 5 minutes | Cook time: 30 minutes | Serves 4

Couscous

- 1 cup whole-wheat couscous
- 1 cup water
- 1 tablespoon extra-virgin olive oil
- 1 teaspoon dried basil
- ¼ teaspoon fine sea salt
- 1 pint cherry or grape tomatoes, halved
- 8 ounces zucchini, halved lengthwise, then sliced crosswise ¼ inch thick
- Salmon
- 1 pound skinless salmon

fillet
- 2 teaspoons extra-virgin olive oil
- 1 tablespoon fresh lemon juice
- 1 garlic clove, minced
- ¼ teaspoon dried oregano
- ¼ teaspoon fine sea salt
- ¼ teaspoon freshly ground black pepper
- 1 tablespoon capers, drained
- Lemon wedges for serving

1. Pour 1 cup water into the Instant Pot. Have ready two-tier stackable stainless-steel containers. 2. To make the couscous: In one of the containers, stir together the couscous, water, oil, basil, and salt. Sprinkle the tomatoes and zucchini over the top. 3. To make the salmon: Place the salmon fillet in the second container. In a small bowl, whisk together the oil, lemon juice, garlic, oregano, salt, pepper, and capers. Spoon the oil mixture over the top of the salmon. 4. Place the container with the couscous and vegetables on the bottom and the salmon container on top. Cover the top container with its lid and then latch the containers together. Grasping the handle, lower the containers into the Instant Pot. 5. Secure the lid and set the Pressure Release to Sealing. Select the Pressure Cook or Manual setting and set the cooking time for 20 minutes at high pressure. (The pot will take about 10 minutes to come up to pressure before the cooking program begins.) 6. When the cooking program ends, let the pressure release naturally for 5 minutes, then move the Pressure Release to Venting to release any remaining steam. Open the pot and, wearing heat-resistant mitts, lift out the stacked containers. Unlatch, unstack, and open the containers, taking care not to get burned by the steam. 7. Using a fork, fluff the couscous and mix in the vegetables. Spoon the couscous onto plates, then use a spatula to cut the salmon into four pieces and place a piece on top of each couscous serving. Serve right away, with lemon wedges on the side.

Dill Salmon Cakes

Prep time: 15 minutes | Cook time: 10 minutes | Serves 4

- 1 pound (454 g) salmon fillet, chopped
- 1 tablespoon chopped dill
- 2 eggs, beaten
- ½ cup almond flour
- 1 tablespoon coconut oil

1. Put the chopped salmon, dill, eggs, and almond flour in the food processor. 2. Blend the mixture until it is smooth. 3. Then make the small balls (cakes) from the salmon mixture. 4. After this, heat up the coconut oil on Sauté mode for 3 minutes. 5. Put the salmon cakes in the instant pot in one layer and cook them on Sauté mode for 2 minutes from each side or until they are light brown.

Cajun Cod Fillet

Prep time: 10 minutes | Cook time: 4 minutes | Serves 2

- 10 ounces (283 g) cod fillet
- 1 tablespoon olive oil
- 1 teaspoon Cajun seasoning
- 2 tablespoons coconut aminos

1. Sprinkle the cod fillet with coconut aminos and Cajun seasoning. 2. Then heat up olive oil in the instant pot on Sauté mode. 3. Add the spiced cod fillet and cook it for 4 minutes from each side. 4. Then cut it into halves and sprinkle with the oily liquid from the instant pot.

Shrimp and Asparagus Risotto

Prep time: 15 minutes | Cook time: 20 minutes | Serves 4

- ¼ cup extra-virgin olive oil, divided
- 8 ounces (227 g) asparagus, trimmed and cut on bias into 1-inch lengths
- ½ onion, chopped fine
- ¼ teaspoon table salt
- 1½ cups Arborio rice
- 3 garlic cloves, minced
- ½ cup dry white wine
- 3 cups chicken or vegetable broth, plus extra as needed
- 1 pound (454 g) large shrimp (26 to 30 per pound), peeled and deveined
- 2 ounces (57 g) Parmesan cheese, grated (1 cup)
- 1 tablespoon lemon juice
- 1 tablespoon minced fresh chives

1. Using highest sauté function, heat 1 tablespoon oil in Instant Pot until shimmering. Add asparagus, partially cover, and cook until just crisp-tender, about 4 minutes. Using slotted spoon, transfer asparagus to bowl; set aside. 2. Add onion, 2 tablespoons oil, and salt to now-empty pot and cook, using highest sauté function, until onion is softened, about 5 minutes. Stir in rice and garlic and cook until grains are translucent around edges, about 3 minutes. Stir in wine and cook until nearly evaporated, about 1 minute. 3. Stir in broth, scraping up any rice that sticks to bottom of pot. Lock lid in place and close pressure release valve. Select high pressure cook function and cook for 7 minutes. 4. Turn off Instant Pot and quick-release pressure. Carefully remove lid, allowing steam to escape away from you. Stir shrimp and asparagus into risotto, cover, and let sit until shrimp are opaque throughout, 5 to 7 minutes. Add Parmesan and remaining 1 tablespoon oil, and stir vigorously until risotto becomes creamy. Adjust consistency with extra hot broth as needed. Stir in lemon juice and season with salt and pepper to taste. Sprinkle individual portions with chives before serving.

Parmesan Salmon Loaf

Prep time: 15 minutes | Cook time: 25 minutes | Serves 6

- 12 ounces (340 g) salmon, boiled and shredded
- 3 eggs, beaten
- ½ cup almond flour
- 1 teaspoon garlic powder
- ¼ cup grated Parmesan
- 1 teaspoon butter, softened
- 1 cup water, for cooking

1. Pour water in the instant pot. 2. Mix up the rest of the ingredients in the mixing bowl and stir until smooth. 3. After this, transfer the salmon mixture in the loaf pan and flatten; insert the pan in the instant pot. Close and seal the lid. 4. Cook the meal on Manual mode (High Pressure) for 25 minutes. 5. When the cooking time is finished, make a quick pressure release and cool the loaf well before serving.

Tuna Spinach Cakes

Prep time: 15 minutes | Cook time: 8 minutes | Serves 4

- 10 ounces (283 g) tuna, shredded
- 1 cup spinach
- 1 egg, beaten
- 1 teaspoon ground coriander
- 2 tablespoon coconut flakes
- 1 tablespoon avocado oil

1. Blend the spinach in the blender until smooth. 2. Then transfer it in the mixing bowl and add tuna, egg, and ground coriander. 3. Add coconut flakes and stir the mass with the help of the spoon. 4. Heat up avocado oil in the instant pot on Sauté mode for 2 minutes. 5. Then make the medium size cakes from the tuna mixture and place them in the hot oil. 6. Cook the tuna cakes on Sauté mode for 3 minutes. Then flip the on another side and cook for 3 minutes more or until they are light brown.

Salmon with Garlicky Broccoli Rabe and White Beans

Prep time: 20 minutes | Cook time: 10 minutes | Serves 4

- 2 tablespoons extra-virgin olive oil, plus extra for drizzling
- 4 garlic cloves, sliced thin
- ½ cup chicken or vegetable broth
- ¼ teaspoon red pepper flakes
- 1 lemon, sliced ¼ inch thick, plus lemon wedges for serving
- 4 (6-ounce / 170-g) skinless salmon fillets, 1½ inches thick
- ½ teaspoon table salt
- ¼ teaspoon pepper
- 1 pound (454 g) broccoli rabe, trimmed and cut into 1-inch pieces
- 1 (15-ounce / 425-g) can cannellini beans, rinsed

1. Using highest sauté function, cook oil and garlic in Instant Pot until garlic is fragrant and light golden brown, about 3 minutes. Using slotted spoon, transfer garlic to paper towel–lined plate and season with salt to taste; set aside for serving. Turn off Instant Pot, then stir in broth and pepper flakes. 2. Fold sheet of aluminum foil into 16 by 6-inch sling. Arrange lemon slices widthwise in 2 rows across center of sling. Sprinkle flesh side of salmon with salt and pepper, then arrange skinned side down on top of lemon slices. Using sling, lower salmon into Instant Pot; allow narrow edges of sling to rest along sides of insert. Lock lid in place and close pressure release valve. Select high pressure cook function and cook for 3 minutes. 3. Turn off Instant Pot and quick-release pressure. Carefully remove lid, allowing steam to escape away from you. Using sling, transfer salmon to large plate. Tent with foil and let rest while preparing broccoli rabe mixture. 4. Stir broccoli rabe and beans into cooking liquid, partially cover, and cook, using highest sauté function, until broccoli rabe is tender, about 5 minutes. Season with salt and pepper to taste. Gently lift and tilt salmon fillets with spatula to remove lemon slices. Serve salmon with broccoli rabe mixture and lemon wedges, sprinkling individual portions with garlic chips and drizzling with extra oil.

Foil-Packet Salmon

Prep time: 2 minutes | Cook time: 7 minutes | Serves 2

- 2 (3-ounce / 85-g) salmon fillets
- ¼ teaspoon garlic powder
- 1 teaspoon salt
- ¼ teaspoon pepper
- ¼ teaspoon dried dill
- ½ lemon
- 1 cup water

1. Place each filet of salmon on a square of foil, skin-side down. 2. Season with garlic powder, salt, and pepper and squeeze the lemon juice over the fish. 3. Cut the lemon into four slices and place two on each filet. Close the foil packets by folding over edges. 4. Add the water to the Instant Pot and insert a trivet. Place the foil packets on the trivet. 5. Secure the lid. Select the Steam mode and set the cooking time for 7 minutes at Low Pressure. 6. Once cooking is complete, do a quick pressure release. Carefully open the lid. 7. Check the internal temperature with a meat thermometer to ensure the thickest part of the filets reached at least 145ºF (63ºC). Salmon should easily flake when fully cooked. Serve immediately.

Salmon with Wild Rice and Orange Salad

Prep time: 20 minutes | Cook time: 18 minutes | Serves 4

- 1 cup wild rice, picked over and rinsed
- 3 tablespoons extra-virgin olive oil, divided
- 1½ teaspoon table salt, for cooking rice
- 2 oranges, plus ⅛ teaspoon grated orange zest
- 4 (6-ounce / 170-g) skinless salmon fillets, 1½ inches thick
- 1 teaspoon ground dried
- Aleppo pepper
- ½ teaspoon table salt
- 1 small shallot, minced
- 1 tablespoon red wine vinegar
- 2 teaspoons Dijon mustard
- 1 teaspoon honey
- 2 carrots, peeled and shredded
- ¼ cup chopped fresh mint

1. Combine 6 cups water, rice, 1 tablespoon oil, and 1½ teaspoons salt in Instant Pot. Lock lid in place and close pressure release valve. Select high pressure cook function and cook for 15 minutes. Turn off Instant Pot and let pressure release naturally for 15 minutes. Quick-release any remaining pressure, then carefully remove lid, allowing steam to escape away from you. Drain rice and set aside to cool slightly. Wipe pot clean with paper towels. 2. Add ½ cup water to now-empty Instant Pot. Fold sheet of aluminum foil into 16 by 6-inch sling. Slice 1 orange ¼ inch thick and shingle widthwise in 3 rows across center of sling. Sprinkle flesh side of salmon with Aleppo pepper and ½ teaspoon salt, then arrange skinned side down on top of orange slices. Using sling, lower salmon into Instant Pot; allow narrow edges of sling to rest along sides of insert. Lock lid in place and close pressure release valve. Select high pressure cook function and cook for 3 minutes. 3. Meanwhile, cut away peel and pith from remaining 1 orange. Quarter orange, then slice crosswise into ¼-inch pieces. Whisk remaining 2 tablespoons oil, shallot, vinegar, mustard, honey, and orange zest together in large bowl. Add rice, orange pieces, carrots, and mint, and gently toss to combine. Season with salt and pepper to taste. 4. Turn off Instant Pot and quick-release pressure. Carefully remove lid, allowing steam to escape away from you. Using sling, transfer salmon to large plate. Gently lift and tilt fillets with spatula to remove orange slices. Serve salmon with salad.

Salmon with Lemon-Garlic Mashed Cauliflower

Prep time: 15 minutes | Cook time: 10 minutes | Serves 4

- 2 tablespoons extra-virgin olive oil
- 4 garlic cloves, peeled and smashed
- ½ cup chicken or vegetable broth
- ¾ teaspoon table salt, divided
- 1 large head cauliflower (3 pounds / 1.4 kg), cored and
- cut into 2-inch florets
- 4 (6-ounce / 170-g) skinless salmon fillets, 1½ inches thick
- ½ teaspoon ras el hanout
- ½ teaspoon grated lemon zest
- 3 scallions, sliced thin
- 1 tablespoon sesame seeds, toasted

1. Using highest sauté function, cook oil and garlic in Instant Pot until garlic is fragrant and light golden brown, about 3 minutes. Turn off Instant Pot, then stir in broth and ¼ teaspoon salt. Arrange cauliflower in pot in even layer. 2. Fold sheet of aluminum foil into 16 by 6-inch sling. Sprinkle flesh side of salmon with ras el hanout and remaining ½ teaspoon salt, then arrange skinned side down in center of sling. Using sling, lower salmon into Instant Pot on top of cauliflower; allow narrow edges of sling to rest along sides of insert. Lock lid in place and close pressure release valve. Select high pressure cook function and cook for 2 minutes. 3. Turn off Instant Pot and quick-release pressure. Carefully remove lid, allowing steam to escape away from you. Using sling, transfer salmon to large plate. Tent with foil and let rest while finishing cauliflower. 4. Using potato masher, mash cauliflower mixture until no large chunks remain. Using highest sauté function, cook cauliflower, stirring often, until slightly thickened, about 3 minutes. Stir in lemon zest and season with salt and pepper to taste. Serve salmon with cauliflower, sprinkling individual portions with scallions and sesame seeds.

Foil-Pack Haddock with Spinach

Prep time: 15 minutes | Cook time: 15 minutes | Serves 4

- 12 ounces (340 g) haddock fillet
- 1 cup spinach
- 1 tablespoon avocado oil
- 1 teaspoon minced garlic
- ½ teaspoon ground coriander
- 1 cup water, for cooking

1. Blend the spinach until smooth and mix up with avocado oil, ground coriander, and minced garlic. 2. Then cut the haddock into 4 fillets and place on the foil. 3. Top the fish fillets with spinach mixture and place them on the rack. 4. Pour water and insert the rack in the instant pot. 5. Close and seal the lid and cook the haddock on Manual (High Pressure) for 15 minutes. 6. Do a quick pressure release.

Trout Casserole

Prep time: 5 minutes | Cook time: 10 minutes | Serves 3

- 1½ cups water
- 1½ tablespoons olive oil
- 3 plum tomatoes, sliced
- ½ teaspoon dried oregano
- 1 teaspoon dried basil
- 3 trout fillets
- ½ teaspoon cayenne pepper, or more to taste
- ⅓ teaspoon black pepper
- Salt, to taste
- 1 bay leaf
- 1 cup shredded Pepper Jack cheese

1. Pour the water into your Instant Pot and insert a trivet. 2. Grease a baking dish with the olive oil. Add the tomatoes slices to the baking dish and sprinkle with the oregano and basil. 3. Add the fish fillets and season with the cayenne pepper, black pepper, and salt. Add the bay leaf. Lower the baking dish onto the trivet. 4. Lock the lid. Select the Manual mode and set the cooking time for 10 minutes at High Pressure. 5. When the timer beeps, perform a quick pressure release. Carefully remove the lid. 6. Scatter the Pepper Jack cheese on top, lock the lid, and allow the cheese to melt. 7. Serve warm.

Salmon Steaks with Garlicky Yogurt

Prep time: 2 minutes | Cook time: 4 minutes | Serves 4

- 1 cup water
- 2 tablespoons olive oil

Garlicky Yogurt:
- 1 (8-ounce / 227-g) container full-fat Greek yogurt
- 4 salmon steaks
- Coarse sea salt and ground black pepper, to taste
- 2 cloves garlic, minced
- 2 tablespoons mayonnaise
- ⅓ teaspoon Dijon mustard

1. Pour the water into the Instant Pot and insert a trivet. 2. Rub the olive oil into the fish and sprinkle with the salt and black pepper on all sides. Put the fish on the trivet. 3. Lock the lid. Select the Manual mode and set the cooking time for 4 minutes at High Pressure. 4. When the timer beeps, perform a quick pressure release. Carefully remove the lid. 5. Meanwhile, stir together all the ingredients for the garlicky yogurt in a bowl. 6. Serve the salmon steaks alongside the garlicky yogurt.

Snapper in Spicy Tomato Sauce

Prep time: 5 minutes | Cook time: 5 minutes | Serves 6

- 2 teaspoons coconut oil, melted
- 1 teaspoon celery seeds
- ½ teaspoon fresh grated ginger
- ½ teaspoon cumin seeds
- 1 yellow onion, chopped
- 2 cloves garlic, minced
- 1½ pounds (680 g) snapper fillets
- ¾ cup vegetable broth
- 1 (4-ounce / 113-g) can fire-roasted diced tomatoes
- 1 bell pepper, sliced
- 1 jalapeño pepper, minced
- Sea salt and ground black pepper, to taste
- ¼ teaspoon chili flakes
- ½ teaspoon turmeric powder

1. Set the Instant Pot to Sauté. Add and heat the sesame oil until hot. Sauté the celery seeds, fresh ginger, and cumin seeds. 2. Add the onion and continue to sauté until softened and fragrant. 3. Mix in the minced garlic and continue to cook for 30 seconds. Add the remaining ingredients and stir well. 4. Lock the lid. Select the Manual mode and set the cooking time for 3 minutes at Low Pressure. 5. When the timer beeps, perform a quick pressure release. Carefully remove the lid. 6. Serve warm

Lemon Salmon with Tomatoes

Prep time: 7 minutes | Cook time: 21 minutes | Serves 4

- 1 tablespoon unsalted butter
- 3 cloves garlic, minced
- ¼ cup lemon juice
- 1¼ cups fresh or canned diced tomatoes
- 1 tablespoon chopped fresh flat-leaf parsley, plus more
- for garnish
- ¼ teaspoon ground black pepper
- 4 (6-ounce / 170-g) skinless salmon fillets
- 1 teaspoon fine sea salt
- Lemon wedges, for garnish

1. Add the butter to your Instant Pot and select the Sauté mode. Once melted, add the garlic (if using) and sauté for 1 minute. 2. Add the roasted garlic, lemon juice, tomatoes, parsley, and pepper. Let simmer for 5 minutes, or until the liquid has reduced a bit. 3. Meanwhile, rinse the salmon and pat dry with a paper towel. Sprinkle on all sides with the salt. 4. Using a spatula, push the reduced sauce to one side of the pot and place the salmon on the other side. Spoon the sauce over the salmon. 5. Sauté uncovered for another 15 minutes, or until the salmon flakes easily with a fork. The timing will depend on the thickness of the fillets. 6. Transfer the salmon to a serving plate. Serve with the sauce and garnish with the parsley and lemon wedges.

Steamed Lobster Tails with Thyme

Prep time: 10 minutes | Cook time: 4 minutes | Serves 4

- 4 lobster tails
- 1 tablespoon butter, softened
- 1 teaspoon dried thyme
- 1 cup water

1. Pour water and insert the steamer rack in the instant pot. 2. Put the lobster tails on the rack and close the lid. 3. Cook the meal on Manual mode (High Pressure) for 4 minutes. Make a quick pressure release. 4. After this, mix up butter and dried thyme. Peel the lobsters and rub them with thyme butter.

Caprese Salmon

Prep time: 10 minutes | Cook time: 15 minutes | Serves 2

- 10 ounces (283 g) salmon fillet (2 fillets)
- 4 ounces (113 g) Mozzarella, sliced
- 4 cherry tomatoes, sliced
- 1 teaspoon erythritol
- 1 teaspoon dried basil
- ½ teaspoon ground black pepper
- 1 tablespoon apple cider vinegar
- 1 tablespoon butter
- 1 cup water, for cooking

1. Grease the mold with butter and put the salmon inside. 2. Sprinkle the fish with erythritol, dried basil, ground black pepper, and apple cider vinegar. 3. Then top the salmon with tomatoes and Mozzarella. 4. Pour water and insert the steamer rack in the instant pot. 5. Put the fish on the rack. 6. Close and seal the lid. 7. Cook the meal on Manual mode at High Pressure for 15 minutes. Make a quick pressure release.

Lemon Butter Mahi Mahi

Prep time: 10 minutes | Cook time: 9 minutes | Serves 4

- 1 pound (454 g) mahi-mahi fillet
- 1 teaspoon grated lemon zest
- 1 tablespoon lemon juice
- 1 tablespoon butter, softened
- ½ teaspoon salt
- 1 cup water, for cooking

1. Cut the fish on 4 servings and sprinkle with lemon zest, lemon juice, salt, and rub with softened butter. 2. Then put the fish in the baking pan in one layer. 3. Pour water and insert the steamer rack in the instant pot. 4. Put the mold with fish on the rack. Close and seal the lid. 5. Cook the Mahi Mahi on Manual mode (High Pressure) for 9 minutes. Make a quick pressure release.

Salmon Fillets and Bok Choy

- 1½ cups water
- 2 tablespoons unsalted butter
- 4 (1-inch thick) salmon fillets
- ½ teaspoon cayenne pepper
- Sea salt and freshly ground

- pepper, to taste
- 2 cups Bok choy, sliced
- 1 cup chicken broth
- 3 cloves garlic, minced
- 1 teaspoon grated lemon zest
- ½ teaspoon dried dill weed

1. Pour the water into your Instant Pot and insert a trivet. 2. Brush the salmon with the melted butter and season with the cayenne pepper, salt, and black pepper on all sides. 3. Lock the lid. Select the Manual mode and set the cooking time for 3 minutes at Low Pressure. 4. When the timer beeps, perform a quick pressure release. Carefully remove the lid. 5. Add the remaining ingredients. 6. Lock the lid. Select the Manual mode and set the cooking time for 5 minutes at High Pressure. 7. When the timer beeps, perform a quick pressure release. Carefully remove the lid. 8. Serve the poached salmon with the veggies on the side.

Lemony Fish and Asparagus

- 2 lemons
- 2 cups cold water
- 2 tablespoons extra-virgin olive oil
- 4 (4-ounce / 113-g) white fish fillets, such as cod or haddock

- 1 teaspoon fine sea salt
- 1 teaspoon ground black pepper
- 1 bundle asparagus, ends trimmed
- 2 tablespoons lemon juice
- Fresh dill, for garnish

1. Grate the zest off the lemons until you have about 1 tablespoon and set the zest aside. Slice the lemons into ⅛-inch slices. 2. Pour the water into the Instant Pot. Add 1 tablespoon of the olive oil to each of two stackable steamer pans. 3. Sprinkle the fish on all sides with the lemon zest, salt, and pepper. 4. Arrange two fillets in each steamer pan and top each with the lemon slices and then the asparagus. Sprinkle the asparagus with the salt and drizzle the lemon juice over the top. 5. Stack the steamer pans in the Instant Pot. Cover the top steamer pan with its lid. 6. Lock the lid. Select the Manual mode and set the cooking time for 3 minutes at High

Pressure. 7. Once cooking is complete, do a natural pressure release for 7 minutes, then release any remaining pressure. Carefully open the lid. 8. Lift the steamer pans out of the Instant Pot. 9. Transfer the fish and asparagus to a serving plate. Garnish with the lemon slices and dill. 10. Serve immediately.

Fish Bake with Veggies

- 1½ cups water
- Cooking spray
- 2 ripe tomatoes, sliced
- 2 cloves garlic, minced
- 1 teaspoon dried oregano
- 1 teaspoon dried basil
- ½ teaspoon dried rosemary
- 1 red onion, sliced

- 1 head cauliflower, cut into florets
- 1 pound (454 g) tilapia fillets, sliced
- Sea salt, to taste
- 1 tablespoon olive oil
- 1 cup crumbled feta cheese
- ⅓ cup Kalamata olives, pitted and halved

1. Pour the water into your Instant Pot and insert a trivet. 2. Spritz a casserole dish with cooking spray. Add the tomato slices to the dish. Scatter the top with the garlic, oregano, basil, and rosemary. 3. Mix in the onion and cauliflower. Arrange the fish fillets on top. Sprinkle with the salt and drizzle with the olive oil. 4. Place the feta cheese and Kalamata olives on top. Lower the dish onto the trivet. 5. Lock the lid. Select the Manual mode and set the cooking time for 5 minutes at High Pressure. 6. When the timer beeps, perform a quick pressure release. Carefully remove the lid. 7. Allow to cool for 5 minutes before serving.

Clam Chowder with Bacon and Celery

- 5 ounces (142 g) clams
- 1 ounce (28 g) bacon, chopped
- 3 ounces (85 g) celery,

- chopped
- ½ cup water
- ½ cup heavy cream

1. Cook the bacon on Sauté mode for 1 minute. 2. Then add clams, celery, water, and heavy cream. 3. Close and seal the lid. 4. Cook the seafood on steam mode (High Pressure) for 3 minutes. Make a quick pressure release. 5. Ladle the clams with the heavy cream mixture in the bowls.

Salade Niçoise with Oil-Packed Tuna

- 8 ounces small red potatoes, quartered
- 8 ounces green beans, trimmed
- 4 large eggs
- french vinaigrette
- 2 tablespoons extra-virgin olive oil
- 2 tablespoons cold-pressed avocado oil
- 2 tablespoons white wine vinegar
- 1 tablespoon water
- 1 teaspoon Dijon mustard
- ½ teaspoon dried oregano
- ¼ teaspoon fine sea salt
- 1 tablespoon minced shallot
- 2 hearts romaine lettuce, leaves separated and torn into bite-size pieces
- ½ cup grape tomatoes, halved
- ¼ cup pitted Niçoise or Greek olives
- One 7 ounces can oil-packed tuna, drained and flaked
- Freshly ground black pepper
- 1 tablespoon chopped fresh flat-leaf parsley

1. Pour 1 cup water into the Instant Pot and place a steamer basket into the pot. Add the potatoes, green beans, and eggs to the basket. 2. Secure the lid and set the Pressure Release to Sealing. Select the Steam setting and set the cooking time for 3 minutes at high pressure. (The pot will take about 15 minutes to come up to pressure before the cooking program begins.) 3. To make the vinaigrette: While the vegetables and eggs are steaming, in a small jar or other small container with a tight-fitting lid, combine the olive oil, avocado oil, vinegar, water, mustard, oregano, salt, and shallot and shake vigorously to emulsify. Set aside. 4. Prepare an ice bath. 5. When the cooking program ends, perform a quick release by moving the Pressure Release to Venting. Open the pot and, wearing heat-resistant mitts, lift out the steamer basket. Using tongs, transfer the eggs and green beans to the ice bath, leaving the potatoes in the steamer basket. 6. While the eggs and green beans are cooling, divide the lettuce, tomatoes, olives, and tuna among four shallow individual bowls. Drain the eggs and green beans. Peel and halve the eggs lengthwise, then arrange them on the salads along with the green beans and potatoes. 7. Spoon the vinaigrette over the salads and sprinkle with the pepper and parsley. Serve right away.

Chapter 5

Snacks and Appetizers

Chapter 5 Snacks and Appetizers

Buffalo Chicken Meatballs

Prep time: 5 minutes | Cook time: 10 minutes | Serves 4

- 1 pound (454 g) ground chicken
- ½ cup almond flour
- 2 tablespoons cream cheese
- 1 packet dry ranch dressing mix
- ½ teaspoon salt
- ¼ teaspoon pepper
- ¼ teaspoon garlic powder
- 1 cup water
- 2 tablespoons butter, melted
- ⅓ cup hot sauce
- ¼ cup crumbled feta cheese
- ¼ cup sliced green onion

1. In large bowl, mix ground chicken, almond flour, cream cheese, ranch, salt, pepper, and garlic powder. Roll mixture into 16 balls. 2. Place meatballs on steam rack and add 1 cup water to Instant Pot. Click lid closed. Press the Meat/Stew button and set time for 10 minutes. 3. Combine butter and hot sauce. When timer beeps, remove meatballs and place in clean large bowl. Toss in hot sauce mixture. Top with sprinkled feta and green onions to serve.

Cauliflower Cheese Balls

Prep time: 5 minutes | Cook time: 21 minutes | Serves 8

- 1 cup water
- 1 head cauliflower, broken into florets
- 1 cup shredded Asiago cheese
- ½ cup grated Parmesan cheese
- 2 eggs, beaten
- 2 tablespoons butter
- 2 tablespoons minced fresh chives
- 1 garlic clove, minced
- ½ teaspoon cayenne pepper
- Coarse sea salt and white pepper, to taste

1. Pour the water into the Instant Pot and insert a steamer basket. Place the cauliflower in the basket. 2. Lock the lid. Select the Manual mode and set the cooking time for 3 minutes at High Pressure. 3. When the timer beeps, perform a quick pressure release. Carefully remove the lid. 4. Transfer the cauliflower to a food processor, along with the remaining ingredients. Pulse until everything is well combined. 5. Form the mixture into bite-sized balls and place them on a baking sheet. 6. Bake in the preheated oven at 400°F (205°C) for 18 minutes until golden brown. Flip the balls halfway through the cooking time. Cool for 5 minutes before serving.

Cabbage and Broccoli Slaw

Prep time: 5 minutes | Cook time: 10 minutes | Serves 6

- 2 cups broccoli slaw
- ½ head cabbage, thinly sliced
- ¼ cup chopped kale
- 4 tablespoons butter
- 1 teaspoon salt
- ¼ teaspoon pepper

1. Press the Sauté button and add all ingredients to Instant Pot. Stir-fry for 7 to 10 minutes until cabbage softens. Serve warm.

Broccoli with Garlic-Herb Cheese Sauce

Prep time: 5 minutes | Cook time: 3 minutes | Serves 4

- ½ cup water
- 1 pound (454 g) broccoli (frozen or fresh)
- ½ cup heavy cream
- 1 tablespoon butter
- ½ cup shredded Cheddar cheese
- 3 tablespoons garlic and herb cheese spread
- Pinch of salt
- Pinch of black pepper

1. Add the water to the pot and place the trivet inside. 2. Put the steamer basket on top of the trivet. Place the broccoli in the basket. 3. Close the lid and seal the vent. Cook on Low Pressure for 1 minute. Quick release the steam. Press Cancel. 4. Carefully remove the steamer basket from the pot and drain the water. If you steamed a full bunch of broccoli, pull the florets off the stem. (Chop the stem into bite-size pieces, it's surprisingly creamy.) 5. Turn the pot to Sauté mode. Add the cream and butter. Stir continuously while the butter melts and the cream warms up. 6. When the cream begins to bubble on the edges, add the Cheddar cheese, cheese spread, salt, and pepper. Whisk continuously until the cheeses are melted and a sauce consistency is reached, 1 to 2 minutes. 7. Top one-fourth of the broccoli with 2 tablespoons cheese sauce.

Creamy Scallion Dip

Prep time: 10 minutes | Cook time: 11 minutes | Serves 4

- 5 ounces (142 g) scallions, diced
- 4 tablespoons cream cheese
- 1 tablespoon chopped fresh parsley
- 1 teaspoon garlic powder
- 2 tablespoons coconut cream
- ½ teaspoon salt
- 1 teaspoon coconut oil

1. Heat up the instant pot on Sauté mode. 2. Then add coconut oil and melt it. 3. Add diced scallions and sauté it for 6 to 7 minutes or until it is light brown. 4. Add cream cheese, parsley, garlic powder, salt, and coconut cream. 5. Close the instant pot lid and cook the scallions dip for 5 minutes on Manual mode (High Pressure). 6. Make a quick pressure release. Blend the dip will it is smooth if desired.

Curried Broccoli Skewers

Prep time: 15 minutes | Cook time: 1 minute | Serves 2

- 1 cup broccoli florets
- ½ teaspoon curry paste
- 2 tablespoons coconut cream
- 1 cup water, for cooking

1. In the shallow bowl mix up curry paste and coconut cream. 2. Then sprinkle the broccoli florets with curry paste mixture and string on the skewers. 3. Pour water and insert the steamer rack in the instant pot. 4. Place the broccoli skewers on the rack. Close and seal the lid. 5. Cook the meal on Manual mode (High Pressure) for 1 minute. 6. Make a quick pressure release.

Lemon-Butter Mushrooms

Prep time: 10 minutes | Cook time: 4 minutes | Serves 2

- 1 cup cremini mushrooms, sliced
- ½ cup water
- 1 tablespoon lemon juice
- 1 teaspoon almond butter
- 1 teaspoon grated lemon zest
- ½ teaspoon salt
- ½ teaspoon dried thyme

1. Combine all the ingredients in the Instant Pot. 2. Secure the lid. Select the Manual mode and set the cooking time for 4 minutes at High Pressure. 3. Once cooking is complete, do a natural pressure release for 5 minutes, then release any remaining pressure. Carefully open the lid. 4. Serve warm.

Creamy Jalapeño Chicken Dip

Prep time: 5 minutes | Cook time: 12 minutes | Serves 10

- 1 pound boneless chicken breast
- 8 ounces low-fat cream cheese
- 3 jalapeños, seeded and
- sliced
- ½ cup water
- 8 ounces reduced-fat shredded cheddar cheese
- ¾ cup low-fat sour cream

1. Place the chicken, cream cheese, jalapeños, and water in the inner pot of the Instant Pot. 2. Secure the lid so it's locked and turn the vent to sealing. 3. Press Manual and set the Instant Pot for 12 minutes on high pressure. 4. When cooking time is up, turn off Instant Pot, do a quick release of the remaining pressure, then remove lid. 5. Shred the chicken between 2 forks, either in the pot or on a cutting board, then place back in the inner pot. 6. Stir in the shredded cheese and sour cream.

Taco Beef Bites

Prep time: 10 minutes | Cook time: 15 minutes | Serves 6

- 10 ounces (283 g) ground beef
- 3 eggs, beaten
- ⅓ cup shredded Mozzarella
- cheese
- 1 teaspoon taco seasoning
- 1 teaspoon sesame oil

1. In the mixing bowl mix up ground beef, eggs, Mozzarella, and taco seasoning. 2. Then make the small meat bites from the mixture. 3. Heat up sesame oil in the instant pot. 4. Put the meat bites in the hot oil and cook them for 5 minutes from each side on Sauté mode.

Zucchini and Cheese Tots

Prep time: 15 minutes | Cook time: 10 minutes | Serves 6

- 4 ounces (113 g) Parmesan, grated
- 4 ounces (113 g) Cheddar cheese, grated
- 1 zucchini, grated
- 1 egg, beaten
- 1 teaspoon dried oregano
- 1 tablespoon coconut oil

1. In the mixing bowl, mix up Parmesan, Cheddar cheese, zucchini, egg, and dried oregano. 2. Make the small tots with the help of the fingertips. 3. Then melt the coconut oil in the instant pot on Sauté mode. 4. Put the prepared zucchini tots in the hot coconut oil and cook them for 3 minutes from each side or until they are light brown. Cool the zucchini tots for 5 minutes.

Chicken and Cabbage Salad

Prep time: 15 minutes | Cook time: 10 minutes | Serves 4

- 12 ounces (340 g) chicken fillet, chopped
- 1 teaspoon Cajun seasoning
- 1 tablespoon coconut oil
- 1 cup chopped Chinese cabbage
- 1 tablespoon avocado oil
- 1 teaspoon sesame seeds

1. Sprinkle the chopped chicken with the Cajun seasoning. 2. Set your Instant Pot to Sauté and heat the coconut oil. Add the chicken and cook for 10 minutes, stirring occasionally. 3. When the chicken is cooked, transfer to a salad bowl. Add the cabbage, avocado oil, and sesame seeds and gently toss to combine. Serve immediately.

Instant Popcorn

Prep time: 1 minutes | Cook time: 5 minutes | Serves 5

- 2 tablespoons coconut oil
- ½ cup popcorn kernels
- ¼ cup margarine spread, melted, optional
- Sea salt to taste

1. Set the Instant Pot to Sauté. 2. Melt the coconut oil in the inner pot, then add the popcorn kernels and stir. 3. Press Adjust to bring the temperature up to high. 4. When the corn starts popping, secure the lid on the Instant Pot. 5. When you no longer hear popping, turn off the Instant Pot, remove the lid, and pour the popcorn into a bowl. 6. Top with the optional melted margarine and season the popcorn with sea salt to your liking.

Jalapeño Poppers with Bacon

Prep time: 10 minutes | Cook time: 3 minutes | Serves 4

- 6 jalapeños
- 4 ounces (113 g) cream cheese
- ¼ cup shredded sharp
- Cheddar cheese
- 1 cup water
- ¼ cup cooked crumbled bacon

1. Cut jalapeños lengthwise and scoop out seeds and membrane, then set aside. 2. In small bowl, mix cream cheese and Cheddar. Spoon into emptied jalapeños. Pour water into Instant Pot and place steamer basket in bottom. 3. Place stuffed jalapeños on steamer rack. Click lid closed. Press the Manual button and adjust time for 3 minutes. When timer beeps, quick-release the pressure. Serve topped with crumbled bacon.

Creamy Mashed Cauliflower

Prep time: 3 minutes | Cook time: 1 minute | Serves 4

- 1 head cauliflower, chopped into florets
- 1 cup water
- 1 clove garlic, finely minced
- 3 tablespoons butter
- 2 tablespoons sour cream
- ½ teaspoon salt
- ¼ teaspoon pepper

1. Place cauliflower on steamer rack. Add water and steamer rack to Instant Pot. Press the Steam button and adjust time to 1 minute. When timer beeps, quick-release the pressure. 2. Place cooked cauliflower into food processor and add remaining ingredients. Blend until smooth and creamy. Serve warm.

Sesame Mushrooms

Prep time: 2 minutes | Cook time: 10 minutes | Serves 6

- 3 tablespoons sesame oil
- ¾ pound (340 g) small button mushrooms
- 1 teaspoon minced garlic
- ½ teaspoon smoked paprika
- ½ teaspoon cayenne pepper
- Salt and ground black pepper, to taste

1. Set your Instant Pot to Sauté and heat the sesame oil. 2. Add the mushrooms and sauté for 4 minutes until just tender, stirring occasionally. 3. Add the remaining ingredients to the Instant Pot and stir to mix well. 4. Lock the lid. Select the Manual mode and set the cooking time for 5 minutes at High Pressure. 5. When the timer beeps, perform a quick pressure release. Carefully remove the lid. 6. Serve warm.

Oregano Sausage Balls

Prep time: 10 minutes | Cook time: 16 minutes | Serves 10

- 15 ounces (425 g) ground pork sausage
- 1 teaspoon dried oregano
- 4 ounces (113 g) Mozzarella, shredded
- 1 cup coconut flour
- 1 garlic clove, grated
- 1 teaspoon coconut oil, melted

1. In the bowl mix up ground pork sausages, dried oregano, shredded Mozzarella, coconut flour, and garlic clove. 2. When the mixture is homogenous, make the balls. 3. After this, pour coconut oil in the instant pot. 4. Arrange the balls in the instant pot and cook them on Sauté mode for 8 minutes from each side.

Cheddar Chips

Prep time: 10 minutes | Cook time: 5 minutes | Serves 4

- 1 cup shredded Cheddar cheese
- 1 tablespoon almond flour

1. Mix up Cheddar cheese and almond flour. 2. Then preheat the instant pot on Sauté mode. 3. Line the instant pot bowl with baking paper. 4. After this, make the small rounds from the cheese in the instant pot (on the baking paper) and close the lid. 5. Cook them for 5 minutes on Sauté mode or until the cheese is melted. 6. Then switch off the instant pot and remove the baking paper with cheese rounds from it. 7. Cool the chips well and remove them from the baking paper.

Red Wine Mushrooms

Prep time: 5 minutes | Cook time: 15 minutes | Serves 2

- 8 ounces (227 g) sliced mushrooms
- ¼ cup dry red wine
- 2 tablespoons beef broth
- ½ teaspoon garlic powder
- ¼ teaspoon Worcestershire sauce
- Pinch of salt
- Pinch of black pepper
- ¼ teaspoon xanthan gum

1. Add the mushrooms, wine, broth, garlic powder, Worcestershire sauce, salt, and pepper to the pot. 2. Close the lid and seal the vent. Cook on High Pressure for 13 minutes. Quick release the steam. Press Cancel. 3. Turn the pot to Sauté mode. Add the xanthan gum and whisk until the juices have thickened, 1 to 2 minutes.

Pancetta Pizza Dip

Prep time: 10 minutes | Cook time: 4 minutes | Serves 10

- 10 ounces (283 g) Pepper Jack cheese
- 10 ounces (283 g) cream cheese
- 10 ounces (283 g) pancetta, chopped
- 1 pound (454 g) tomatoes, puréed
- 1 cup green olives, pitted and halved
- 1 teaspoon dried oregano
- ½ teaspoon garlic powder
- 1 cup chicken broth
- 4 ounces (113 g) Mozzarella cheese, thinly sliced

1. Mix together the Pepper Jack cheese, cream cheese, pancetta, tomatoes, olives, oregano, and garlic powder in the Instant Pot. Pour in the chicken broth. 2. Lock the lid. Select the Manual mode and set the cooking time for 4 minutes at High Pressure. 3. When the timer beeps, perform a quick pressure release. Carefully remove the lid. 4. Scatter the Mozzarella cheese on top. Cover and allow to sit in the residual heat. Serve warm.

Bok Choy Salad Boats with Shrimp

Prep time: 8 minutes | Cook time: 2 minutes | Serves 8

- 26 shrimp, cleaned and deveined
- 2 tablespoons fresh lemon juice
- 1 cup water
- Sea salt and ground black pepper, to taste
- 4 ounces (113 g) feta cheese, crumbled
- 2 tomatoes, diced
- ⅓ cup olives, pitted and sliced
- 4 tablespoons olive oil
- 2 tablespoons apple cider vinegar
- 8 Bok choy leaves
- 2 tablespoons fresh basil leaves, snipped
- 2 tablespoons chopped fresh mint leaves

1. Toss the shrimp and lemon juice in the Instant Pot until well coated. Pour in the water. 2. Lock the lid. Select the Manual mode and set the cooking time for 2 minutes at Low Pressure. 3. When the timer beeps, perform a quick pressure release. Carefully remove the lid. 4. Season the shrimp with salt and pepper to taste, then let them cool completely. 5. Toss the shrimp with the feta cheese, tomatoes, olives, olive oil, and vinegar until well incorporated. 6. Divide the salad evenly onto each Bok choy leaf and place them on a serving plate. Scatter the basil and mint leaves on top and serve immediately.

Brussels Sprouts with Aioli Sauce

Prep time: 5 minutes | Cook time: 7 minutes | Serves 4

- 1 tablespoon butter
- ½ cup chopped scallions

Aioli Sauce:

- ¼ cup mayonnaise
- 1 tablespoon fresh lemon juice
- ¾ pound (340 g) Brussels sprouts
- 1 garlic clove, minced
- ½ teaspoon Dijon mustard

1. Set your Instant Pot to Sauté and melt the butter. 2. Add the scallions and sauté for 2 minutes until softened. Add the Brussels sprouts and cook for another 1 minute. 3. Lock the lid. Select the Manual mode and set the cooking time for 4 minutes at High Pressure. 4. Meanwhile, whisk together all the ingredients for the Aioli sauce in a small bowl until well incorporated. 5. When the timer beeps, perform a quick pressure release. Carefully remove the lid. 6. Serve the Brussels sprouts with the Aioli sauce on the side.

Cayenne Beef Bites

Prep time: 5 minutes | Cook time: 23 minutes | Serves 6

- 2 tablespoons olive oil
- 1 pound (454 g) beef steak, cut into cubes
- 1 cup beef bone broth
- ¼ cup dry white wine
- 1 teaspoon cayenne pepper
- ½ teaspoon dried marjoram
- Sea salt and ground black pepper, to taste

1. Set your Instant Pot to Sauté and heat the olive oil. 2. Add the beef and sauté for 2 to 3 minutes, stirring occasionally. 3. Add the remaining ingredients to the Instant Pot and combine well. 4. Lock the lid. Select the Manual mode and set the cooking time for 20 minutes at High Pressure. 5. When the timer beeps, perform a natural pressure release for 10 minutes, then release any remaining pressure. Carefully remove the lid. 6. Remove the beef from the Instant Pot to a platter and serve warm.

Creole Pancetta and Cheese Balls

Prep time: 5 minutes | Cook time: 5 minutes | Serves 6

- 1 cup water
- 6 eggs
- 4 slices pancetta, chopped
- ⅓ cup grated Cheddar cheese
- ¼ cup cream cheese
- ¼ cup mayonnaise
- 1 teaspoon Creole seasonings
- Sea salt and ground black pepper, to taste

1. Pour the water into the Instant Pot and insert a steamer basket. Place the eggs in the basket. 2. Lock the lid. Select the Manual mode and set the cooking time for 5 minutes at Low Pressure. 3. When the timer beeps, perform a quick pressure release. Carefully remove the lid. 4. Allow the eggs to cool for 10 to 15 minutes. Peel the eggs and chop them, then transfer to a bowl. Add the remaining ingredients and stir to combine well. 5. Shape the mixture into balls with your hands. Serve chilled.

Parmesan Chicken Balls with Chives

Prep time: 10 minutes | Cook time: 15 minutes | Serves 4

- 1 teaspoon coconut oil, softened
- 1 cup ground chicken
- ¼ cup chicken broth
- 1 tablespoon chopped
- chives
- 1 teaspoon cayenne pepper
- 3 ounces (85 g) Parmesan cheese, grated

1. Set your Instant Pot to Sauté and heat the coconut oil. 2. Add the remaining ingredients except the cheese to the Instant Pot and stir to mix well. 3. Secure the lid. Select the Manual mode and set the cooking time for 15 minutes at High Pressure. 4. Once cooking is complete, do a quick pressure release. Carefully open the lid. 5. Add the grated cheese and stir until combined. Form the balls from the cooked chicken mixture and allow to cool for 10 minutes, then serve.

Colby Cheese and Pepper Dip

Prep time: 5 minutes | Cook time: 5 minutes | Serves 8

- 1 tablespoon butter
- 2 red bell peppers, sliced
- 2 cups shredded Colby cheese
- 1 cup cream cheese, room temperature
- 1 cup chicken broth
- 2 garlic cloves, minced
- 1 teaspoon red Aleppo pepper flakes
- 1 teaspoon sumac
- Salt and ground black pepper, to taste

1. Set your Instant Pot to Sauté and melt the butter. 2. Add the bell peppers and sauté for about 2 minutes until just tender. 3. Add the remaining ingredients to the Instant Pot and gently stir to incorporate. 4. Lock the lid. Select the Manual mode and set the cooking time for 3 minutes at High Pressure. 5. When the timer beeps, perform a quick pressure release. Carefully remove the lid. 6. Allow to cool for 5 minutes and serve warm.

Garlic Meatballs

Prep time: 20 minutes | Cook time: 15 minutes | Serves 6

- 7 ounces (198 g) ground beef
- 7 ounces (198 g) ground pork
- 1 teaspoon minced garlic
- 3 tablespoons water
- 1 teaspoon chili flakes
- 1 teaspoon dried parsley
- 1 tablespoon coconut oil
- ¼ cup beef broth

1. In the mixing bowl, mix up ground beef, ground pork, minced garlic, water, chili flakes, and dried parsley. 2. Make the medium size meatballs from the mixture. 3. After this, heat up coconut oil in the instant pot on Sauté mode. 4. Put the meatballs in the hot coconut oil in one layer and cook them for 2 minutes from each side. 5. Then add beef broth and close the lid. 6. Cook the meatballs for 10 minutes on Manual mode (High Pressure). 7. Then make a quick pressure release and transfer the meatballs on the plate.

Cauliflower Fritters with Cheese

Prep time: 10 minutes | Cook time: 8 minutes | Serves 4

- 1 cup cauliflower, boiled
- 2 eggs, beaten
- 2 tablespoons almond flour
- 2 ounces (57 g) Cheddar cheese, shredded
- ½ teaspoon garlic powder
- 1 tablespoon avocado oil

1. In a medium bowl, mash the cauliflower. Add the beaten eggs, flour, cheese, and garlic powder and stir until well incorporated. Make the fritters from the cauliflower mixture. 2. Set your Instant Pot to Sauté and heat the avocado oil. 3. Add the fritters to the hot oil and cook each side for 3 minutes until golden brown. 4. Serve hot.

Roasted Garlic Bulbs

Prep time: 2 minutes | Cook time: 25 minutes | Serves 4

- 4 bulbs garlic
- 1 tablespoon avocado oil
- 1 teaspoon salt
- Pinch of black pepper
- 1 cup water

1. Slice the pointy tops off the bulbs of garlic to expose the cloves. 2. Drizzle the avocado oil on top of the garlic and sprinkle with the salt and pepper. 3. Place the bulbs in the steamer basket, cut-side up. Alternatively, you may place them on a piece of aluminum foil with the sides pulled up and resting on top of the trivet. Place the steamer basket in the pot. 4. Close the lid and seal the vent. Cook on High Pressure for 25 minutes. Quick release the steam. 5. Let the garlic cool completely before removing the bulbs from the pot. 6. Hold the stem end (bottom) of the bulb and squeeze out all the garlic. Mash the cloves with a fork to make a paste.

Asparagus with Creamy Dip

Prep time: 5 minutes | Cook time: 1 minute | Serves 6

- 1 cup water
- 1½ pounds (680 g) asparagus spears, trimmed
- Dipping Sauce:
- ½ cup mayonnaise
- ½ cup sour cream
- 2 tablespoons chopped scallions
- 2 tablespoons fresh chervil
- 1 teaspoon minced garlic
- Salt, to taste

1. Pour the water into the Instant Pot and insert a steamer basket.

Place the asparagus in the basket. 2. Lock the lid. Select the Manual mode and set the cooking time for 1 minute at High Pressure. 3. When the timer beeps, perform a quick pressure release. Carefully remove the lid. Transfer the asparagus to a plate. 4. Whisk together the remaining ingredients to make your dipping sauce. Serve the asparagus with the dipping sauce on the side.

Candied Pecans

Prep time: 5 minutes | Cook time: 20 minutes | Serves 10

- 4 cups raw pecans
- 1½ teaspoons liquid stevia
- ½ cup plus 1 tablespoon water, divided
- 1 teaspoon vanilla extract
- 1 teaspoon cinnamon
- ¼ teaspoon nutmeg
- ⅛ teaspoon ground ginger
- ⅛ teaspoon sea salt

1. Place the raw pecans, liquid stevia, 1 tablespoon water, vanilla, cinnamon, nutmeg, ground ginger, and sea salt into the inner pot of the Instant Pot. 2. Press the Sauté button on the Instant Pot and sauté the pecans and other ingredients until the pecans are soft. 3. Pour in the ½ cup water and secure the lid to the locked position. Set the vent to sealing. 4. Press Manual and set the Instant Pot for 15 minutes. 5. Preheat the oven to 350°F. 6. When cooking time is up, turn off the Instant Pot, then do a quick release. 7. Spread the pecans onto a greased, lined baking sheet. 8. Bake the pecans for 5 minutes or less in the oven, checking on them frequently so they do not burn.

Lemon-Cheese Cauliflower Bites

Prep time: 5 minutes | Cook time: 8 minutes | Serves 6

- 1 cup water
- 1 pound (454 g) cauliflower, broken into florets
- Sea salt and ground black pepper, to taste
- 2 tablespoons extra-virgin olive oil
- 2 tablespoons lemon juice
- 1 cup grated Cheddar cheese

1. Pour the water into the Instant Pot and insert a steamer basket. Place the cauliflower florets in the basket. 2. Lock the lid. Select the Manual mode and set the cooking time for 3 minutes at Low Pressure. 3. When the timer beeps, perform a quick pressure release. Carefully remove the lid. 4. Season the cauliflower with salt and pepper. Drizzle with olive oil and lemon juice. Sprinkle the grated cheese all over the cauliflower. 5. Press the Sauté button to heat the Instant Pot. Allow to cook for about 5 minutes, or until the cheese melts. Serve warm.

Crispy Brussels Sprouts with Bacon

Prep time: 5 minutes | Cook time: 10 minutes | Serves 4

- ½ pound (227 g) bacon
- 1 pound (454 g) Brussels sprouts
- 4 tablespoons butter
- 1 teaspoon salt
- ½ teaspoon pepper
- ½ cup water

1. Press the Sauté button and press the Adjust button to lower heat to Less. Add bacon to Instant Pot and fry for 3 to 5 minutes or until fat begins to render. Press the Cancel button. 2. Press the Sauté button, with heat set to Normal, and continue frying bacon until crispy. While bacon is frying, wash Brussels sprouts and remove damaged outer leaves. Cut in half or quarters. 3. When bacon is done, remove and set aside. Add Brussels sprouts to hot bacon grease and add butter. Sprinkle with salt and pepper. Sauté for 8 to 10 minutes until caramelized and crispy, adding a few tablespoons of water at a time as needed to deglaze pan. Serve warm.

Hummus with Chickpeas and Tahini Sauce

Prep time: 10 minutes | Cook time: 55 minutes | Makes 4 cups

- 4 cups water
- 1 cup dried chickpeas
- 2½ teaspoons fine sea salt
- ½ cup tahini
- 3 tablespoons fresh lemon juice
- 1 garlic clove
- ¼ teaspoon ground cumin

1. Combine the water, chickpeas, and 1 teaspoon of the salt in the Instant Pot and stir to dissolve the salt. 2. Secure the lid and set the Pressure Release to Sealing. Select the Bean/Chili, Pressure Cook, or Manual setting and set the cooking time for 40 minutes at high pressure. (The pot will take about 15 minutes to come up to pressure before the cooking program begins.) 3. When the cooking program ends, let the pressure release naturally for 15 minutes, then move the Pressure Release to Venting to release any remaining steam. 4. Place a colander over a bowl. Open the pot and, wearing heat-resistant mitts, lift out the inner pot and drain the beans in the colander. Return the chickpeas to the inner pot and place it back in the Instant Pot housing on the Keep Warm setting. Reserve the cooking liquid. 5. In a blender or food processor, combine 1 cup of the cooking liquid, the tahini, lemon juice, garlic, cumin, and 1 teaspoon salt. Blend or process on high speed, stopping to scrape down the sides of the container as needed, for about 30 seconds, until smooth and a little fluffy. Scoop out and set aside ½ cup of this sauce for the topping. 6. Set aside ½ cup of the chickpeas for the topping. Add the remaining chickpeas to the tahini sauce in the blender or food processor along with ½ cup of the cooking liquid and the remaining ½ teaspoon salt. Blend or process on high speed, stopping to scrape down the sides of the container as needed, for about 1 minute, until very smooth. 7. Transfer the hummus to a shallow serving bowl. Spoon the reserved tahini mixture over the top, then sprinkle on the reserved chickpeas. The hummus will keep in an airtight container in the refrigerator for up to 3 days. Serve at room temperature or chilled.

Creamy Spinach Dip

Prep time: 13 minutes | Cook time: 5 minutes | Serves 11

- 8 ounces low-fat cream cheese
- 1 cup low-fat sour cream
- ½ cup finely chopped onion
- ½ cup no-sodium vegetable broth
- 5 cloves garlic, minced
- ½ teaspoon salt
- ¼ teaspoon black pepper
- 10 ounces frozen spinach
- 12 ounces reduced-fat shredded Monterey Jack cheese
- 12 ounces reduced-fat shredded Parmesan cheese

1. Add cream cheese, sour cream, onion, vegetable broth, garlic, salt, pepper, and spinach to the inner pot of the Instant Pot. 2. Secure lid, make sure vent is set to sealing, and set to the Bean/Chili setting on high pressure for 5 minutes. 3. When done, do a manual release. 4. Add the cheeses and mix well until creamy and well combined.

Porcupine Meatballs

Prep time: 20 minutes | Cook time: 15 minutes | Serves 8

- 1 pound ground sirloin or turkey
- ½ cup raw brown rice, parboiled
- 1 egg
- ¼ cup finely minced onion
- 1 or 2 cloves garlic, minced
- ¼ teaspoon dried basil and/or oregano, optional
- 10¾-ounce can reduced-fat condensed tomato soup
- ½ soup can of water

1. Mix all ingredients, except tomato soup and water, in a bowl to combine well. 2. Form into balls about 1½-inch in diameter. 3. Mix tomato soup and water in the inner pot of the Instant Pot, then add the meatballs. 4. Secure the lid and make sure the vent is turned to sealing. 5. Press the Meat button and set for 15 minutes on high pressure. 6. Allow the pressure to release naturally after cook time is up.

Mayo Chicken Celery

Prep time: 15 minutes | Cook time: 15 minutes | Serves 4

- 14 ounces (397 g) chicken breast, skinless, boneless
- 1 cup water
- 4 celery stalks
- 1 teaspoon salt
- ½ teaspoon onion powder
- 1 teaspoon mayonnaise

1. Combine all the ingredients except the mayo in the Instant Pot. 2. Secure the lid. Select the Manual mode and set the cooking time for 15 minutes at High Pressure. 3. Once cooking is complete, do a natural pressure release for 6 minutes, then release any remaining pressure. Carefully open the lid. 4. Remove the chicken and shred with two forks, then return to the Instant Pot. 5. Add the mayo and stir well. Serve immediately.

Green Goddess White Bean Dip

Prep time: 1 minutes | Cook time: 45 minutes | Makes 3 cups

- 1 cup dried navy, great Northern, or cannellini beans
- 4 cups water
- 2 teaspoons fine sea salt
- 3 tablespoons fresh lemon juice
- ¼ cup extra-virgin olive oil,
- plus 1 tablespoon
- ¼ cup firmly packed fresh flat-leaf parsley leaves
- 1 bunch chives, chopped
- Leaves from 2 tarragon sprigs
- Freshly ground black pepper

1. Combine the beans, water, and 1 teaspoon of the salt in the Instant Pot and stir to dissolve the salt. 2. Secure the lid and set the Pressure Release to Sealing. Select the Bean/Chili, Pressure Cook, or Manual setting and set the cooking time for 30 minutes at high pressure if using navy or Great Northern beans or 40 minutes at high pressure if using cannellini beans. (The pot will take about 15 minutes to come up to pressure before the cooking program begins.) 3. When the cooking program ends, let the pressure release naturally for 15 minutes, then move the Pressure Release to Venting to release any remaining steam. Open the pot and scoop out and reserve ½ cup of the cooking liquid. Wearing heat-resistant mitts, lift out the inner pot and drain the beans in a colander. 4. In a food processor or blender, combine the beans, ½ cup cooking liquid, lemon juice, ¼ cup olive oil, ½ teaspoon parsley, chives, tarragon, remaining 1 teaspoon salt, and ½ teaspoon pepper. Process or blend on medium speed, stopping to scrape down the sides of the container as needed, for about 1 minute, until the mixture is smooth. 5. Transfer the dip to a serving bowl. Drizzle with the remaining 1 tablespoon olive oil and sprinkle with a few grinds of pepper. The dip will keep in an airtight container in the refrigerator for up to 1 week. Serve at room temperature or chilled.

Broccoli Cheese Dip

Prep time: 5 minutes | Cook time: 10 minutes | Serves 6

- 4 tablespoons butter
- ½ medium onion, diced
- 1½ cups chopped broccoli
- 8 ounces (227 g) cream cheese
- ½ cup mayonnaise
- ½ cup chicken broth
- 1 cup shredded Cheddar cheese

1. Press the Sauté button and then press the Adjust button to set heat to Less. Add butter to Instant Pot. Add onion and sauté until softened, about 5 minutes. Press the Cancel button. 2. Add broccoli, cream cheese, mayo, and broth to pot. Press the Manual button and adjust time for 4 minutes. 3. When timer beeps, quick-release the pressure and stir in Cheddar. Serve warm.

Lemon Artichokes

Prep time: 5 minutes | Cook time: 5 to 15 minutes | Serves 4

- 4 artichokes
- 1 cup water
- 2 tablespoons lemon juice
- 1 teaspoon salt

1. Wash and trim artichokes by cutting off the stems flush with the bottoms of the artichokes and by cutting ¾–1 inch off the tops. Stand upright in the bottom of the inner pot of the Instant Pot. 2. Pour water, lemon juice, and salt over artichokes. 3. Secure the lid and make sure the vent is set to sealing. On Manual, set the Instant Pot for 15 minutes for large artichokes, 10 minutes for medium artichokes, or 5 minutes for small artichokes. 4. When cook time is up, perform a quick release by releasing the pressure manually.

Parmesan Artichoke

Prep time: 1 minute | Cook time: 30 minutes | Serves 2

- 1 large artichoke
- 1 cup water
- ¼ cup grated Parmesan cheese
- ¼ teaspoon salt
- ¼ teaspoon red pepper flakes

1. Trim artichoke. Remove stem, outer leaves and top. Gently spread leaves. 2. Add water to Instant Pot and place steam rack on bottom. Place artichoke on steam rack and sprinkle with Parmesan, salt, and red pepper flakes. Click lid closed. Press the Steam button and adjust time for 30 minutes. 3. When timer beeps, allow a 15-minute natural release and then quick-release the remaining pressure. Enjoy warm topped with additional Parmesan.

Chapter 6

Vegetables and Sides

Chapter 6 Vegetables and Sides

Italian Wild Mushrooms

Prep time: 30 minutes | Cook time: 3 minutes | Serves 10

- 2 tablespoons canola oil
- 2 large onions, chopped
- 4 garlic cloves, minced
- 3 large red bell peppers, chopped
- 3 large green bell peppers, chopped
- 12 ounces package oyster mushrooms, cleaned and
- chopped
- 3 fresh bay leaves
- 10 fresh basil leaves, chopped
- 1 teaspoon salt
- 1½ teaspoons pepper
- 28 ounces can Italian plum tomatoes, crushed or chopped

1. Press Sauté on the Instant Pot and add in the oil. Once the oil is heated, add the onions, garlic, peppers, and mushroom to the oil. Sauté just until mushrooms begin to turn brown. 2. Add remaining ingredients. Stir well. 3. Secure the lid and make sure vent is set to sealing. Press Manual and set time for 3 minutes. 4. When cook time is up, release the pressure manually. Discard bay leaves.

Braised Radishes with Sugar Snap Peas and Dukkah

Prep time: 20 minutes | Cook time: 5 minutes | Serves 4

- ¼ cup extra-virgin olive oil, divided
- 1 shallot, sliced thin
- 3 garlic cloves, sliced thin
- 1½ pounds (680 g) radishes, 2 cups greens reserved, radishes trimmed and halved if small or quartered if large
- ½ cup water
- ½ teaspoon table salt
- 8 ounces (227 g) sugar snap peas, strings removed, sliced thin on bias
- 8 ounces (227 g) cremini mushrooms, trimmed and sliced thin
- 2 teaspoons grated lemon zest plus 1 teaspoon juice
- 1 cup plain Greek yogurt
- ½ cup fresh cilantro leaves
- 3 tablespoons dukkah

1. Using highest sauté function, heat 2 tablespoons oil in Instant Pot until shimmering. Add shallot and cook until softened, about 2 minutes. Stir in garlic and cook until fragrant, about 30 seconds. Stir in radishes, water, and salt. Lock lid in place and close pressure release valve. Select high pressure cook function and cook for 1 minute. 2. Turn off Instant Pot and quick-release pressure. Carefully remove lid, allowing steam to escape away from you. Stir in snap peas, cover, and let sit until heated through, about 3 minutes. Add radish greens, mushrooms, lemon zest and juice, and remaining 2 tablespoons oil and gently toss to combine. Season with salt and pepper to taste. 3. Spread ¼ cup yogurt over bottom of 4 individual serving plates. Using slotted spoon, arrange vegetable mixture on top and sprinkle with cilantro and dukkah. Serve.

Braised Whole Cauliflower with North African Spices

Prep time: 15 minutes | Cook time: 10 minutes | Serves 4

- 2 tablespoons extra-virgin olive oil
- 6 garlic cloves, minced
- 3 anchovy fillets, rinsed and minced (optional)
- 2 teaspoons ras el hanout
- ⅛ teaspoon red pepper flakes
- 1 (28-ounce / 794-g) can
- whole peeled tomatoes, drained with juice reserved, chopped coarse
- 1 large head cauliflower (3 pounds / 1.4 kg)
- ½ cup pitted brine-cured green olives, chopped coarse
- ¼ cup golden raisins
- ¼ cup fresh cilantro leaves

¼ cup pine nuts, toasted

1. Using highest sauté function, cook oil, garlic, anchovies (if using), ras el hanout, and pepper flakes in Instant Pot until fragrant, about 3 minutes. Turn off Instant Pot, then stir in tomatoes and reserved juice. 2. Trim outer leaves of cauliflower and cut stem flush with bottom florets. Using paring knife, cut 4-inch-deep cross in stem. Nestle cauliflower stem side down into pot and spoon some of sauce over top. Lock lid in place and close pressure release valve. Select high pressure cook function and cook for 3 minutes. 3. Turn off Instant Pot and quick-release pressure. Carefully remove lid, allowing steam to escape away from you. Using tongs and slotted spoon, transfer cauliflower to serving dish and tent with aluminum foil. Stir olives and raisins into sauce and cook, using highest sauté function, until sauce has thickened slightly, about 5 minutes. Season with salt and pepper to taste. Cut cauliflower into wedges and spoon some of sauce over top. Sprinkle with cilantro and pine nuts. Serve, passing remaining sauce separately.

Spaghetti Squash Noodles with Tomatoes

Prep time: 15 minutes | Cook time: 14 to 16 minutes | Serves 4

- 1 medium spaghetti squash
- 1 cup water
- 2 tablespoons olive oil
- 1 small yellow onion, diced
- 6 garlic cloves, minced
- 2 teaspoons crushed red pepper flakes
- 2 teaspoons dried oregano
- 1 cup sliced cherry tomatoes
- 1 teaspoon kosher salt
- ½ teaspoon freshly ground black pepper
- 1 (14.5-ounce / 411-g) can sugar-free crushed tomatoes
- ¼ cup capers
- 1 tablespoon caper brine
- ½ cup sliced olives

1. With a sharp knife, halve the spaghetti squash crosswise. Using a spoon, scoop out the seeds and sticky gunk in the middle of each half. 2. Pour the water into the Instant Pot and place the trivet in the pot with the handles facing up. Arrange the squash halves, cut side facing up, on the trivet. 3. Lock the lid. Select the Manual mode and set the cooking time for 7 minutes on High Pressure. When the timer goes off, use a quick pressure release. Carefully open the lid. 4. Remove the trivet and pour out the water that has collected in the squash cavities. Using the tines of a fork, separate the cooked strands into spaghetti-like pieces and set aside in a bowl. 5. Pour the water out of the pot. Select the Sauté mode and heat the oil. 6. Add the onion to the pot and sauté for 3 minutes. Add the garlic, pepper flakes and oregano to the pot and sauté for 1 minute. 7. Stir in the cherry tomatoes, salt and black pepper and cook for 2 minutes, or until the tomatoes are tender. 8. Pour in the crushed tomatoes, capers, caper brine and olives and bring the mixture to a boil. Continue to cook for 2 to 3 minutes to allow the flavors to meld. 9. Stir in the spaghetti squash noodles and cook for 1 to 2 minutes to warm everything through. 10. Transfer the dish to a serving platter and serve.

Chinese-Style Pe-Tsai with Onion

Prep time: 5 minutes | Cook time: 8 minutes | Serves 4

- 2 tablespoons sesame oil
- 1 yellow onion, chopped
- 1 pound (454 g) pe-tsai cabbage, shredded
- ¼ cup rice wine vinegar
- 1 tablespoon coconut
- aminos
- 1 teaspoon finely minced garlic
- ½ teaspoon salt
- ¼ teaspoon Szechuan pepper

1. Set the Instant Pot on the Sauté mode and heat the sesame oil. Add the onion to the pot and sauté for 5 minutes, or until tender.

Stir in the remaining ingredients. 2. Lock the lid. Select the Manual mode and set the cooking time for 3 minutes on High Pressure. When the timer goes off, perform a quick pressure release. Carefully open the lid. 3. Transfer the cabbage mixture to a bowl and serve immediately.

Chanterelle Mushrooms with Cheddar Cheese

Prep time: 10 minutes | Cook time: 5 minutes | Serves 4

- 1 tablespoon olive oil
- 2 cloves garlic, minced
- 1 (1-inch) ginger root, grated
- 16 ounces (454 g) Chanterelle mushrooms, brushed clean and sliced
- ½ cup unsweetened tomato purée
- ½ cup water
- 2 tablespoons dry white wine
- 1 teaspoon dried basil
- ½ teaspoon dried thyme
- ½ teaspoon dried dill weed
- ⅓ teaspoon freshly ground black pepper
- Kosher salt, to taste
- 1 cup shredded Cheddar cheese

1. Press the Sauté button on the Instant Pot and heat the olive oil. Add the garlic and grated ginger to the pot and sauté for 1 minute, or until fragrant. Stir in the remaining ingredients, except for the cheese. 2. Lock the lid. Select the Manual mode and set the cooking time for 5 minutes on Low Pressure. When the timer goes off, perform a quick pressure release. Carefully open the lid.. 3. Serve topped with the shredded cheese.

Green Cabbage Turmeric Stew

Prep time: 5 minutes | Cook time: 4 minutes | Serves 4

- 2 tablespoons olive oil
- ½ cup sliced yellow onion
- 1 teaspoon crushed garlic
- Sea salt and freshly ground black pepper, to taste
- 1 teaspoon turmeric powder
- 1 serrano pepper, chopped
- 1 pound (454 g) green cabbage, shredded
- 1 celery stalk, chopped
- 2 tablespoons rice wine
- 1 cup roasted vegetable broth

1. Place all of the above ingredients in the Instant Pot. 2. Secure the lid. Choose Manual mode and High Pressure; cook for 4 minutes. Once cooking is complete, use a quick pressure release; carefully remove the lid. 3. Divide between individual bowls and serve warm. Bon appétit!

Cauliflower Curry

- 1 pound (454 g) cauliflower, chopped
- 3 ounces (85 g) scallions, chopped
- 1 cup coconut milk
- ¼ cup crushed tomatoes
- 1 tablespoon coconut oil
- 1 teaspoon garam masala
- 1 teaspoon ground turmeric

1. Add all the ingredients to the Instant Pot and stir to combine. 2. Lock the lid. Select the Manual mode and set the cooking time for 3 minutes at High Pressure. When the timer goes off, use a natural pressure release for 5 minutes, then release any remaining pressure. Carefully open the lid. 3. Stir the cooked dish well before serving.

Instant Pot Zucchini Sticks

- 2 zucchinis, trimmed and cut into sticks
- 2 teaspoons olive oil
- ½ teaspoon white pepper
- ½ teaspoon salt
- 1 cup water

1. Place the zucchini sticks in the Instant Pot pan and sprinkle with the olive oil, white pepper and salt. 2. Pour the water and put the trivet in the pot. Place the pan on the trivet. 3. Lock the lid. Select the Manual setting and set the cooking time for 8 minutes at High Pressure. Once the timer goes off, use a quick pressure release. Carefully open the lid. 4. Remove the zucchinis from the pot and serve.

Masala Cauliflower

- 2 tablespoons olive oil
- ½ cup chopped scallions
- 2 cloves garlic, pressed
- 1 tablespoon garam masala
- 1 teaspoon curry powder
- 1 red chili pepper, minced
- ½ teaspoon ground cumin
- Sea salt and ground black pepper, to taste
- 1 tablespoon chopped fresh coriander
- 2 tomatoes, puréed
- 1 pound (454 g) cauliflower, broken into florets
- ½ cup water
- ½ cup almond yogurt

1. Press the Sauté button to heat up your Instant Pot. Now, heat the oil and sauté the scallions for 1 minute. 2. Add garlic and continue to cook an additional 30 seconds or until aromatic. 3. Add garam masala, curry powder, chili pepper, cumin, salt, black pepper, coriander, tomatoes, cauliflower, and water. 4. Secure the lid. Choose Manual mode and High Pressure; cook for 3 minutes. Once cooking is complete, use a quick pressure release; carefully remove the lid. 5. Pour in the almond yogurt, stir well and serve warm. Bon appétit!

Corn on the Cob

- 2 large ears fresh corn
- Olive oil for misting
- Salt, to taste (optional)

1. Shuck corn, remove silks, and wash. 2. Cut or break each ear in half crosswise. 3. Spray corn with olive oil. 4. Air fry at 390°F (199°C) for 12 to 15 minutes or until browned as much as you like. 5. Serve plain or with coarsely ground salt.

Garlicky Broccoli with Roasted Almonds

- 6 cups broccoli florets
- 1 cup water
- 1½ tablespoons olive oil
- 8 garlic cloves, thinly sliced
- 2 shallots, thinly sliced
- ½ teaspoon crushed red pepper flakes
- Grated zest and juice of 1 medium lemon
- ½ teaspoon kosher salt
- Freshly ground black pepper, to taste
- ¼ cup chopped roasted almonds
- ¼ cup finely slivered fresh basil

1. Pour the water into the Instant Pot. Place the broccoli florets in a steamer basket and lower into the pot. 2. Close and secure the lid. Select the Steam setting and set the cooking time for 2 minutes at Low Pressure. Once the timer goes off, use a quick pressure release. Carefully open the lid. 3. Transfer the broccoli to a large bowl filled with cold water and ice. Once cooled, drain the broccoli and pat dry. 4. Select the Sauté mode on the Instant Pot and heat the olive oil. Add the garlic to the pot and sauté for 30 seconds, tossing constantly. Add the shallots and pepper flakes to the pot and sauté for 1 minute. 5. Stir in the cooked broccoli, lemon juice, salt and black pepper. Toss the ingredients together and cook for 1 minute. 6. Transfer the broccoli to a serving platter and sprinkle with the chopped almonds, lemon zest and basil. Serve immediately.

Thyme Cabbage

Prep time: 10 minutes | Cook time: 5 minutes | Serves 4

- 1 pound (454 g) white cabbage
- 2 tablespoons butter
- 1 teaspoon dried thyme
- ½ teaspoon salt
- 1 cup water

1. Cut the white cabbage on medium size petals and sprinkle with the butter, dried thyme and salt. Place the cabbage petals in the Instant Pot pan. 2. Pour the water and insert the trivet in the Instant Pot. Put the pan on the trivet. 3. Set the lid in place. Select the Manual mode and set the cooking time for 5 minutes on High Pressure. When the timer goes off, do a quick pressure release. Carefully open the lid. 4. Serve immediately.

Spiced Winter Squash with Halloumi and Shaved Brussels Sprouts

Prep time: 20 minutes | Cook time: 15 minutes | Serves 4

- 3 tablespoons extra-virgin olive oil, divided
- 2 tablespoons lemon juice
- 2 garlic cloves, minced, divided
- ⅛ teaspoon plus ½ teaspoon table salt, divided
- 8 ounces (227 g) Brussels sprouts, trimmed, halved, and sliced very thin
- 1 (8-ounce / 227-g) block halloumi cheese, sliced crosswise into ¾-inch-thick slabs
- 4 scallions, white parts minced, green parts sliced
- thin on bias
- ½ teaspoon ground cardamom
- ¼ teaspoon ground cumin
- ⅛ teaspoon cayenne pepper
- 2 pounds (907 g) butternut squash, peeled, seeded, and cut into 1-inch pieces
- ½ cup chicken or vegetable broth
- 2 teaspoons honey
- ¼ cup dried cherries
- 2 tablespoons roasted pepitas

1. Whisk 1 tablespoon oil, lemon juice, ¼ teaspoon garlic, and ⅛ teaspoon salt together in bowl. Add Brussels sprouts and toss to coat; let sit until ready to serve. 2. Using highest sauté function, heat remaining 2 tablespoons oil in Instant Pot until shimmering. Arrange halloumi around edges of pot and cook until browned, about 3 minutes per side; transfer to plate. Add scallion whites to fat left in pot and cook until softened, about 2 minutes. Stir in remaining garlic, cardamom, cumin, and cayenne and cook until fragrant, about 30 seconds. Stir in squash, broth, and remaining ½ teaspoon salt. Lock lid in place and close pressure release valve. Select high pressure cook function and cook for 6 minutes. 3.

Turn off Instant Pot and quick-release pressure. Carefully remove lid, allowing steam to escape away from you. Using highest sauté function, continue to cook squash mixture, stirring occasionally until liquid is almost completely evaporated, about 5 minutes. Turn off Instant Pot. Using potato masher, mash squash until mostly smooth. Season with salt and pepper to taste. 4. Spread portion of squash over bottom of individual serving plates. Top with Brussels sprouts and halloumi. Drizzle with honey and sprinkle with cherries, pepitas, and scallion greens. Serve.

Curried Cauliflower and Tomatoes

Prep time: 10 minutes | Cook time: 2 minutes | Serves 4 to 6

- 1 medium head cauliflower, cut into bite-size pieces
- 1 (14-ounce / 397-g) can sugar-free diced tomatoes, undrained
- 1 bell pepper, thinly sliced
- 1 (14-ounce / 397-g) can full-fat coconut milk
- ½ to 1 cup water
- 2 tablespoons red curry paste
- 1 teaspoon salt
- 1 teaspoon garlic powder
- ½ teaspoon onion powder
- ½ teaspoon ground ginger
- ¼ teaspoon chili powder
- Freshly ground black pepper, to taste

1. Add all the ingredients, except for the black pepper, to the Instant Pot and stir to combine. 2. Lock the lid. Select the Manual setting and set the cooking time for 2 minutes at High Pressure. Once the timer goes off, use a quick pressure release. Carefully open the lid. 3. Sprinkle the black pepper and stir well. Serve immediately.

Potatoes with Parsley

Prep time: 10 minutes | Cook time: 5 minutes | Serves 4

- 3 tablespoons margarine, divided
- 2 pounds medium red potatoes (about 2 ounces each), halved lengthwise
- 1 clove garlic, minced
- ½ teaspoon salt
- ½ cup low-sodium chicken broth
- 2 tablespoons chopped fresh parsley

1. Place 1 tablespoon margarine in the inner pot of the Instant Pot and select Sauté. 2. After margarine is melted, add potatoes, garlic, and salt, stirring well. 3. Sauté 4 minutes, stirring frequently. 4. Add chicken broth and stir well. 5. Seal lid, make sure vent is on sealing, then select Manual for 5 minutes on high pressure. 6. When cooking time is up, manually release the pressure. 7. Strain potatoes, toss with remaining 2 tablespoons margarine and chopped parsley, and serve immediately.

Broccoli and Mushroom Bake

Prep time: 10 minutes | Cook time: 3 minutes | Serves 4

- ½ cup sunflower seeds, soaked overnight
- 2 tablespoons sesame seeds
- 1 cup water
- 1 cup unsweetened almond milk
- ¼ teaspoon grated nutmeg
- ½ teaspoon sea salt
- 1 tablespoon nutritional yeast
- 2 tablespoons rice vinegar
- 1 pound (454 g) broccoli, broken into florets
- ½ cup chopped spring onions
- 10 ounces (283 g) white fresh mushrooms, sliced
- Sea salt and white pepper, to taste
- 1 tablespoon cayenne pepper
- ¼ teaspoon dried dill
- ¼ teaspoon ground bay leaf

1. Add sunflower seeds, sesame seeds, water, milk, nutmeg, ½ teaspoon of sea salt, nutritional yeast, and vinegar to your blender. 2. Blend until smooth and uniform. 3. Spritz a casserole dish with a nonstick cooking spray. Add broccoli, spring onions and mushrooms. 4. Sprinkle with salt, white pepper, cayenne pepper, dill, and ground bay leaf. Pour the prepared vegan béchamel over your casserole. 5. Add 1 cup of water and a metal rack to your Instant Pot. Place the dish on the rack. 6. Secure the lid. Choose Manual mode and High Pressure; cook for 3 minutes. Once cooking is complete, use a quick pressure release; carefully remove the lid. 7. Allow the dish to stand for 5 to 10 minutes before slicing and serving. Bon appétit!

Vinegary Broccoli with Cheese

Prep time: 5 minutes | Cook time: 5 minutes | Serves 4

- 1 pound (454 g) broccoli, cut into florets
- 1 cup water
- 2 garlic cloves, minced
- 1 cup crumbled Cottage cheese
- 2 tablespoons balsamic vinegar
- 1 teaspoon cumin seeds
- 1 teaspoon mustard seeds
- Salt and pepper, to taste

1. Pour the water into the Instant Pot and put the steamer basket in the pot. Place the broccoli in the steamer basket. 2. Close and secure the lid. Select the Manual setting and set the cooking time for 5 minutes at High Pressure. Once the timer goes off, do a quick pressure release. Carefully open the lid. 3. Stir in the remaining ingredients. 4. Serve immediately.

Sauerkraut and Mushroom Casserole

Prep time: 6 minutes | Cook time: 15 minutes | Serves 6

- 1 tablespoon olive oil
- 1 celery rib, diced
- ½ cup chopped leeks
- 2 pounds (907 g) canned sauerkraut, drained
- 6 ounces (170 g) brown
- mushrooms, sliced
- 1 teaspoon caraway seeds
- 1 teaspoon brown mustard
- 1 bay leaf
- 1 cup dry white wine

1. Press the Sauté button to heat up your Instant Pot. Now, heat the oil and cook celery and leeks until softened. 2. Add the sauerkraut and mushrooms and cook for 2 minutes more. 3. Add the remaining ingredients and stir to combine well. 4. Secure the lid. Choose Manual mode and High Pressure; cook for 10 minutes. Once cooking is complete, use a natural pressure release; carefully remove the lid. Bon appétit!

Indian Okra

Prep time: 8 minutes | Cook time: 7 minutes | Serves 6

- 1 pound (454 g) young okra
- 4 tablespoons ghee or avocado oil
- ½ teaspoon cumin seeds
- ¼ teaspoon ground turmeric
- Pinch of ground cinnamon
- ½ medium onion, diced
- 2 cloves garlic, minced
- 2 teaspoons minced fresh ginger
- 1 serrano chile, seeded and ribs removed, minced
- 1 small tomato, diced
- ½ teaspoon sea salt
- ¼ teaspoon cayenne pepper (optional)
- 1 cup vegetable stock or filtered water

1. Rinse and thoroughly dry the okra. Slice it on a diagonal into slices ½ to ¾ inch thick, discarding the stems. 2. Set the Instant Pot to Sauté. Once hot, add the ghee and heat until melted. Stir in the cumin seeds, turmeric, and cinnamon and cook until they are fragrant, about 1 minute. This may cause the cumin seeds to jump and pop. Add the onion and cook, stirring frequently, until soft and translucent, about 3 minutes. Add the garlic, ginger, and serrano chile and sauté for an additional minute. Press Cancel. 3. Stir in the tomato, okra, salt, cayenne (if using), and stock. Secure the lid and set the steam release valve to Sealing. Press the Manual button and set the cook time to 2 minutes. 4. When the Instant Pot beeps, carefully switch the steam release valve to Venting to quick-release the pressure. When fully released, open the lid. Stir gently and allow the okra to rest on the Keep Warm setting for a few minutes before serving.

Braised Cabbage with Ginger

Prep time: 10 minutes | Cook time: 8 minutes | Serves 6

- 1 tablespoon avocado oil
- 1 tablespoon butter or ghee (or more avocado oil)
- ½ medium onion, diced
- 1 medium bell pepper (any color), diced
- 1 teaspoon sea salt
- ½ teaspoon ground black
- pepper
- 1 clove garlic, minced
- 1-inch piece fresh ginger, grated
- 1 pound (454 g) green or red cabbage, cored and leaves chopped
- ½ cup bone broth or vegetable broth

1. Set the Instant Pot to Sauté and heat the oil and butter together. When the butter has stopped foaming, add the onion, bell pepper, salt, and black pepper. Sauté, stirring frequently, until just softened, about 3 minutes. Add the garlic and ginger and cook 1 minute longer. Add the cabbage and stir to combine. Pour in the broth. 2. Secure the lid and set the steam release valve to Sealing. Press the Manual button and set the cook time to 2 minutes. 3. When the Instant Pot beeps, carefully switch the steam release valve to Venting to quick-release the pressure. When fully released, open the lid. Stir the cabbage and transfer it to a serving dish. Serve warm.

Lemon Garlic Asparagus

Prep time: 6 minutes | Cook time: 5 minutes | Serves 4

- 1 large bunch asparagus, woody ends cut off (medium-thick spears if possible)
- 1 cup water
- 2 tablespoons salted butter
- 2 large cloves garlic, minced
- 2 teaspoons fresh lemon juice (from ½ lemon)
- ¾ cup finely shredded Parmesan cheese (optional)
- Salt, to taste

1. Cut the asparagus spears on a diagonal into 3 equal pieces, or trim the whole spears to fit your Instant Pot. 2. Pour the water into the Instant Pot. Place a metal steaming basket inside. Place the asparagus in the basket. Secure the lid and set the steam release valve to Sealing. Press the Manual button and set the cook time to 1 minute for tender (for softer, increase to 2 minutes; for crisp, decrease to 0). While it cooks, prepare a bowl with ice water. 3. When the Instant Pot beeps, carefully switch the steam release valve to Venting to quick-release the pressure. When fully released, open the lid and use tongs to transfer the asparagus to the ice bath. Let it sit for a minute, then drain and place the asparagus on a clean kitchen towel and pat dry. 4. Carefully remove the pot insert.

Remove the steaming basket, drain the water, and wipe the pot insert dry. 5. Return the pot insert to the Instant Pot and press the Sauté button. Put the butter in the pot. When it has melted and starts to foam, add the garlic and sauté, stirring, for 1 minute. 6. Return the asparagus to the pot and stir well to coat it with the garlic-butter mixture. Add the lemon juice. Sauté until it reaches the desired doneness, about 1 minute more. 7. Transfer the asparagus to a serving bowl and stir in the Parmesan. Taste the asparagus and add salt to taste. Serve warm.

Almond Butter Zucchini Noodles

Prep time: 10 minutes | Cook time: 4 minutes | Serves 4

- 2 tablespoons coconut oil
- 1 yellow onion, chopped
- 2 zucchini, julienned
- 1 cup shredded Chinese cabbage
- 2 garlic cloves, minced
- 2 tablespoons almond butter
- Sea salt and freshly ground black pepper, to taste
- 1 teaspoon cayenne pepper

1. Press the Sauté button to heat up your Instant Pot. Heat the coconut oil and sweat the onion for 2 minutes. 2. Add the other ingredients. 3. Secure the lid. Choose Manual mode and High Pressure; cook for 2 minutes. Once cooking is complete, use a quick pressure release; carefully remove the lid. Bon appétit!

Lemon Cabbage and Tempeh

Prep time: 8 minutes | Cook time: 10 minutes | Serves 3

- 2 tablespoons sesame oil
- ½ cup chopped scallions
- 2 cups shredded cabbage
- 6 ounces (170 g) tempeh, cubed
- 1 tablespoon coconut aminos
- 1 cup vegetable stock
- 2 garlic cloves, minced
- 1 tablespoon lemon juice
- Salt and pepper, to taste
- ¼ teaspoon paprika
- ¼ cup roughly chopped fresh cilantro

1. Press the Sauté button to heat up your Instant Pot. Heat the sesame oil and sauté the scallions until tender and fragrant. 2. Then, add the cabbage, tempeh, coconut aminos, vegetable stock, garlic, lemon juice, salt, pepper, and paprika. 3. Secure the lid. Choose Manual mode and Low Pressure; cook for 3 minutes. Once cooking is complete, use a quick pressure release; carefully remove the lid. 4. Press the Sauté button to thicken the sauce if desired. Divide between serving bowls, garnish with fresh cilantro, and serve warm. Bon appétit!

Best Brown Rice

Prep time: 5 minutes | Cook time: 22 minutes | Serves 6 to 12

- 2 cups brown rice
- 2½ cups water

1. Rinse brown rice in a fine-mesh strainer. 2. Add rice and water to the inner pot of the Instant Pot. 3. Secure the lid and make sure vent is on sealing. 4. Use Manual setting and select 22 minutes cooking time on high pressure. 5. When cooking time is done, let the pressure release naturally for 10 minutes, then press Cancel and manually release any remaining pressure.

Gobi Masala

Prep time: 5 minutes | Cook time: 4 to 5 minutes | Serves 4 to 6

- 1 tablespoon olive oil
- 1 teaspoon cumin seeds
- 1 white onion, diced
- 1 garlic clove, minced
- 1 head cauliflower, chopped
- 1 tablespoon ground coriander
- 1 teaspoon ground cumin
- ½ teaspoon garam masala
- ½ teaspoon salt
- 1 cup water

1. Set the Instant Pot to the Sauté mode and heat the olive oil. Add the cumin seeds to the pot and sauté for 30 seconds, stirring constantly. Add the onion and sauté for 2 to 3 minutes, stirring constantly. Add the garlic and sauté for 30 seconds, stirring frequently. 2. Stir in the remaining ingredients. 3. Lock the lid. Select the Manual mode and set the cooking time for 1 minute on High Pressure. When the timer goes off, perform a quick pressure release. Carefully open the lid. 4. Serve immediately.

Mushroom Stroganoff with Vodka

Prep time: 8 minutes | Cook time: 8 minutes | Serves 4

- 2 tablespoons olive oil
- ½ teaspoon crushed caraway seeds
- ½ cup chopped onion
- 2 garlic cloves, smashed
- ¼ cup vodka
- ¾ pound (340 g) button
- mushrooms, chopped
- 1 celery stalk, chopped
- 1 ripe tomato, puréed
- 1 teaspoon mustard seeds
- Sea salt and freshly ground pepper, to taste
- 2 cups vegetable broth

1. Press the Sauté button to heat up your Instant Pot. Now, heat the oil and sauté caraway seeds until fragrant, about 40 seconds.

2. Then, add the onion and garlic, and continue sautéing for 1 to 2 minutes more, stirring frequently. 3. After that, add the remaining ingredients and stir to combine. 4. Secure the lid. Choose Manual mode and High Pressure; cook for 5 minutes. Once cooking is complete, use a quick pressure release; carefully remove the lid. 5. Ladle into individual bowls and serve warm. Bon appétit!

Asparagus and Mushroom Soup

Prep time: 10 minutes | Cook time: 7 minutes | Serves 4

- 2 tablespoons coconut oil
- ½ cup chopped shallots
- 2 cloves garlic, minced
- 1 pound (454 g) asparagus, washed, trimmed, and chopped
- 4 ounces (113 g) button mushrooms, sliced
- 4 cups vegetable broth
- 2 tablespoons balsamic vinegar
- Himalayan salt, to taste
- ¼ teaspoon ground black pepper
- ¼ teaspoon paprika
- ¼ cup vegan sour cream

1. Press the Sauté button to heat up your Instant Pot. Heat the oil and cook the shallots and garlic for 2 to 3 minutes. 2. Add the remaining ingredients, except for sour cream, to the Instant Pot. 3. Secure the lid. Choose Manual mode and High Pressure; cook for 4 minutes. Once cooking is complete, use a quick pressure release; carefully remove the lid. 4. Spoon into four soup bowls; add a dollop of sour cream to each serving and serve immediately. Bon appétit!

Spicy Cauliflower Head

Prep time: 5 minutes | Cook time: 7 minutes | Serves 4

- 13 ounces (369 g) cauliflower head
- 1 cup water
- 1 tablespoon coconut cream
- 1 tablespoon avocado oil
- 1 teaspoon ground paprika
- 1 teaspoon ground turmeric
- ½ teaspoon ground cumin
- ½ teaspoon salt

1. Pour the water in the Instant Pot and insert the trivet. 2. In the mixing bowl, stir together the coconut cream, avocado oil, paprika, turmeric, cumin and salt. 3. Carefully brush the cauliflower head with the coconut cream mixture. Sprinkle the remaining coconut cream mixture over the cauliflower. 4. Transfer the cauliflower head onto the trivet. 5. Lock the lid. Select the Manual mode and set the cooking time for 7 minutes at High Pressure. When the timer goes off, use a natural pressure release for 10 minutes, then release any remaining pressure. Carefully open the lid. 6. Serve immediately.

Spaghetti Squash

1 spaghetti squash (about 2 pounds)

1. Cut the spaghetti squash in half crosswise and use a large spoon to remove the seeds. 2. Pour 1 cup of water into the electric pressure cooker and insert a wire rack or trivet. 3. Place the squash halves on the rack, cut-side up. 4. Close and lock the lid of the pressure cooker. Set the valve to sealing. 5. Cook on high pressure for 7 minutes. 6. When the cooking is complete, hit Cancel and quick release the pressure. 7. Once the pin drops, unlock and remove the lid. 8. With tongs, remove the squash from the pot and transfer it to a plate. When it is cool enough to handle, scrape the squash with the tines of a fork to remove the strands. Discard the skin.

Lemon Broccoli

- 2 cups broccoli florets
- 1 tablespoon ground paprika
- 1 tablespoon lemon juice
- 1 teaspoon grated lemon zest
- 1 teaspoon olive oil
- ½ teaspoon chili powder
- 1 cup water

1. Pour the water in the Instant Pot and insert the trivet. 2. In the Instant Pot pan, stir together the remaining ingredients. 3. Place the pan on the trivet. 4. Set the lid in place. Select the Manual mode and set the cooking time for 4 minutes on High Pressure. When the timer goes off, do a quick pressure release. Carefully open the lid. 5. Serve immediately.

Individual Asparagus and Goat Cheese Frittatas

- 1 tablespoon extra-virgin olive oil
- 8 ounces (227 g) asparagus, trimmed and sliced ¼ inch thick
- 1 red bell pepper, stemmed, seeded, and chopped
- 2 shallots, minced
- 2 ounces (57 g) goat cheese, crumbled (½ cup)
- 1 tablespoon minced fresh tarragon
- 1 teaspoon grated lemon zest
- 8 large eggs
- ½ teaspoon table salt

1. Using highest sauté function, heat oil in Instant Pot until shimmering. Add asparagus, bell pepper, and shallots; cook until softened, about 5 minutes. Turn off Instant Pot and transfer vegetables to bowl. Stir in goat cheese, tarragon, and lemon zest. 2. Arrange trivet included with Instant Pot in base of now-empty insert and add 1 cup water. Spray four 6-ounce ramekins with vegetable oil spray. Beat eggs, ¼ cup water, and salt in large bowl until thoroughly combined. Divide vegetable mixture between prepared ramekins, then pour egg mixture over top (you may have some left over). Set ramekins on trivet. Lock lid in place and close pressure release valve. Select high pressure cook function and cook for 10 minutes. 3. Turn off Instant Pot and quick-release pressure. Carefully remove lid, allowing steam to escape away from you. Using tongs, transfer ramekins to wire rack and let cool slightly. Run paring knife around inside edge of ramekins to loosen frittatas, then invert onto individual serving plates. Serve.

Cauliflower Rice Curry

- 1 (9-ounce / 255-g) head cauliflower, chopped
- ½ teaspoon garlic powder
- ½ teaspoon freshly ground black pepper
- ½ teaspoon ground turmeric
- ½ teaspoon curry powder
- ½ teaspoon kosher salt
- ½ teaspoon fresh paprika
- ¼ small onion, thinly sliced

1. Pour 1 cup of filtered water into the inner pot of the Instant Pot, then insert the trivet. In a well-greased, Instant Pot-friendly dish, add the cauliflower. Sprinkle the garlic powder, black pepper, turmeric, curry powder, salt, paprika, and onion over top. 2. Place the dish onto the trivet, and cover loosely with aluminum foil. Close the lid, set the pressure release to Sealing and select Manual. Set the Instant Pot to 2 minutes on High Pressure, and let cook. 3. Once cooked, perform a quick release. 4. Open the Instant Pot, and remove the dish. Serve, and enjoy!

Parmesan Zoodles

- 1 large zucchini, trimmed and spiralized
- 1 tablespoon butter
- 1 garlic clove, diced
- ½ teaspoon chili flakes
- 3 ounces (85 g) Parmesan cheese, grated

1. Set the Instant Pot on the Sauté mode and melt the butter. Add the garlic and chili flakes to the pot. Sauté for 2 minutes, or until fragrant. 2. Stir in the zucchini spirals and sauté for 2 minutes, or until tender. 3. Add the grated Parmesan cheese to the pot and stir well. Continue to cook it for 1 minute, or until the cheese melts. 4. Transfer to a plate and serve immediately

Lemony Brussels Sprouts with Poppy Seeds

- 1 pound (454 g) Brussels sprouts
- 2 tablespoons avocado oil, divided
- 1 cup vegetable broth or chicken bone broth
- 1 tablespoon minced garlic
- ½ teaspoon kosher salt
- Freshly ground black pepper, to taste
- ½ medium lemon
- ½ tablespoon poppy seeds

1. Trim the Brussels sprouts by cutting off the stem ends and removing any loose outer leaves. Cut each in half lengthwise (through the stem). 2. Set the electric pressure cooker to the Sauté/More setting. When the pot is hot, pour in 1 tablespoon of the avocado oil. 3. Add half of the Brussels sprouts to the pot, cut-side down, and let them brown for 3 to 5 minutes without disturbing. Transfer to a bowl and add the remaining tablespoon of avocado oil and the remaining Brussels sprouts to the pot. Hit Cancel and return all of the Brussels sprouts to the pot. 4. Add the broth, garlic, salt, and a few grinds of pepper. Stir to distribute the seasonings. 5. Close and lock the lid of the pressure cooker. Set the valve to sealing. 6. Cook on high pressure for 2 minutes. 7. While the Brussels sprouts are cooking, zest the lemon, then cut it into quarters. 8. When the cooking is complete, hit Cancel and quick release the pressure. 9. Once the pin drops, unlock and remove the lid. 10. Using a slotted spoon, transfer the Brussels sprouts to a serving bowl. Toss with the lemon zest, a squeeze of lemon juice, and the poppy seeds. Serve immediately.

Chapter *7*

Stews and Soups

Chapter 7 Stews and Soups

Butternut Squash Soup

Prep time: 30 minutes | Cook time: 15 minutes | Serves 4

- 2 tablespoons margarine
- 1 large onion, chopped
- 2 cloves garlic, minced
- 1 teaspoon thyme
- ½ teaspoon sage
- Salt and pepper to taste
- 2 large butternut squash, peeled, seeded, and cubed (about 4 pounds)
- 4 cups low-sodium chicken stock

1. In the inner pot of the Instant Pot, melt the margarine using Sauté function. 2. Add onion and garlic and cook until soft, 3 to 5 minutes. 3. Add thyme and sage and cook another minute. Season with salt and pepper. 4. Stir in butternut squash and add chicken stock. 5. Secure the lid and make sure vent is at sealing. Using Manual setting, cook squash and seasonings 10 minutes, using high pressure. 6. When time is up, do a quick release of the pressure. 7. Puree the soup in a food processor or use immersion blender right in the inner pot. If soup is too thick, add more stock. Adjust salt and pepper as needed.

Chicken Cauliflower Rice Soup

Prep time: 5 minutes | Cook time: 20 minutes | Serves 4

- 4 tablespoons butter
- ¼ cup diced onion
- 2 stalks celery, chopped
- ½ cup fresh spinach
- ½ teaspoon salt
- ¼ teaspoon pepper
- ¼ teaspoon dried thyme
- ¼ teaspoon dried parsley
- 1 bay leaf
- 2 cups chicken broth
- 2 cups diced cooked chicken
- ¾ cup uncooked cauliflower rice
- ½ teaspoon xanthan gum (optional)

1. Press the Sauté button and add butter to Instant Pot. Add onions and sauté until translucent. Place celery and spinach into Instant Pot and sauté for 2 to 3 minutes until spinach is wilted. Press the Cancel button. 2. Sprinkle seasoning into Instant Pot and add bay leaf, broth, and cooked chicken. Click lid closed. Press the Soup button and adjust time for 10 minutes. 3. When timer beeps, quick-release the pressure and stir in cauliflower rice. Leave Instant Pot on Keep Warm setting to finish cooking cauliflower rice additional 10 minutes. Serve warm. 4. For a thicker soup, stir in xanthan gum.

Jalapeño Popper Chicken Soup

Prep time: 5 minutes | Cook time: 25 minutes | Serves 4

- 2 tablespoons butter
- ½ medium diced onion
- ¼ cup sliced pickled jalapeños
- ¼ cup cooked crumbled bacon
- 2 cups chicken broth
- 2 cups cooked diced chicken
- 4 ounces (113 g) cream cheese
- 1 teaspoon salt
- ½ teaspoon pepper
- ¼ teaspoon garlic powder
- ⅓ cup heavy cream
- 1 cup shredded sharp Cheddar cheese

1. Press the Sauté button. Add butter, onion, and sliced jalapeños to Instant Pot. Sauté for 5 minutes, until onions are translucent. Add bacon and press the Cancel button. 2. Add broth, cooked chicken, cream cheese, salt, pepper, and garlic to Instant Pot. Click lid closed. Press the Soup button and adjust time for 20 minutes. 3. When timer beeps, quick-release the steam. Stir in heavy cream and Cheddar. Continue stirring until cheese is fully melted. Serve warm.

Beef and Cauliflower Soup

Prep time: 10 minutes | Cook time: 14 minutes | Serves 4

- 1 cup ground beef
- ½ cup cauliflower, shredded
- 1 teaspoon unsweetened tomato purée
- ¼ cup coconut milk
- 1 teaspoon minced garlic
- 1 teaspoon dried oregano
- ½ teaspoon salt
- 4 cups water

1. Put all ingredients in the Instant Pot and stir well. 2. Close the lid. Select Manual mode and set cooking time for 14 minutes on High Pressure. 3. When timer beeps, make a quick pressure release and open the lid. 4. Blend with an immersion blender until smooth. 5. Serve warm.

Kale Curry Soup

Prep time: 10 minutes | Cook time: 15 minutes | Serves 3

- 2 cups kale
- 1 teaspoon almond butter
- 1 tablespoon fresh cilantro
- ½ cup ground chicken
- 1 teaspoon curry paste
- ½ cup heavy cream
- 1 cup chicken stock
- ½ teaspoon salt

1. Put the kale in the Instant Pot. 2. Add the almond butter, cilantro, and ground chicken. Sauté the mixture for 5 minutes. 3. Meanwhile, mix the curry paste and heavy cream in the Instant Pot until creamy. 4. Add chicken stock and salt, and close the lid. 5. Select Manual mode and set cooking time for 10 minutes on High Pressure. 6. When timer beeps, make a quick pressure release. Open the lid. 7. Serve warm.

Tomato-Basil Parmesan Soup

Prep time: 5 minutes | Cook time: 12 minutes | Serves 12

- 2 tablespoons unsalted butter or coconut oil
- ½ cup finely diced onions
- Cloves squeezed from 1 head roasted garlic , or 2 cloves garlic, minced
- 1 tablespoon dried basil leaves
- 1 teaspoon dried oregano leaves
- 1 (8 ounces / 227 g) package cream cheese, softened
- 4 cups chicken broth
- 2 (14½ ounces / 411 g) cans diced tomatoes
- 1 cup shredded Parmesan cheese, plus more for garnish
- 1 teaspoon fine sea salt
- ¼ teaspoon ground black pepper
- Fresh basil leaves, for garnish

1. Place the butter in the Instant Pot and press Sauté. Once melted, add the onions, garlic, basil, and oregano and cook, stirring often, for 4 minutes, or until the onions are soft. Press Cancel to stop the Sauté. 2. Add the cream cheese and whisk to loosen. (If you don't use a whisk to loosen the cream cheese, you will end up with clumps in your soup.) Slowly whisk in the broth. Add the tomatoes, Parmesan, salt, and pepper and stir to combine. 3. Seal the lid, press Manual, and set the timer for 8 minutes. Once finished, turn the valve to venting for a quick release. 4. Remove the lid and purée the soup with a stick blender, or transfer the soup to a regular blender or food processor and process until smooth. If using a regular blender, you may need to blend the soup in two batches; if you overfill the blender jar, the soup will not purée properly. 5. Season with salt and pepper to taste, if desired. Ladle the soup into bowls and garnish with more Parmesan and basil leaves.

Easy Southern Brunswick Stew

Prep time: 20 minutes | Cook time: 8 minutes | Serves 12

- 2 pounds pork butt, visible fat removed
- 17-ounce can white corn
- 1¼ cups ketchup
- 2 cups diced, cooked potatoes
- 10-ounce package frozen peas
- 2 10¾-ounce cans reduced-sodium tomato soup
- Hot sauce to taste, optional

1. Place pork in the Instant Pot and secure the lid. 2. Press the Slow Cook setting and cook on low 6–8 hours. 3. When cook time is over, remove the meat from the bone and shred, removing and discarding all visible fat. 4. Combine all the meat and remaining ingredients (except the hot sauce) in the inner pot of the Instant Pot. 5. Secure the lid once more and cook in Slow Cook mode on low for 30 minutes more. Add hot sauce if you wish.

Broccoli and Bacon Cheese Soup

Prep time: 6 minutes | Cook time: 10 minutes | Serves 6

- 3 tablespoons butter
- 2 stalks celery, diced
- ½ yellow onion, diced
- 3 garlic cloves, minced
- 3½ cups chicken stock
- 4 cups chopped fresh broccoli florets
- 3 ounces (85 g) block-style cream cheese, softened and cubed
- ½ teaspoon ground nutmeg
- ½ teaspoon sea salt
- 1 teaspoon ground black pepper
- 3 cups shredded Cheddar cheese
- ½ cup shredded Monterey Jack cheese
- 2 cups heavy cream
- 4 slices cooked bacon, crumbled
- 1 tablespoon finely chopped chives

1. Select Sauté mode. Once the Instant Pot is hot, add the butter and heat until the butter is melted. 2. Add the celery, onions, and garlic. Continue sautéing for 5 minutes or until the vegetables are softened. 3. Add the chicken stock and broccoli florets to the pot. Bring the liquid to a boil. 4. Lock the lid,. Select Manual mode and set cooking time for 5 minutes on High Pressure. 5. When cooking is complete, allow the pressure to release naturally for 10 minutes and then release the remaining pressure. 6. Open the lid and add the cream cheese, nutmeg, sea salt, and black pepper. Stir to combine. 7. Select Sauté mode. Bring the soup to a boil and then slowly stir in the Cheddar and Jack cheeses. Once the cheese has melted, stir in the heavy cream. 8. Ladle the soup into serving bowls and top with bacon and chives. Serve hot.

Creamy Chicken Wild Rice Soup

Prep time: 15 minutes | Cook time: 15 minutes | Serves 5

- 2 tablespoons margarine
- ½ cup yellow onion, diced
- ¾ cup carrots, diced
- ¾ cup sliced mushrooms (about 3–4 mushrooms)
- ½ pound chicken breast, diced into 1-inch cubes
- 6.2-ounce box Uncle Ben's Long Grain & Wild Rice

Fast Cook

- 2 14-ounce cans low-sodium chicken broth
- 1 cup skim milk
- 1 cup evaporated skim milk
- 2 ounces fat-free cream cheese
- 2 tablespoons cornstarch

1. Select the Sauté feature and add the margarine, onion, carrots, and mushrooms to the inner pot. Sauté for about 5 minutes until onions are translucent and soft. 2. Add the cubed chicken and seasoning packet from the Uncle Ben's box and stir to combine. 3. Add the rice and chicken broth. Select Manual, high pressure, then lock the lid and make sure the vent is set to sealing. Set the time for 5 minutes. 4. After the cooking time ends, allow it to stay on Keep Warm for 5 minutes and then quick release the pressure. 5. Remove the lid; change the setting to the Sauté function again. 6. Add the skim milk, evaporated milk, and cream cheese. Stir to melt. 7. In a small bowl, mix the cornstarch with a little bit of water to dissolve, then add to the soup to thicken.

All-Purpose Chicken Broth

Prep time: 10 minutes | Cook time: 1 hour 25 minutes | Makes 3 quarts

- 3 pounds (1.4 kg) chicken wings
- 1 tablespoon vegetable oil
- 1 onion, chopped
- 3 garlic cloves, lightly

crushed and peeled
- 12 cups water, divided
- ½ teaspoon table salt
- 3 bay leaves

1. Pat chicken wings dry with paper towels. Using highest sauté function, heat oil in Instant Pot for 5 minutes (or until just smoking). Brown half of chicken wings on all sides, about 10 minutes; transfer to bowl. Repeat with remaining chicken wings; transfer to bowl. 2. Add onion to fat left in pot and cook until softened and well browned, 8 to 10 minutes. Stir in garlic and cook until fragrant, about 30 seconds. Stir in 1 cup water, scraping up any browned bits. Stir in remaining 11 cups water, salt, bay leaves, and chicken and any accumulated juices. 3. Lock lid in place and close pressure release valve. Select high pressure cook function and cook for 1 hour. Turn off Instant Pot and let pressure release naturally for 15 minutes. Quick-release any remaining pressure,

then carefully remove lid, allowing steam to escape away from you. 4. Strain broth through fine-mesh strainer into large container, pressing on solids to extract as much liquid as possible; discard solids. Using wide, shallow spoon, skim excess fat from surface of broth. (Broth can be refrigerated for up to 4 days or frozen for up to 2 months.)

Broccoli and Red Feta Soup

Prep time: 10 minutes | Cook time: 25 minutes | Serves 4

- 1 cup broccoli, chopped
- ½ cup coconut cream
- 1 teaspoon unsweetened tomato purée
- 4 cups beef broth
- 1 teaspoon chili flakes
- 6 ounces (170 g) feta, crumbled

1. Put broccoli, coconut cream, tomato purée, and beef broth in the Instant Pot. Sprinkle with chili flakes and stir to mix well. 2. Close the lid and select Manual mode. Set cooking time for 8 minutes on High Pressure. 3. When timer beeps, make a quick pressure release and open the lid. 4. Add the feta cheese and stir the soup on Sauté mode for 5 minutes or until the cheese melt. 5. Serve immediately.

Buttercup Squash Soup

Prep time: 15 minutes | Cook time: 10 minutes | Serves 6

- 2 tablespoons extra-virgin olive oil
- 1 medium onion, chopped
- 4 to 5 cups Vegetable Broth or Chicken Bone Broth
- 1½ pounds buttercup

squash, peeled, seeded, and cut into 1-inch chunks
- ½ teaspoon kosher salt
- ¼ teaspoon ground white pepper
- Whole nutmeg, for grating

1. Set the electric pressure cooker to the Sauté setting. When the pot is hot, pour in the olive oil. 2. Add the onion and sauté for 3 to 5 minutes, until it begins to soften. Hit Cancel. 3. Add the broth, squash, salt, and pepper to the pot and stir. (If you want a thicker soup, use 4 cups of broth. If you want a thinner, drinkable soup, use 5 cups.) 4. Close and lock the lid of the pressure cooker. Set the valve to sealing. 5. Cook on high pressure for 10 minutes. 6. When the cooking is complete, hit Cancel and allow the pressure to release naturally. 7. Once the pin drops, unlock and remove the lid. 8. Use an immersion blender to purée the soup right in the pot. If you don't have an immersion blender, transfer the soup to a blender or food processor and purée. (Follow the instructions that came with your machine for blending hot foods.) 9. Pour the soup into serving bowls and grate nutmeg on top.

Chicken and Asparagus Soup

- 1 tablespoon unsalted butter (or coconut oil for dairy-free)
- ¼ cup finely chopped onions
- 2 cloves garlic, minced
- 1 (14-ounce / 397-g) can full-fat coconut milk
- 1 (14-ounce / 397-g) can sugar-free tomato sauce
- 1 cup chicken broth
- 1 tablespoon red curry paste
- 1 teaspoon fine sea salt
- ½ teaspoon ground black pepper
- 2 pounds (907 g) boneless, skinless chicken breasts, cut into ½-inch chunks
- 2 cups asparagus, trimmed and cut into 2-inch pieces
- Fresh cilantro leaves, for garnish
- Lime wedges, for garnish

1. Place the butter in the Instant Pot and press Sauté. Once melted, add the onions and garlic and sauté for 4 minutes, or until the onions are soft. Press Cancel to stop the Sauté. 2. Add the coconut milk, tomato sauce, broth, curry paste, salt, and pepper and whisk to combine well. Stir in the chicken and asparagus. 3. Seal the lid, press Manual, and set the timer for 7 minutes. Once finished, turn the valve to venting for a quick release. 4. Remove the lid and stir well. Taste and adjust the seasoning to your liking. Ladle the soup into bowls and garnish with cilantro. Serve with lime wedges or a squirt of lime juice.

Favorite Chili

- 1 pound extra-lean ground beef
- 1 teaspoon salt
- ½ teaspoons black pepper
- 1 tablespoon olive oil
- 1 small onion, chopped
- 2 cloves garlic, minced
- 1 green pepper, chopped
- 2 tablespoons chili powder
- ½ teaspoons cumin
- 1 cup water
- 16-ounce can chili beans
- 15-ounce can low-sodium crushed tomatoes

1. Press Sauté button and adjust once to Sauté More function. Wait until indicator says "hot." 2. Season the ground beef with salt and black pepper. 3. Add the olive oil into the inner pot. Coat the whole bottom of the pot with the oil. 4. Add ground beef into the inner pot. The ground beef will start to release moisture. Allow the ground beef to brown and crisp slightly, stirring occasionally to break it up. Taste and adjust the seasoning with more salt and ground black pepper. 5. Add diced onion, minced garlic, chopped pepper, chili powder, and cumin. Sauté for about 5 minutes, until the spices start to release their fragrance. Stir frequently. 6. Add water and 1 can of chili beans, not drained. Mix well. Pour in 1 can of crushed tomatoes. 7. Close and secure lid, making sure vent is set to sealing, and pressure cook on Manual at high pressure for 10 minutes. 8. Let the pressure release naturally when cooking time is up. Open the lid carefully.

Avocado and Serrano Chile Soup

- 2 avocados
- 1 small fresh tomatillo, quartered
- 2 cups chicken broth
- 2 tablespoons avocado oil
- 1 tablespoon butter
- 2 tablespoons finely minced onion
- 1 clove garlic, minced
- ½ Serrano chile, deseeded and ribs removed, minced, plus thin slices for garnish
- ¼ teaspoon sea salt
- Pinch of ground white pepper
- ½ cup full-fat coconut milk
- Fresh cilantro sprigs, for garnish

1. Scoop the avocado flesh into a food processor. Add the tomatillo and chicken broth and purée until smooth. Set aside. 2. Set the Instant Pot to Sauté mode and add the avocado oil and butter. When the butter melts, add the onion and garlic and sauté for a minute or until softened. Add the Serrano chile and sauté for 1 minute more. 3. Pour the puréed avocado mixture into the pot, add the salt and pepper, and stir to combine. 4. Secure the lid. Press the Manual button and set cooking time for 5 minutes on High Pressure. 5. When timer beeps, use a quick pressure release. Open the lid and stir in the coconut milk. 6. Serve hot topped with thin slices of Serrano chile, and cilantro sprigs.

Beef and Spinach Stew

- 1 pound (454 g) beef sirloin, chopped
- 2 cups spinach, chopped
- 3 cups chicken broth
- 1 cup coconut milk
- 1 teaspoon allspices
- 1 teaspoon coconut aminos

1. Put all ingredients in the Instant Pot. Stir to mix well. 2. Close the lid. Set the Manual mode and set cooking time for 30 minutes on High Pressure. 3. When timer beeps, use a natural pressure release for 10 minutes, then release any remaining pressure. Open the lid. 4. Blend with an immersion blender until smooth. 5. Serve warm.

Curried Chicken Soup

- 1 pound (454 g) boneless, skinless chicken thighs
- 1½ cups unsweetened coconut milk
- ½ onion, finely diced
- 3 or 4 garlic cloves, crushed
- 1 (2-inch) piece ginger, finely chopped
- 1 cup sliced mushrooms,
- such as cremini and shiitake
- 4 ounces (113 g) baby spinach
- 1 teaspoon salt
- ½ teaspoon ground turmeric
- ½ teaspoon cayenne
- 1 teaspoon garam masala
- ¼ cup chopped fresh cilantro

1. In the inner cooking pot of your Instant Pot, add the chicken, coconut milk, onion, garlic, ginger, mushrooms, spinach, salt, turmeric, cayenne, garam masala, and cilantro. 2. Lock the lid into place. Select Manual and adjust the pressure to High. Cook for 10 minutes. When the cooking is complete, let the pressure release naturally. Unlock the lid. 3. Use tongs to transfer the chicken to a bowl. Shred the chicken, then stir it back into the soup. 4. Eat and rejoice.

Chicken and Mushroom Soup

- 1 onion, cut into thin slices
- 3 garlic cloves, minced
- 2 cups chopped mushrooms
- 1 yellow summer squash, chopped
- 1 pound (454 g) boneless, skinless chicken breast, cut into large chunks
- 2½ cups chicken broth
- 1 teaspoon salt
- 1 teaspoon freshly ground black pepper
- 1 teaspoon Italian seasoning or poultry seasoning
- 1 cup heavy (whipping) cream

1. Put the onion, garlic, mushrooms, squash, chicken, chicken broth, salt, pepper, and Italian seasoning in the inner cooking pot of the Instant Pot. 2. Lock the lid into place. Select Manual and adjust the pressure to High. Cook for 15 minutes. When the cooking is complete, let the pressure release naturally for 10 minutes, then quick-release any remaining pressure. Unlock the lid. 3. Using tongs, transfer the chicken pieces to a bowl and set aside. 4. Tilt the pot slightly. Using an immersion blender, roughly purée the vegetables, leaving a few intact for texture and visual appeal. 5. Shred the chicken and stir it back in to the soup. 6. Add the cream and stir well. Serve.

Beef and Eggplant Tagine

- 1 pound (454 g) beef fillet, chopped
- 1 eggplant, chopped
- 6 ounces (170 g) scallions, chopped
- 4 cups beef broth
- 1 teaspoon ground allspices
- 1 teaspoon erythritol
- 1 teaspoon coconut oil

1. Put all ingredients in the Instant Pot. Stir to mix well. 2. Close the lid. Select Manual mode and set cooking time for 25 minutes on High Pressure. 3. When timer beeps, use a natural pressure release for 15 minutes, then release any remaining pressure. Open the lid. 4. Serve warm.

Venison and Tomato Stew

- 1 tablespoon unsalted butter
- 1 cup diced onions
- 2 cups button mushrooms, sliced in half
- 2 large stalks celery, cut into ¼-inch pieces
- Cloves squeezed from 2 heads roasted garlic or 4 cloves garlic, minced
- 2 pounds (907 g) boneless venison or beef roast, cut into 4 large pieces
- 5 cups beef broth
- 1 (14½-ounce / 411-g) can
- diced tomatoes
- 1 teaspoon fine sea salt
- 1 teaspoon ground black pepper
- ½ teaspoon dried rosemary, or 1 teaspoon fresh rosemary, finely chopped
- ½ teaspoon dried thyme leaves, or 1 teaspoon fresh thyme leaves, finely chopped
- ½ head cauliflower, cut into large florets
- Fresh thyme leaves, for garnish

1. Place the butter in the Instant Pot and press Sauté. Once melted, add the onions and sauté for 4 minutes, or until soft. 2. Add the mushrooms, celery, and garlic and sauté for another 3 minutes, or until the mushrooms are golden brown. Press Cancel to stop the Sauté. Add the roast, broth, tomatoes, salt, pepper, rosemary, and thyme. 3. Seal the lid, press Manual, and set the timer for 30 minutes. Once finished, turn the valve to venting for a quick release. 4. Add the cauliflower. Seal the lid, press Manual, and set the timer for 5 minutes. Once finished, let the pressure release naturally. 5. Remove the lid and shred the meat with two forks. Taste the liquid and add more salt, if needed. Ladle the stew into bowls. Garnish with thyme leaves.

Creamy Sweet Potato Soup

Prep time: 15 minutes | Cook time: 10 minutes | Serves 6

- 2 tablespoons avocado oil
- 1 small onion, chopped
- 2 celery stalks, chopped
- 2 teaspoons minced garlic
- 1 teaspoon kosher salt
- ½ teaspoon freshly ground black pepper
- 1 teaspoon ground turmeric
- ½ teaspoon ground cinnamon
- 2 pounds sweet potatoes, peeled and cut into 1-inch cubes
- 3 cups Vegetable Broth or Chicken Bone Broth
- Plain Greek yogurt, to garnish (optional)
- Chopped fresh parsley, to garnish (optional)
- Pumpkin seeds (pepitas), to garnish (optional)

1. Set the electric pressure cooker to the Sauté setting. When the pot is hot, pour in the avocado oil. 2. Sauté the onion and celery for 3 to 5 minutes or until the vegetables begin to soften. 3. Stir in the garlic, salt, pepper, turmeric, and cinnamon. Hit Cancel. 4. Stir in the sweet potatoes and broth. 5. Close and lock the lid of the pressure cooker. Set the valve to sealing. 6. Cook on high pressure for 10 minutes. 7. When the cooking is complete, hit Cancel and allow the pressure to release naturally. 8. Once the pin drops, unlock and remove the lid. 9. Use an immersion blender to purée the soup right in the pot. If you don't have an immersion blender, transfer the soup to a blender or food processor and purée. (Follow the instructions that came with your machine for blending hot foods.) 10. Spoon into bowls and serve topped with Greek yogurt, parsley, and/or pumpkin seeds (if using).

Bacon Broccoli Soup

Prep time: 12 minutes | Cook time: 12 minutes | Serves 6

- 2 large heads broccoli
- 2 strips bacon, chopped
- 2 tablespoons unsalted butter
- ¼ cup diced onions
- Cloves squeezed from 1 head roasted garlic, or 2 cloves garlic, minced
- 3 cups chicken broth or beef broth
- 6 ounces (170 g) extra-sharp Cheddar cheese, shredded (about 1½ cups)
- 2 ounces (57 g) cream cheese, softened
- ½ teaspoon fine sea salt
- ¼ teaspoon ground black pepper
- Pinch of ground nutmeg

1. Cut the broccoli florets off the stems, leaving as much of the stems intact as possible. Reserve the florets for another recipe. Trim the bottom end of each stem so that it is flat. Using a spiral slicer, cut the stems into "noodles." 2. Place the bacon in the Instant Pot and press Sauté. Cook, stirring occasionally, for 4 minutes, or until crisp. Remove the bacon with a slotted spoon and set aside on a paper towel-lined plate to drain, leaving the drippings in the pot. 3. Add the butter and onions to the Instant Pot and cook for 4 minutes, or until the onions are soft. Add the garlic (and, if using raw garlic, sauté for another minute). Add the broth, Cheddar cheese, cream cheese, salt, pepper, and nutmeg and sauté until the cheeses are melted, about 3 minutes. Press Cancel to stop the Sauté. 4. Use a stick blender to purée the soup until smooth. Alternatively, you can pour the soup into a regular blender or food processor and purée until smooth, then return it to the Instant Pot. If using a regular blender, you may need to blend the soup in two batches; if you overfill the blender jar, the soup will not purée properly. 5. Add the broccoli noodles to the puréed soup in the Instant Pot. Seal the lid, press Manual, and set the timer for 1 minute. Once finished, let the pressure release naturally. 6. Remove the lid and stir well. Ladle the soup into bowls and sprinkle some of the bacon on top of each serving.

Cauliflower Soup

Prep time: 10 minutes | Cook time: 6 minutes | Serves 4

- 2 cups chopped cauliflower
- 2 tablespoons fresh cilantro
- 1 cup coconut cream
- 2 cups beef broth
- 3 ounces (85 g) Provolone cheese, chopped

1. Put cauliflower, cilantro, coconut cream, beef broth, and cheese in the Instant Pot. Stir to mix well. 2. Select Manual mode and set cooking time for 6 minutes on High Pressure. 3. When timer beeps, allow a natural pressure release for 4 minutes, then release any remaining pressure. Open the lid. 4. Blend the soup and ladle in bowls to serve.

Pork and Daikon Stew

Prep time: 15 minutes | Cook time: 3 minutes | Serves 6

- 1 pound (454 g) pork tenderloin, chopped
- 1 ounce (28 g) green onions, chopped
- ½ cup daikon, chopped
- 1 lemon slice
- 1 tablespoon heavy cream
- 1 tablespoon butter
- 1 teaspoon ground black pepper
- 3 cups water

1. Put all ingredients in the Instant Pot and stir to mix with a spatula. 2. Seal the lid. Set Manual mode and set cooking time for 20 minutes on High Pressure. 3. When cooking is complete, use a natural pressure release for 15 minutes, then release any remaining pressure. Open the lid. 4. Serve warm.

Chicken Poblano Pepper Soup

- 1 cup diced onion
- 3 poblano peppers, chopped
- 5 garlic cloves
- 2 cups diced cauliflower
- 1½ pounds (680 g) chicken breast, cut into large chunks
- ¼ cup chopped fresh cilantro
- 1 teaspoon ground coriander
- 1 teaspoon ground cumin
- 1 to 2 teaspoons salt
- 2 cups water
- 2 ounces (57 g) cream cheese, cut into small chunks
- 1 cup sour cream

1. To the inner cooking pot of the Instant Pot, add the onion, poblanos, garlic, cauliflower, chicken, cilantro, coriander, cumin, salt, and water. 2. Lock the lid into place. Select Manual and adjust the pressure to High. Cook for 15 minutes. When the cooking is complete, let the pressure release naturally for 10 minutes, then quick-release any remaining pressure. Unlock the lid. 3. Remove the chicken with tongs and place in a bowl. 4. Tilting the pot, use an immersion blender to roughly purée the vegetable mixture. It should still be slightly chunky. 5. Turn the Instant Pot to Sauté and adjust to high heat. When the broth is hot and bubbling, add the cream cheese and stir until it melts. Use a whisk to blend in the cream cheese if needed. 6. Shred the chicken and stir it back into the pot. Once it is heated through, serve, topped with sour cream, and enjoy.

Pancetta and Jalapeño Soup

- 3 ounces (85 g) pancetta, chopped
- 1 teaspoon coconut oil
- 2 jalapeño peppers, sliced
- ½ teaspoon garlic powder
- ½ teaspoon smoked paprika
- ½ cup heavy cream
- 2 cups water
- ½ cup Monterey Jack cheese, shredded

1. Toss the pancetta in the Instant Pot, then add the coconut oil and cook for 4 minutes on Sauté mode. Stir constantly. 2. Add the sliced jalapeños, garlic powder, and smoked paprika. Sauté for 1 more minute. 3. Pour in the heavy cream and water. Add the Monterey Jack cheese and stir to mix well. 4. Close the lid and select Manual mode and set cooking time on High Pressure. 5. When timer beeps, make a quick pressure release. Open the lid. 6. Serve warm.

Blue Cheese Mushroom Soup

- 2 cups chopped white mushrooms
- 3 tablespoons cream cheese
- 4 ounces (113 g) scallions, diced
- 4 cups chicken broth
- 1 teaspoon olive oil
- ½ teaspoon ground cumin
- 1 teaspoon salt
- 2 ounces (57 g) blue cheese, crumbled

1. Combine the mushrooms, cream cheese, scallions, chicken broth, olive oil, and ground cumin in the Instant Pot. 2. Seal the lid. Select Manual mode and set cooking time for 20 minutes on High Pressure. 3. When timer beeps, use a quick pressure release and open the lid. 4. Add the salt and blend the soup with an immersion blender. 5. Ladle the soup in the bowls and top with blue cheese. Serve warm.

Bacon, Leek, and Cauliflower Soup

- 6 slices bacon
- 1 leek, remove the dark green end and roots, sliced in half lengthwise, rinsed, cut into ½-inch-thick slices crosswise
- ½ medium yellow onion, sliced
- 4 cloves garlic, minced
- 3 cups chicken broth
- 1 large head cauliflower, roughly chopped into florets
- 1 cup water
- 1 teaspoon kosher salt
- 1 teaspoon ground black pepper
- ⅔ cup shredded sharp Cheddar cheese, divided
- ½ cup heavy whipping cream

1. Set the Instant Pot to Sauté mode. When heated, place the bacon on the bottom of the pot and cook for 5 minutes or until crispy. 2. Transfer the bacon slices to a plate. Let stand until cool enough to handle, crumble it with forks. 3. Add the leek and onion to the bacon fat remaining in the pot. Sauté for 5 minutes or until fragrant and the onion begins to caramelize. Add the garlic and sauté for 30 seconds more or until fragrant. 4. Stir in the chicken broth, cauliflower florets, water, salt, pepper, and three-quarters of the crumbled bacon. 5. Secure the lid. Press the Manual button and set cooking time for 3 minutes on High Pressure. 6. When timer beeps, perform a quick pressure release. Open the lid. 7. Stir in ½ cup of the Cheddar and the cream. Use an immersion blender to purée the soup until smooth. 8. Ladle into bowls and garnish with the remaining Cheddar and crumbled bacon. Serve immediately.

Beef and Mushroom Stew

Prep time: 15 minutes | Cook time: 30 minutes | Serves 4

- 2 tablespoons coconut oil
- 1 pound (454 g) cubed chuck roast
- 1 cup sliced button mushrooms
- ½ medium onion, chopped
- 2 cups beef broth
- ½ cup chopped celery
- 1 tablespoon sugar-free tomato paste
- 1 teaspoon thyme
- 2 garlic cloves, minced
- ½ teaspoon xanthan gum

1. Press the Sauté button and add coconut oil to Instant Pot. Brown cubes of chuck roast until golden, working in batches if necessary. (If the pan is overcrowded, they will not brown properly.) Set aside after browning is completed. 2. Add mushrooms and onions to pot. Sauté until mushrooms begin to brown and onions are translucent. Press the Cancel button. 3. Add broth to Instant Pot. Use wooden spoon to scrape bits from bottom if necessary. Add celery, tomato paste, thyme, and garlic. Click lid closed. Press the Manual button and adjust time for 35 minutes. When timer beeps, allow a natural release. 4. When pressure valve drops, stir in xanthan gum and allow to thicken. Serve warm.

Spiced Chicken Soup with Squash and Chickpeas

Prep time: 15 minutes | Cook time: 30 minutes | Serves 6 to 8

- 2 tablespoons extra-virgin olive oil
- 1 onion, chopped
- 1¾ teaspoons table salt
- 2 tablespoons tomato paste
- 4 garlic cloves, minced
- 1 tablespoon ground coriander
- 1½ teaspoons ground cumin
- 1 teaspoon ground cardamom
- ½ teaspoon ground allspice
- ¼ teaspoon cayenne pepper
- 7 cups water, divided
- 2 (12 ounces / 340 g) bone-in split chicken breasts, trimmed
- 4 (5 to 7 ounces / 142 to 198 g) bone-in chicken thighs, trimmed
- 1½ pounds (680 g) butternut squash, peeled, seeded, and cut into 1½-inch pieces (4 cups)
- 1 (15 ounces / 425 g) can chickpeas, rinsed
- ½ cup chopped fresh cilantro

1. Using highest sauté function, heat oil in Instant Pot until shimmering. Add onion and salt and cook until onion is softened, about 5 minutes. Stir in tomato paste, garlic, coriander, cumin, cardamom, allspice, and cayenne and cook until fragrant, about 30 seconds. Stir in 5 cups water, scraping up any browned bits. Nestle chicken breasts and thighs in pot, then arrange squash evenly around chicken. 2. Lock lid in place and close pressure release valve. Select high pressure cook function and cook for 20 minutes. Turn off Instant Pot and quick-release pressure. Carefully remove lid, allowing steam to escape away from you. 3. Transfer chicken to cutting board, let cool slightly, then shred into bite-size pieces using 2 forks; discard skin and bones. 4. Using wide, shallow spoon, skim excess fat from surface of soup, then break squash into bite-size pieces. Stir chicken and any accumulated juices, chickpeas, and remaining 2 cups water into soup and let sit until heated through, about 3 minutes. Stir in cilantro and season with salt and pepper to taste. Serve.

Beef Stew with Eggplant and Potatoes

Prep time: 15 minutes | Cook time: 50 minutes | Serves 6 to 8

- 2 pounds (907 g) boneless short ribs, trimmed and cut into 1-inch pieces
- 1½ teaspoons table salt, divided
- 2 tablespoons extra-virgin olive oil
- 1 onion, chopped fine
- 3 tablespoons tomato paste
- ¼ cup all-purpose flour
- 3 garlic cloves, minced
- 1 tablespoon ground cumin
- 1 teaspoon ground turmeric
- 1 teaspoon ground cardamom
- ¾ teaspoon ground cinnamon
- 4 cups chicken broth
- 1 cup water
- 1 pound (454 g) eggplant, cut into 1-inch pieces
- 1 pound (454 g) Yukon Gold potatoes, unpeeled, cut into 1-inch pieces
- ½ cup chopped fresh mint or parsley

1. Pat beef dry with paper towels and sprinkle with 1 teaspoon salt. Using highest sauté function, heat oil in Instant Pot for 5 minutes (or until just smoking). Brown half of beef on all sides, 7 to 9 minutes; transfer to bowl. Set aside remaining uncooked beef. 2. Add onion to fat left in pot and cook, using highest sauté function, until softened, about 5 minutes. Stir in tomato paste, flour, garlic, cumin, turmeric, cardamom, cinnamon, and remaining ½ teaspoon salt. Cook until fragrant, about 1 minute. Slowly whisk in broth and water, scraping up any browned bits. Stir in eggplant and potatoes. Nestle remaining uncooked beef into pot along with browned beef, and add any accumulated juices. 3. Lock lid in place and close pressure release valve. Select high pressure cook function and cook for 30 minutes. Turn off Instant Pot and quick-release pressure. Carefully remove lid, allowing steam to escape away from you. 4. Using wide, shallow spoon, skim excess fat from surface of stew. Stir in mint and season with salt and pepper to taste. Serve.

Bacon Curry Soup

Prep time: 10 minutes | Cook time: 20 minutes | Serves 4

- 3 ounces (85 g) bacon, chopped
- 1 tablespoon chopped scallions
- 1 teaspoon curry powder
- 1 cup coconut milk
- 3 cups beef broth
- 1 cup Cheddar cheese, shredded

1. Heat the the Instant Pot on Sauté mode for 3 minutes and add bacon. Cook for 5 minutes. Flip constantly. 2. Add the scallions and curry powder. Sauté for 5 minutes more. 3. Pour in the coconut milk and beef broth. Add the Cheddar cheese and stir to mix well. 4. Select Manual mode and set cooking time for 10 minutes on High Pressure. 5. When timer beeps, use a quick pressure release. Open the lid. 6. Blend the soup with an immersion blender until smooth. Serve warm.

Savory Beef Stew with Mushrooms and Turnips

Prep time: 0 minutes | Cook time: 55 minutes | Serves 6

- 1½ pounds beef stew meat
- ¾ teaspoon fine sea salt
- ¾ teaspoon freshly ground black pepper
- 1 tablespoon cold-pressed avocado oil
- 3 garlic cloves, minced
- 1 yellow onion, diced
- 2 celery stalks, diced
- 8 ounces cremini mushrooms, quartered
- 1 cup low-sodium roasted beef bone broth
- 2 tablespoons Worcestershire sauce
- 1 tablespoon Dijon mustard
- 1 teaspoon dried rosemary, crumbled
- 1 bay leaf
- 3 tablespoons tomato paste
- 8 ounces carrots, cut into 1-inch-thick rounds
- 1 pound turnips, cut into 1-inch pieces
- 1 pound parsnips, halved lengthwise, then cut crosswise into 1-inch pieces

1. Sprinkle the beef all over with the salt and pepper. 2. Select the Sauté setting on the Instant Pot and heat the oil and garlic for 2 minutes, until the garlic is bubbling but not browned. Add the onion, celery, and mushrooms and sauté for 5 minutes, until the onion begins to soften and the mushrooms are giving up their liquid. Stir in the broth, Worcestershire sauce, mustard, rosemary, and bay leaf. Stir in the beef. Add the tomato paste in a dollop on top. Do not stir it in. 3. Secure the lid and set the Pressure Release to Sealing. Press the Cancel button to reset the cooking program, then select the Meat/Stew, Pressure Cook, or Manual setting and set the cooking time for 20 minutes at high pressure. (The pot will take about 10 minutes to come up to pressure before the cooking program begins.) 4. When the cooking program ends, perform a quick pressure release by moving the Pressure Release to Venting, or let the pressure release naturally. Open the pot, remove and discard the bay leaf, and stir in the tomato paste. Place the carrots, turnips, and parsnips on top of the meat. 5. Secure the lid and set the Pressure Release to Sealing. Press the Cancel button to reset the cooking program, then select the Pressure Cook or Manual setting and set the cooking time for 3 minutes at low pressure. (The pot will take about 15 minutes to come up to pressure before the cooking program begins.) 6. When the cooking program ends, perform a quick pressure release by moving the Pressure Release to Venting. Open the pot and stir to combine all of the ingredients. 7. Ladle the stew into bowls and serve hot.

Garlic Beef Soup

Prep time: 12 minutes | Cook time: 42 minutes | Serves 8

- 10 strips bacon, chopped
- 1 medium white onion, chopped
- Cloves squeezed from 3 heads roasted garlic, or 6 cloves garlic, minced
- 1 to 2 jalapeño peppers, seeded and chopped (optional)
- 2 pounds (907 g) boneless

For Garnish:

- 1 avocado, peeled, pitted, and diced
- 2 radishes, very thinly sliced

- beef chuck roast, cut into 4 equal-sized pieces
- 5 cups beef broth
- 1 cup chopped fresh cilantro, plus more for garnish
- 2 teaspoons fine sea salt
- 1 teaspoon ground black pepper

- 2 tablespoons chopped fresh chives

1. Place the bacon in the Instant Pot and press Sauté. Cook, stirring occasionally, for 4 minutes, or until the bacon is crisp. Remove the bacon with a slotted spoon, leaving the drippings in the pot. Set the bacon on a paper towel-lined plate to drain. 2. Add the onion, garlic, and jalapeños, if using, to the Instant Pot and sauté for 3 minutes, or until the onion is soft. Press Cancel to stop the Sauté. 3. Add the beef, broth, cilantro, salt, and pepper. Stir to combine. 4. Seal the lid, press Manual, and set the timer for 35 minutes. Once finished, let the pressure release naturally. 5. Remove the lid and shred the beef with two forks. Taste the liquid and add more salt, if needed. 6. Ladle the soup into bowls. Garnish with the reserved bacon, avocado, radishes, chives, and more cilantro.

Beef and Okra Stew

Prep time: 15 minutes | Cook time: 25 minutes | Serves 3

- 8 ounces (227 g) beef sirloin, chopped
- ¼ teaspoon cumin seeds
- 1 teaspoon dried basil
- 1 tablespoon avocado oil
- ¼ cup coconut cream
- 1 cup water
- 6 ounces (170 g) okra, chopped

1. Sprinkle the beef sirloin with cumin seeds and dried basil and put in the Instant Pot. 2. Add avocado oil and roast the meat on Sauté mode for 5 minutes. Flip occasionally. 3. Add coconut cream, water, and okra. 4. Close the lid and select Manual mode. Set cooking time for 25 minutes on High Pressure. 5. When timer beeps, use a natural pressure release for 10 minutes, the release any remaining pressure. Open the lid. 6. Serve warm.

Beef, Mushroom, and Wild Rice Soup

Prep time: 0 minutes | Cook time: 55 minutes | Serves 6

- 2 tablespoons extra-virgin olive oil or unsalted butter
- 2 garlic cloves, minced
- 8 ounces shiitake mushrooms, stems removed and sliced
- 1 teaspoon fine sea salt
- 2 carrots, diced
- 2 celery stalks, diced
- 1 yellow onion, diced
- 1 teaspoon dried thyme
- 1½ pounds beef stew meat, larger pieces halved, or beef chuck, trimmed of fat and cut into ¾-inch pieces
- 4 cups low-sodium roasted beef bone broth
- 1 cup wild rice, rinsed
- 1 tablespoon Worcestershire sauce
- 2 tablespoons tomato paste

1. Select the Sauté setting on the Instant Pot and heat the oil and garlic for about 1 minute, until the garlic is bubbling but not browned. Add the mushrooms and salt and sauté for 5 minutes, until the mushrooms have wilted and given up some of their liquid. Add the carrots, celery, and onion and sauté for 4 minutes, until the onion begins to soften. Add the thyme and beef and sauté for 3 minutes more, until the beef is mostly opaque on the outside. Stir in the broth, rice, Worcestershire sauce, and tomato paste, using a wooden spoon to nudge any browned bits from the bottom of the pot. 2. Secure the lid and set the Pressure Release to Sealing. Press the Cancel button to reset the cooking program, then select the Pressure Cook or Manual setting and set the cooking time for 25 minutes at high pressure. (The pot will take about 15 minutes to come up to pressure before the cooking program begins.) 3.

When the cooking program ends, let the pressure release naturally for at least 15 minutes, then move the Pressure Release to Venting to release any remaining steam. Open the pot. Ladle the soup into bowls and serve hot.

Chicken and Kale Soup

Prep time: 5 minutes | Cook time: 5 minutes | Serves 4

- 2 cups chopped cooked chicken breast
- 12 ounces (340 g) frozen kale
- 1 onion, chopped
- 2 cups water
- 1 tablespoon powdered chicken broth base
- ½ teaspoon ground cinnamon
- Pinch ground cloves
- 2 teaspoons minced garlic
- 1 teaspoon freshly ground black pepper
- 1 teaspoon salt
- 2 cups full-fat coconut milk

1. Put the chicken, kale, onion, water, chicken broth base, cinnamon, cloves, garlic, pepper, and salt in the inner cooking pot of the Instant Pot. 2. Lock the lid into place. Select Manual and adjust the pressure to High. Cook for 5 minutes. When the cooking is complete, let the pressure release naturally for 10 minutes, then quick-release any remaining pressure. Unlock the lid. 3. Stir in the coconut milk. Taste and adjust any seasonings as needed before serving.

Vegetarian Chili

Prep time: 25 minutes | Cook time: 10 minutes | Serves 6

- 2 teaspoons olive oil
- 3 garlic cloves, minced
- 2 onions, chopped
- 1 green bell pepper, chopped
- 1 cup textured vegetable protein (T.V.P.)
- 1-pound can beans of your choice, drained
- 1 jalapeño pepper, seeds removed, chopped
- 28-ounce can diced Italian tomatoes
- 1 bay leaf
- 1 tablespoon dried oregano
- ½ teaspoons salt
- ¼ teaspoons pepper

1. Set the Instant Pot to the Sauté function. As it's heating, add the olive oil, garlic, onions, and bell pepper. Stir constantly for about 5 minutes as it all cooks. Press Cancel. 2. Place all of the remaining ingredients into the inner pot of the Instant pot and stir. 3. Secure the lid and make sure vent is set to sealing. Cook on Manual mode for 10 minutes. 4. When cook time is up, let the steam release naturally for 5 minutes and then manually release the rest.

Italian Vegetable Soup

Prep time: 20 minutes | Cook time: 5 to 9 hours | Serves 6

- 3 small carrots, sliced
- 1 small onion, chopped
- 2 small potatoes, diced
- 2 tablespoons chopped parsley
- 1 garlic clove, minced
- 3 teaspoons sodium-free beef bouillon powder
- 1¼ teaspoons dried basil
- ¼ teaspoon pepper
- 16-ounce can red kidney beans, undrained
- 3 cups water
- 14½-ounce can stewed tomatoes, with juice
- 1 cup diced, extra-lean, lower-sodium cooked ham

1. In the inner pot of the Instant Pot, layer the carrots, onion, potatoes, parsley, garlic, beef bouillon, basil, pepper, and kidney beans. Do not stir. Add water. 2. Secure the lid and cook on the Low Slow Cook mode for 8–9 hours, or on high 4½–5½ hours, until vegetables are tender. 3. Remove the lid and stir in the tomatoes and ham. Secure the lid again and cook on high Slow Cook mode for 10–15 minutes more.

Pasta e Fagioli with Ground Beef

Prep time: 0 minutes | Cook time: 30 minutes | Serves 8

- 2 tablespoons extra-virgin olive oil
- 4 garlic cloves, minced
- 1 yellow onion, diced
- 2 large carrots, diced
- 4 celery stalks, diced
- 1½ pounds 95 percent extra-lean ground beef
- 4 cups low-sodium vegetable broth
- 2 teaspoons Italian seasoning
- ½ teaspoon freshly ground black pepper
- 1¼ cups chickpea-based elbow pasta or whole-wheat elbow pasta
- 1½ cups drained cooked kidney beans, or one 15-ounce can kidney beans, rinsed and drained
- One 28-ounce can whole San Marzano tomatoes and their liquid
- 2 tablespoons chopped fresh flat-leaf parsley

1. Select the Sauté setting on the Instant Pot and heat the oil and garlic for 2 minutes, until the garlic is bubbling but not browned. Add the onion, carrots, and celery and sauté for 5 minutes, until the onion begins to soften. Add the beef and sauté, using a wooden spoon or spatula to break up the meat as it cooks, for 5 minutes; it's fine if some streaks of pink remain, the beef does not need to be cooked through. 2. Stir in the broth, Italian seasoning, pepper, and pasta, making sure all of the pasta is submerged in the liquid. Add the beans and stir to mix. Add the tomatoes and their liquid, crushing the tomatoes with your hands as you add them to the pot. Do not stir them in. 3. Secure the lid and set the Pressure Release to Sealing. Press the Cancel button to reset the cooking program, then select the Pressure Cook or Manual setting and set the cooking time for 2 minutes at low pressure. (The pot will take about 15 minutes to come up to pressure before the cooking program begins.) 4. When the cooking program ends, let the pressure release naturally for 10 minutes, then move the Pressure Release to Venting to release any remaining steam. Open the pot and stir the soup to mix all of the ingredients. 5. Ladle the soup into bowls, sprinkle with the parsley, and serve right away.

Gigante Bean Soup with Celery and Olives

Prep time: 30 minutes | Cook time: 12 minutes | Serves 6 to 8

- 1½ tablespoons table salt, for brining
- 1 pound (454 g) dried gigante beans, picked over and rinsed
- 2 tablespoons extra-virgin olive oil, plus extra for drizzling
- 5 celery ribs, cut into ½-inch pieces, plus ½ cup leaves, minced
- 1 onion, chopped
- ½ teaspoon table salt
- 4 garlic cloves, minced
- 4 cups vegetable or chicken broth
- 4 cups water
- 2 bay leaves
- ½ cup pitted kalamata olives, chopped
- 2 tablespoons minced fresh marjoram or oregano
- Lemon wedges

1. Dissolve 1½ tablespoons salt in 2 quarts cold water in large container. Add beans and soak at room temperature for at least 8 hours or up to 24 hours. Drain and rinse well. 2. Using highest sauté function, heat oil in Instant Pot until shimmering. Add celery pieces, onion, and ½ teaspoon salt and cook until vegetables are softened, about 5 minutes. Stir in garlic and cook until fragrant, about 30 seconds. Stir in broth, water, beans, and bay leaves. 3. Lock lid in place and close pressure release valve. Select high pressure cook function and cook for 6 minutes. Turn off Instant Pot and let pressure release naturally for 15 minutes. Quick-release any remaining pressure, then carefully remove lid, allowing steam to escape away from you. 4. Combine celery leaves, olives, and marjoram in bowl. Discard bay leaves. Season soup with salt and pepper to taste. Top individual portions with celery-olive mixture and drizzle with extra oil. Serve with lemon wedges.

Cabbage Roll Soup

Prep time: 10 minutes | Cook time: 8 minutes | Serves 4

- ½ pound (227 g) 84% lean ground pork
- ½ pound (227 g) 85% lean ground beef
- ½ medium onion, diced
- ½ medium head cabbage, thinly sliced
- 2 tablespoons sugar-free tomato paste
- ½ cup diced tomatoes
- 2 cups chicken broth
- 1 teaspoon salt
- ½ teaspoon thyme
- ½ teaspoon garlic powder
- ¼ teaspoon pepper

1. Press the Sauté button and add beef and pork to Instant Pot. Brown meat until no pink remains. Add onion and continue cooking until onions are fragrant and soft. Press the Cancel button. 2. Add remaining ingredients to Instant Pot. Press the Manual button and adjust time for 8 minutes. 3. When timer beeps, allow a 15-minute natural release and then quick-release the remaining pressure. Serve warm.

Sicilian Fish Stew

Prep time: 10 minutes | Cook time: 10 minutes | Serves 4 to 6

- 2 tablespoons extra-virgin olive oil
- 2 onions, chopped fine
- 1 teaspoon table salt
- ½ teaspoon pepper
- 1 teaspoon minced fresh thyme or ¼ teaspoon dried
- Pinch red pepper flakes
- 4 garlic cloves, minced, divided
- 1 (28-ounce / 794-g) can whole peeled tomatoes, drained with juice reserved, chopped coarse
- 1 (8-ounce / 227-g) bottle clam juice
- ¼ cup dry white wine
- ¼ cup golden raisins
- 2 tablespoons capers, rinsed
- 1½ pounds (680 g) skinless swordfish steak, 1 to 1½ inches thick, cut into 1-inch pieces
- ¼ cup pine nuts, toasted
- ¼ cup minced fresh mint
- 1 teaspoon grated orange zest

1. Using highest sauté function, heat oil in Instant Pot until shimmering. Add onions, salt, and pepper and cook until onions are softened, about 5 minutes. Stir in thyme, pepper flakes, and three-quarters of garlic and cook until fragrant, about 30 seconds. Stir in tomatoes and reserved juice, clam juice, wine, raisins, and capers. Nestle swordfish into pot and spoon some cooking liquid over top. 2. Lock lid in place and close pressure release valve. Select high pressure cook function and cook for 1 minute. Turn off Instant Pot and quick-release pressure. Carefully remove lid, allowing steam to escape away from you. 3. Combine pine nuts, mint, orange zest, and remaining garlic in bowl. Season stew with salt and pepper to taste. Sprinkle individual portions with pine nut mixture before serving.

Garlicky Chicken Soup

Prep time: 5 minutes | Cook time: 20 minutes | Serves 6

- 10 roasted garlic cloves
- ½ medium onion, diced
- 4 tablespoons butter
- 4 cups chicken broth
- ½ teaspoon salt
- ¼ teaspoon pepper
- 1 teaspoon thyme
- 1 pound (454 g) boneless, skinless chicken thighs, cubed
- ½ cup heavy cream
- 2 ounces (57 g) cream cheese

1. In small bowl, mash roasted garlic into paste. Press the Sauté button and add garlic, onion, and butter to Instant Pot. Sauté for 2 to 3 minutes until onion begins to soften. Press the Cancel button. 2. Add Chicken Broth, salt, pepper, thyme, and chicken to Instant Pot. Click lid closed. Press the Manual button and adjust time for 20 minutes. 3. When timer beeps, quick-release the pressure. Stir in heavy cream and cream cheese until smooth. Serve warm.

Salmon and Tomatillos Stew

Prep time: 15 minutes | Cook time: 12 minutes | Serves 2

- 10 ounces (283 g) salmon fillet, chopped
- 2 tomatillos, chopped
- ½ teaspoon ground turmeric
- 1 cup coconut cream
- 1 teaspoon ground paprika
- ½ teaspoon salt

1. Put all ingredients in the Instant Pot. Stir to mix well. 2. Close the lid. Select Manual mode and set cooking time for 12 minutes on Low Pressure. 3. When timer beeps, use a quick pressure release. Open the lid. 4. Serve warm.

Chapter *8*

Desserts

Chapter 8 Desserts

Cardamom Rolls with Cream Cheese

Prep time: 20 minutes | Cook time: 18 minutes | Serves 5

- ½ cup coconut flour
- 1 tablespoon ground cardamom
- 2 tablespoon Swerve
- 1 egg, whisked
- ¼ cup almond milk
- 1 tablespoon butter, softened
- 1 tablespoon cream cheese
- ⅓ cup water

1. Combine together coconut flour, almond milk, and softened butter. 2. Knead the smooth dough. 3. Roll up the dough with the help of the rolling pin. 4. Then combine together Swerve and ground cardamom. 5. Sprinkle the surface of the dough with the ground cardamom mixture. 6. Roll the dough into one big roll and cut them into servings. 7. Place the rolls into the instant pot round mold. 8. Pour water in the instant pot (⅓ cup) and insert the mold inside. 9. Set Manual mode (High Pressure) for 18 minutes. 10. Then use the natural pressure release method for 15 minutes. 11. Chill the rolls to the room temperature and spread with cream cheese.

Southern Almond Pie

Prep time: 10 minutes | Cook time: 35 minutes | Serves 12

- 2 cups almond flour
- 1½ cups powdered erythritol
- 1 teaspoon baking powder
- Pinch of salt
- ½ cup sour cream
- 4 tablespoons butter, melted
- 1 egg
- 1 teaspoon vanilla extract
- Cooking spray
- 1½ teaspoons ground cinnamon
- 1½ teaspoons Swerve
- 1 cup water

1. In a large bowl, whisk together the almond flour, powdered erythritol, baking powder, and salt. 2. Add the sour cream, butter, egg, and vanilla and whisk until well combined. The batter will be very thick, almost like cookie dough. 3. Grease the baking dish with cooking spray. Line with parchment paper, if desired. 4.

Transfer the batter to the dish and level with an offset spatula. 5. In a small bowl, combine the cinnamon and Swerve. Sprinkle over the top of the batter. 6. Cover the dish tightly with aluminum foil. Add the water to the pot. Set the dish on the trivet and carefully lower it into the pot. 7. Set the lid in place. Select the Manual mode and set the cooking time for 35 minutes on High Pressure. When the timer goes off, do a quick pressure release. Carefully open the lid. 8. Remove the trivet and pie from the pot. Remove the foil from the pan. The pie should be set but soft, and the top should be slightly cracked. 9. Cool completely before cutting.

Pumpkin Walnut Cheesecake

Prep time: 15 minutes | Cook time: 50 minutes | Serves 6

- 2 cups walnuts
- 3 tablespoons melted butter
- 1 teaspoon cinnamon
- 16 ounces (454 g) cream cheese, softened
- 1 cup powdered erythritol
- ⅓ cup heavy cream
- ⅔ cup pumpkin purée
- 2 teaspoons pumpkin spice
- 1 teaspoon vanilla extract
- 2 eggs
- 1 cup water

1. Preheat oven to 350ºF (180ºC). Add walnuts, butter, and cinnamon to food processor. Pulse until ball forms. Scrape down sides as necessary. Dough should hold together in ball. 2. Press into greased 7-inch springform pan. Bake for 10 minutes or until it begins to brown. Remove and set aside. While crust is baking, make cheesecake filling. 3. In large bowl, stir cream cheese until completely smooth. Using rubber spatula, mix in erythritol, heavy cream, pumpkin purée, pumpkin spice, and vanilla. 4. In small bowl, whisk eggs. Slowly add them into large bowl, folding gently until just combined. 5. Pour mixture into crust and cover with foil. Pour water into Instant Pot and place steam rack on bottom. Place pan onto steam rack and click lid closed. Press the Cake button and press the Adjust button to set heat to More. Set timer for 40 minutes. 6. When timer beeps, allow a full natural release. When pressure indicator drops, carefully remove pan and place on counter. Remove foil. Let cool for additional hour and then refrigerate. Serve chilled.

Cocoa Cookies

Prep time: 15 minutes | Cook time: 25 minutes | Serves 4

- ½ cup coconut flour
- 3 tablespoons cream cheese
- 1 teaspoon cocoa powder
- 1 tablespoon erythritol
- ¼ teaspoon baking powder
- 1 teaspoon apple cider vinegar
- 1 tablespoon butter
- 1 cup water, for cooking

1. Make the dough: Mix up coconut flour, cream cheese, cocoa powder, erythritol, baking powder, apple cider vinegar, and butter. Knead the dough, 2. Then transfer the dough in the baking pan and flatten it in the shape of a cookie. 3. Pour water and insert the steamer rack in the instant pot. 4. Put the pan with a cookie in the instant pot. Close and seal the lid. 5. Cook the cookie on Manual (High Pressure) for 25 minutes. Make a quick pressure release. Cool the cookie well.

Vanilla Cream Pie

Prep time: 20 minutes | Cook time: 35 minutes | Serves 12

- 1 cup heavy cream
- 3 eggs, beaten
- 1 teaspoon vanilla extract
- ¼ cup erythritol
- 1 cup coconut flour
- 1 tablespoon butter, melted
- 1 cup water, for cooking

1. In the mixing bowl, mix up coconut flour, erythritol, vanilla extract, eggs, and heavy cream. 2. Grease the baking pan with melted butter. 3. Pour the coconut mixture in the baking pan. 4. Pour water and insert the steamer rack in the instant pot. 5. Place the pie on the rack. Close and seal the lid. 6. Cook the pie on Manual mode (High Pressure) for 35 minutes. 7. Allow the natural pressure release for 10 minutes.

Strawberry Cheesecake

Prep time: 20 minutes | Cook time: 10 minutes | Serves 2

- 1 tablespoon gelatin
- 4 tablespoon water (for gelatin)
- 4 tablespoon cream cheese
- 1 strawberry, chopped
- ¼ cup coconut milk
- 1 tablespoon Swerve

1. Mix up gelatin and water and leave the mixture for 10 minutes. 2. Meanwhile, pour coconut milk in the instant pot. 3. Bring it to boil on Sauté mode, about 10 minutes. 4. Meanwhile, mash the strawberry and mix it up with cream cheese. 5. Add the mixture in the hot coconut milk and stir until smooth. 6. Cool the liquid for 10 minutes and add gelatin. Whisk it until gelatin is melted. 7. Then pour the cheesecake in the mold and freeze in the freezer for 3 hours.

Pumpkin Pie Spice Pots De Crème

Prep time: 5 minutes | Cook time: 7 minutes | Serves 4

- 2 cups heavy cream (or full-fat coconut milk for dairy-free)
- 4 large egg yolks
- ¼ cup Swerve, or more to taste
- 2 teaspoons pumpkin pie spice
- 1 teaspoon vanilla extract
- Pinch of fine sea salt
- 1 cup cold water

1. Heat the cream in a pan over medium-high heat until hot, about 2 minutes. 2. Place the remaining ingredients except the water in a medium bowl and stir until smooth. 3. Slowly pour in the hot cream while stirring. Taste and adjust the sweetness to your liking. Scoop the mixture into four ramekins with a spatula. Cover the ramekins with aluminum foil. 4. Place a trivet in the Instant Pot and pour in the water. Place the ramekins on the trivet. 5. Lock the lid. Select the Manual mode and set the cooking time for 5 minutes at High Pressure. 6. When the timer beeps, use a quick pressure release. Carefully remove the lid. 7. Remove the foil and set the foil aside. Let the pots de crème cool for 15 minutes. Cover the ramekins with the foil again and place in the refrigerator to chill completely, about 2 hours. 8. Serve.

Chai Pear-Fig Compote

Prep time: 20 minutes | Cook time: 3 minutes | Serves 4

- 1 vanilla chai tea bag
- 1 (3-inch) cinnamon stick
- 1 strip lemon peel (about 2-by-½ inches)
- 1½ pounds pears, peeled and chopped (about 3 cups)
- ½ cup chopped dried figs
- 2 tablespoons raisins

1. Pour 1 cup of water into the electric pressure cooker and hit Sauté/More. When the water comes to a boil, add the tea bag and cinnamon stick. Hit Cancel. Let the tea steep for 5 minutes, then remove and discard the tea bag. 2. Add the lemon peel, pears, figs, and raisins to the pot. 3. Close and lock the lid of the pressure cooker. Set the valve to sealing. 4. Cook on high pressure for 3 minutes. 5. When the cooking is complete, hit Cancel and quick release the pressure. 6. Once the pin drops, unlock and remove the lid. 7. Remove the lemon peel and cinnamon stick. Serve warm or cool to room temperature and refrigerate.

Chipotle Black Bean Brownies

Prep time: 15 minutes | Cook time: 30 minutes | Serves 8

- Nonstick cooking spray
- ½ cup dark chocolate chips, divided
- ¾ cup cooked calypso beans or black beans
- ½ cup extra-virgin olive oil
- 2 large eggs
- ¼ cup unsweetened dark chocolate cocoa powder
- ⅓ cup honey
- 1 teaspoon vanilla extract
- ⅓ cup white wheat flour
- ½ teaspoon chipotle chili powder
- ½ teaspoon ground cinnamon
- ½ teaspoon baking powder
- ½ teaspoon kosher salt

1. Spray a 7-inch Bundt pan with nonstick cooking spray. 2. Place half of the chocolate chips in a small bowl and microwave them for 30 seconds. Stir and repeat, if necessary, until the chips have completely melted. 3. In a food processor, blend the beans and oil together. Add the melted chocolate chips, eggs, cocoa powder, honey, and vanilla. Blend until the mixture is smooth. 4. In a large bowl, whisk together the flour, chili powder, cinnamon, baking powder, and salt. Pour the bean mixture from the food processor into the bowl and stir with a wooden spoon until well combined. Stir in the remaining chocolate chips. 5. Pour the batter into the prepared Bundt pan. Cover loosely with foil. 6. Pour 1 cup of water into the electric pressure cooker. 7. Place the Bundt pan onto the wire rack and lower it into the pressure cooker. 8. Close and lock the lid of the pressure cooker. Set the valve to sealing. 9. Cook on high pressure for 30 minutes. 10. When the cooking is complete, hit Cancel and quick release the pressure. 11. Once the pin drops, unlock and remove the lid. 12. Carefully transfer the pan to a cooling rack for about 10 minutes, then invert the cake onto the rack and let it cool completely. 13. Cut into slices and serve.

Chocolate Fondue

Prep time: 5 minutes | Cook time: 2 minutes | Serves 4

- 2 ounces (57 g) unsweetened baking chocolate, finely chopped, divided
- 1 cup heavy cream, divided
- ⅓ cup Swerve, divided
- Fine sea salt
- 1 cup cold water
- Special Equipment:
- Set of fondue forks or wooden skewers

1. Divide the chocolate, cream, and sweetener evenly among four ramekins. Add a pinch of salt to each one and stir well. Cover the ramekins with aluminum foil. 2. Place a trivet in the bottom of your Instant Pot and pour in the water. Place the ramekins on the trivet.

3. Lock the lid. Select the Manual mode and set the cooking time for 2 minutes at High Pressure. 4. When the timer beeps, perform a natural pressure release for 10 minutes. Carefully remove the lid. 5. Use tongs to remove the ramekins from the pot. Use a fork to stir the fondue until smooth. 6. Use immediately.

Fudgy Walnut Brownies

Prep time: 10 minutes | Cook time: 1 hour | Serves 12

- ¾ cup walnut halves and pieces
- ½ cup unsalted butter, melted and cooled
- 4 large eggs
- 1½ teaspoons instant coffee crystals
- 1½ teaspoons vanilla extract
- 1 cup Lakanto Monkfruit Sweetener Golden
- ¼ teaspoon fine sea salt
- ¾ cup almond flour
- ¾ cup natural cocoa powder
- ¾ cup stevia-sweetened chocolate chips

1. In a dry small skillet over medium heat, toast the walnuts, stirring often, for about 5 minutes, until golden. Transfer the walnuts to a bowl to cool. 2. Pour 1 cup water into the Instant Pot. Line the base of a 7 by 3-inch round cake pan with a circle of parchment paper. Butter the sides of the pan and the parchment or coat with nonstick cooking spray. 3. Pour the butter into a medium bowl. One at a time, whisk in the eggs, then whisk in the coffee crystals, vanilla, sweetener, and salt. Finally, whisk in the flour and cocoa powder just until combined. Using a rubber spatula, fold in the chocolate chips and walnuts. 4. Transfer the batter to the prepared pan and, using the spatula, spread it in an even layer. Cover the pan tightly with aluminum foil. Place the pan on a long-handled silicone steam rack, then, holding the handles of the steam rack, lower it into the Instant Pot. 5. Secure the lid and set the Pressure Release to Sealing. Select the Cake, Pressure Cook, or Manual setting and set the cooking time for 45 minutes at high pressure. (The pot will take about 10 minutes to come up to pressure before the cooking program begins.) 6. When the cooking program ends, let the pressure release naturally for 10 minutes, then move the Pressure Release to Venting to release any remaining steam. Open the pot and, wearing heat-resistant mitts, grasp the handles of the steam rack and lift it out of the pot. Uncover the pan, taking care not to get burned by the steam or to drip condensation onto the brownies. Let the brownies cool in the pan on a cooling rack for about 2 hours, to room temperature. 7. Run a butter knife around the edge of the pan to make sure the brownies are not sticking to the pan sides. Invert the brownies onto the rack, lift off the pan, and peel off the parchment paper. Invert the brownies onto a serving plate and cut into twelve wedges. The brownies will keep, stored in an airtight container in the refrigerator for up to 5 days, or in the freezer for up to 4 months.

Greek Yogurt Strawberry Pops

Prep time: 5 minutes | Cook time: 0 minutes | Serves 6

2 ripe bananas, peeled, cut into ½-inch pieces, and frozen
½ cup plain 2 percent Greek yogurt
1 cup chopped fresh strawberries

1. In a food processor, combine the bananas and yogurt and process at high speed for 2 minutes, until mostly smooth (it's okay if a few small chunks remain). Scrape down the sides of the bowl, add the strawberries, and process for 1 minute, until smooth. 2. Divide the mixture evenly among six ice-pop molds. Tap each mold on a countertop a few times to get rid of any air pockets, then place an ice-pop stick into each mold and transfer the molds to the freezer. Freeze for at least 4 hours, or until frozen solid. 3. To unmold each ice pop, run it under cold running water for 5 seconds, taking care not to get water inside the mold, then remove the ice pop from the mold. Eat the ice pops right away or store in a ziplock plastic freezer bag in the freezer for up to 2 months.

Traditional Cheesecake

Prep time: 30 minutes | Cook time: 45 minutes | Serves 8

For Crust:

- 1½ cups almond flour
- 4 tablespoons butter, melted
- 1 tablespoon Swerve
- 1 tablespoon granulated erythritol
- ½ teaspoon ground cinnamon

For Filling:

- 16 ounces (454 g) cream cheese, softened
- ½ cup granulated erythritol
- 2 eggs
- 1 teaspoon vanilla extract
- ½ teaspoon lemon extract
- 1½ cups water

1. To make the crust: In a medium bowl, combine the almond flour, butter, Swerve, erythritol, and cinnamon. Use a fork to press it all together. When completed, the mixture should resemble wet sand. 2. Spray the springform pan with cooking spray and line the bottom with parchment paper. 3. Press the crust evenly into the pan. Work the crust up the sides of the pan, about halfway from the top, and make sure there are no bare spots on the bottom. 4. Place the crust in the freezer for 20 minutes while you make the filling. 5. To make the filling: In the bowl of a stand mixer using the whip attachment, combine the cream cheese and erythritol on medium speed until the cream cheese is light and fluffy, 2 to 3 minutes. 6. Add the eggs, vanilla extract, and lemon extract. Mix until well combined. 7. Remove the crust from the freezer and pour in the filling. Cover the pan tightly with aluminum foil and place it on the trivet. 8. Add the

water to the pot and carefully lower the trivet into the pot. 9. Close the lid. Select Manual mode and set cooking time for 45 minutes on High Pressure. 10. When timer beeps, use a quick pressure release and open the lid. 11. Remove the trivet and cheesecake from the pot. Remove the foil from the pan. The center of the cheesecake should still be slightly jiggly. If the cheesecake is still very jiggly in the center, cook for an additional 5 minutes on High pressure until the appropriate doneness is reached. 12. Let the cheesecake cool for 30 minutes on the counter before placing it in the refrigerator to set. Leave the cheesecake in the refrigerator for at least 6 hours before removing the sides of the pan, slicing, and serving.

Candied Mixed Nuts

Prep time: 5 minutes | Cook time: 15 minutes | Serves 8

- 1 cup pecan halves
- 1 cup chopped walnuts
- ⅓ cup Swerve, or more to taste
- ⅓ cup grass-fed butter
- 1 teaspoon ground cinnamon

1. Preheat your oven to 350°F (180°C), and line a baking sheet with aluminum foil. 2. While your oven is warming, pour ½ cup of filtered water into the inner pot of the Instant Pot, followed by the pecans, walnuts, Swerve, butter, and cinnamon. Stir nut mixture, close the lid, and then set the pressure valve to Sealing. Use the Manual mode to cook at High Pressure, for 5 minutes. 3. Once cooked, perform a quick release by carefully switching the pressure valve to Venting, and strain the nuts. Pour the nuts onto the baking sheet, spreading them out in an even layer. Place in the oven for 5 to 10 minutes (or until crisp, being careful not to overcook). Cool before serving. Store leftovers in the refrigerator or freezer.

Apple Crunch

Prep time: 13 minutes | Cook time: 2 minutes | Serves 4

- 3 apples, peeled, cored, and sliced (about 1½ pounds)
- 1 teaspoon pure maple syrup
- 1 teaspoon apple pie spice
- or ground cinnamon
- ¼ cup unsweetened apple juice, apple cider, or water
- ¼ cup low-sugar granola

1. In the electric pressure cooker, combine the apples, maple syrup, apple pie spice, and apple juice. 2. Close and lock the lid of the pressure cooker. Set the valve to sealing. 3. Cook on high pressure for 2 minutes. 4. When the cooking is complete, hit Cancel and quick release the pressure. 5. Once the pin drops, unlock and remove the lid. 6. Spoon the apples into 4 serving bowls and sprinkle each with 1 tablespoon of granola.

Chocolate Chip Brownies

Prep time: 10 minutes | Cook time: 33 minutes | Serves 8

- 1½ cups almond flour
- ⅓ cup unsweetened cocoa powder
- ¾ cup granulated erythritol
- 1 teaspoon baking powder
- 2 eggs
- 1 tablespoon vanilla extract
- 5 tablespoons butter, melted
- ¼ cup sugar-free chocolate chips
- ½ cup water

1. In a large bowl, add the almond flour, cocoa powder, erythritol, and baking powder. Use a hand mixer on low speed to combine and smooth out any lumps. 2. Add the eggs and vanilla and mix until well combined. 3. Add the butter and mix on low speed until well combined. Scrape the bottom and sides of the bowl and mix again if needed. Fold in the chocolate chips. 4. Grease a baking dish with cooking spray. Pour the batter into the dish and smooth with a spatula. Cover tightly with aluminum foil. 5. Pour the water into the pot. Place the trivet in the pot and carefully lower the baking dish onto the trivet. 6. Close the lid. Select Manual mode and set cooking time for 33 minutes on High Pressure. 7. When timer beeps, use a quick pressure release and open the lid. 8. Use the handles to carefully remove the trivet from the pot. Remove the foil from the dish. 9. Let the brownies cool for 10 minutes before turning out onto a plate.

Traditional Kentucky Butter Cake

Prep time: 5 minutes | Cook time: 35 minutes | Serves 4

- 2 cups almond flour
- ¾ cup granulated erythritol
- 1½ teaspoons baking powder
- 4 eggs
- 1 tablespoon vanilla extract
- ½ cup butter, melted
- Cooking spray
- ½ cup water

1. In a medium bowl, whisk together the almond flour, erythritol, and baking powder. Whisk well to remove any lumps. 2. Add the eggs and vanilla and whisk until combined. 3. Add the butter and whisk until the batter is mostly smooth and well combined. 4. Grease the pan with cooking spray and pour in the batter. Cover tightly with aluminum foil. 5. Add the water to the pot. Place the Bundt pan on the trivet and carefully lower it into the pot using. 6. Set the lid in place. Select the Manual mode and set the cooking time for 35 minutes on High Pressure. When the timer goes off, do a quick pressure release. Carefully open the lid. 7. Remove the pan from the pot. Let the cake cool in the pan before flipping out onto a plate.

Coconut Cupcakes

Prep time: 5 minutes | Cook time: 10 minutes | Serves 6

- 4 eggs, beaten
- 4 tablespoons coconut milk
- 4 tablespoons coconut flour
- ½ teaspoon vanilla extract
- 2 tablespoons erythritol
- 1 teaspoon baking powder
- 1 cup water

1. In the mixing bowl, mix up eggs, coconut milk, coconut flour, vanilla extract, erythritol, and baking powder. 2. Then pour the batter in the cupcake molds. 3. Pour the water and insert the trivet in the instant pot. 4. Place the cupcakes on the trivet. 5. Lock the lid. Select the Manual mode and set the cooking time for 10 minutes on High Pressure. Once the timer goes off, perform a natural pressure release for 5 minutes, then release any remaining pressure. Carefully open the lid. 6. Serve immediately.

Chocolate Chip Banana Cake

Prep time: 15 minutes | Cook time: 25 minutes | Serves 8

- Nonstick cooking spray
- 3 ripe bananas
- ½ cup buttermilk
- 3 tablespoons honey
- 1 teaspoon vanilla extract
- 2 large eggs, lightly beaten
- 3 tablespoons extra-virgin olive oil
- 1½ cups whole wheat pastry flour
- ⅛ teaspoon ground nutmeg
- 1 teaspoon ground cinnamon
- ¼ teaspoon salt
- 1 teaspoon baking soda
- ⅓ cup dark chocolate chips

1. Spray a 7-inch Bundt pan with nonstick cooking spray. 2. In a large bowl, mash the bananas. Add the buttermilk, honey, vanilla, eggs, and olive oil, and mix well. 3. In a medium bowl, whisk together the flour, nutmeg, cinnamon, salt, and baking soda. 4. Add the flour mixture to the banana mixture and mix well. Stir in the chocolate chips. Pour the batter into the prepared Bundt pan. Cover the pan with foil. 5. Pour 1 cup of water into the electric pressure cooker. Place the pan on the wire rack and lower it into the pressure cooker. 6. Close and lock the lid of the pressure cooker. Set the valve to sealing. 7. Cook on high pressure for 25 minutes. 8. When the cooking is complete, hit Cancel and quick release the pressure. 9. Once the pin drops, unlock and remove the lid. 10. Carefully transfer the pan to a cooling rack, uncover, and let it cool for 10 minutes. 11. Invert the cake onto the rack and let it cool for about an hour. 12. Slice and serve the cake.

Goat Cheese–Stuffed Pears

- 2 ounces goat cheese, at room temperature
- 2 teaspoons pure maple syrup
- 2 ripe, firm pears, halved lengthwise and cored
- 2 tablespoons chopped pistachios, toasted

1. Pour 1 cup of water into the electric pressure cooker and insert a wire rack or trivet. 2. In a small bowl, combine the goat cheese and maple syrup. 3. Spoon the goat cheese mixture into the cored pear halves. Place the pears on the rack inside the pot, cut-side up. 4. Close and lock the lid of the pressure cooker. Set the valve to sealing. 5. Cook on high pressure for 2 minutes. 6. When the cooking is complete, hit Cancel and quick release the pressure. 7. Once the pin drops, unlock and remove the lid. 8. Using tongs, carefully transfer the pears to serving plates. 9. Sprinkle with pistachios and serve immediately.

Nutmeg Cupcakes

Cake:

- 2 cups blanched almond flour
- 2 tablespoons grass-fed butter, softened
- 2 eggs
- ½ cup unsweetened almond

milk
- ½ cup Swerve, or more to taste
- ½ teaspoon ground nutmeg
- ½ teaspoon baking powder

Frosting:

- 4 ounces (113 g) full-fat cream cheese, softened
- 4 tablespoons grass-fed butter, softened
- 2 cups heavy whipping cream
- 1 teaspoon vanilla extract
- ½ cup Swerve, or more to taste
- 6 tablespoons sugar-free chocolate chips (optional)

1. Pour 1 cup of filtered water into the inner pot of the Instant Pot, then insert the trivet. In a large bowl, combine the flour, butter, eggs, almond milk, Swerve, nutmeg, and baking powder. Mix thoroughly. Working in batches if needed, transfer this mixture into a well-greased, Instant Pot-friendly muffin (or egg bites) mold. 2. Place the molds onto the trivet, and cover loosely with aluminum foil. Close the lid, set the pressure release to Sealing, and select Manual. Set the Instant Pot to 30 minutes on High Pressure, and let cook. 3. While you wait, in a large bowl, combine the cream cheese, butter, whipping cream, vanilla, Swerve, and chocolate chips. Use an electric hand mixer until you achieve a light and fluffy texture. Place frosting in refrigerator. 4. Once the cupcakes are cooked, let the pressure release naturally, for about 10 minutes. Then, switch the pressure release to Venting. Open the Instant Pot, and remove the food. Let cool, top each cupcake evenly with a scoop of frosting.

Lush Chocolate Cake

For Cake:

- 2 cups almond flour
- ⅓ cup unsweetened cocoa powder
- 1½ teaspoons baking powder
- 1 cup granulated erythritol
- Pinch of salt
- 4 eggs
- 1 teaspoon vanilla extract
- ½ cup butter, melted and cooled
- 6 tablespoons strong coffee, cooled
- ½ cup water

For Frosting:

- 4 ounces (113 g) cream cheese, softened
- ½ cup butter, softened
- ¼ teaspoon vanilla extract
- 2½ tablespoons powdered erythritol
- 2 tablespoons unsweetened cocoa powder

1. To make the cake: In a large bowl, whisk together the almond flour, cocoa powder, baking powder, granulated erythritol, and salt. Whisk well to remove any lumps. 2. Add the eggs and vanilla and mix with a hand mixer until combined. 3. With the mixer still on low speed, slowly add the melted butter and mix until well combined. 4. Add the coffee and mix on low speed until the batter is thoroughly combined. Scrape the sides and bottom of the bowl to make sure everything is well mixed. 5. Spray the cake pan with cooking spray. Pour the batter into the pan. Cover tightly with aluminum foil. 6. Add the water to the pot. Place the cake pan on the trivet and carefully lower then pan into the pot. 7. Close the lid. Select Manual mode and set cooking time for 35 minutes on High Pressure. 8. When timer beeps, use a quick pressure release and open the lid. 9. Carefully remove the cake pan from the pot and place on a wire rack to cool. Flip the cake onto a plate once it is cool enough to touch. Cool completely before frosting. 10. To make the frosting: In a medium bowl, use the mixer to whip the cream cheese, butter, and vanilla until light and fluffy, 1 to 2 minutes. With the mixer running, slowly add the powdered erythritol and cocoa powder. Mix until everything is well combined. 11. Once the cake is completely cooled, spread the frosting on the top and down the sides.

Thai Pandan Coconut Custard

Prep time: 10 minutes | Cook time: 30 minutes | Serves 4

- Nonstick cooking spray
- 1 cup unsweetened coconut milk
- 3 eggs
- ⅓ cup Swerve
- 3 to 4 drops pandan extract, or use vanilla extract if you must

1. Grease a 6-inch heatproof bowl with the cooking spray. 2. In a large bowl, whisk together the coconut milk, eggs, Swerve, and pandan extract. Pour the mixture into the prepared bowl and cover it with aluminum foil. 3. Pour 2 cups of water into the inner cooking pot of the Instant Pot, then place a trivet in the pot. Place the bowl on the trivet. 4. Lock the lid into place. Select Manual and adjust the pressure to High. Cook for 30 minutes. When the cooking is complete, let the pressure release naturally. Unlock the lid. 5. Remove the bowl from the pot and remove the foil. A knife inserted into the custard should come out clean. Cool in the refrigerator for 6 to 8 hours, or until the custard is set.

Pecan Pumpkin Pie

Prep time: 5 minutes | Cook time: 40 minutes | Serves 5 to 6

Base:
- 2 tablespoons grass-fed butter, softened

Topping:
- ½ cup Swerve, or more to taste
- ⅓ cup heavy whipping cream
- ½ teaspoon ground cinnamon
- ½ teaspoon ginger, finely
- 1 cup blanched almond flour
- ½ cup chopped pecans

grated
- ½ teaspoon ground nutmeg
- ½ teaspoon ground cloves
- 1 (14-ounce / 397-g) can organic pumpkin purée
- 1 egg

1. Pour 1 cup of filtered water into the inner pot of the Instant Pot, then insert the trivet. Using an electric mixer, combine the butter, almond flour, and pecans. Mix thoroughly. Transfer this mixture into a well-greased, Instant Pot-friendly pan, and form a crust at the bottom of the pan, with a slight coating of the mixture also on the sides. Freeze for 15 minutes. In a large bowl, thoroughly combine the topping ingredients. 2. Take the pan from the freezer, add the topping evenly, and then place the pan onto the trivet. Cover loosely with aluminum foil. Close the lid, set the pressure release to Sealing, and select Manual. Set the Instant Pot to 40 minutes on High Pressure, and let cook. 3. Once cooked, let the pressure naturally disperse from the Instant Pot for about 10 minutes, then carefully switch the pressure release to Venting. 4. Open the Instant

Pot and remove the pan. Cool in the refrigerator for 4 to 5 hours, serve, and enjoy!

Coconut Squares

Prep time: 15 minutes | Cook time: 4 minutes | Serves 2

- ⅓ cup coconut flakes
- 1 tablespoon butter
- 1 egg, beaten
- 1 cup water, for cooking

1. Mix up together coconut flakes, butter, and egg. 2. Then put the mixture into the square shape mold and flatten well. 3. Pour water and insert the steamer rack in the instant pot. 4. Put the mold with dessert on the rack. Close and seal the lid. 5. Cook the meal on Manual mode (High Pressure) for 4 minutes. Make a quick pressure release. 6. Cool the cooked dessert little and cut into the squares.

Vanilla Butter Curd

Prep time: 5 minutes | Cook time: 6 hours | Serves 3

- 4 egg yolks, whisked
- 2 tablespoon butter
- 1 tablespoon erythritol
- ½ cup organic almond milk
- 1 teaspoon vanilla extract

1. Set the instant pot to Sauté mode and when the "Hot" is displayed, add butter. 2. Melt the butter but not boil it and add whisked egg yolks, almond milk, and vanilla extract. 3. Add erythritol. Whisk the mixture. 4. Cook the meal on Low for 6 hours.

Almond Pie with Coconut

Prep time: 5 minutes | Cook time: 41 minutes | Serves 8

- 1 cup almond flour
- ½ cup coconut milk
- 1 teaspoon vanilla extract
- 2 tablespoons butter,
- softened
- 1 tablespoon Truvia
- ¼ cup shredded coconut
- 1 cup water

1. In the mixing bowl, mix up almond flour, coconut milk, vanilla extract, butter, Truvia, and shredded coconut. 2. When the mixture is smooth, transfer it in the baking pan and flatten. 3. Pour water and insert the trivet in the instant pot. 4. Put the baking pan with cake on the trivet. 5. Lock the lid. Select the Manual mode and set the cooking time for 41 minutes on High Pressure. Once the timer goes off, perform a natural pressure release for 10 minutes, then release any remaining pressure. Carefully open the lid. 6. Serve immediately.

Keto Brownies

Prep time: 15 minutes | Cook time: 15 minutes | Serves 8

- 1 cup coconut flour
- 1 tablespoon cocoa powder
- 1 tablespoon coconut oil
- 1 teaspoon vanilla extract
- 1 teaspoon baking powder
- 1 teaspoon apple cider vinegar
- ⅓ cup butter, melted
- 1 tablespoon erythritol
- 1 cup water, for cooking

1. In the mixing bowl, mix up erythritol, melted butter, apple cider vinegar, baking powder, vanilla extract, coconut oil, cocoa powder, and coconut flour. 2. Whisk the mixture until smooth and pour it in the baking pan. Flatten the surface of the batter. 3. Pour water and insert the steamer rack in the instant pot. 4. Put the pan with brownie batter on the rack. Close and seal the lid. 5. Cook the brownie on Manual mode (High Pressure) for 15 minutes. 6. Then allow the natural pressure release for 5 minutes. 7. Cut the cooked brownies into the bars.

Cinnamon Roll Cheesecake

Prep time: 15 minutes | Cook time: 35 minutes | Serves 12

Crust:

- 3½ tablespoons unsalted butter or coconut oil
- 1½ ounces (43 g) unsweetened baking chocolate, chopped
- 1 large egg, beaten

Filling:

- 4 (8-ounce / 227-g) packages cream cheese, softened
- ¾ cup Swerve
- ½ cup unsweetened almond milk (or hemp milk for nut-free)

Cinnamon Swirl:

- 6 tablespoons (¾ stick) unsalted butter (or butter flavored coconut oil for dairy-free)
- ½ cup Swerve
- Seeds scraped from ½ vanilla bean (about 8 inches

- ⅓ cup Swerve
- 2 teaspoons ground cinnamon
- 1 teaspoon vanilla extract
- ¼ teaspoon fine sea salt

- 1 teaspoon vanilla extract
- ¼ teaspoon almond extract (omit for nut-free)
- ¼ teaspoon fine sea salt
- 3 large eggs

long), or 1 teaspoon vanilla extract
- 1 tablespoon ground cinnamon
- ¼ teaspoon fine sea salt
- 1 cup cold water

1. Line a baking pan with two layers of aluminum foil. 2. Make the crust: Melt the butter in a pan over medium-low heat. Slowly add the chocolate and stir until melted. Stir in the egg, sweetener, cinnamon, vanilla extract, and salt. 3. Transfer the crust mixture to the prepared baking pan, spreading it with your hands to cover the bottom completely. 4. Make the filling: In the bowl of a stand mixer, add the cream cheese, sweetener, milk, extracts, and salt and mix until well blended. Add the eggs, one at a time, mixing on low speed after each addition just until blended. Then blend until the filling is smooth. Pour half of the filling over the crust. 5. Make the cinnamon swirl: Heat the butter over high heat in a pan until the butter froths and brown flecks appear, stirring occasionally. Stir in the sweetener, vanilla seeds, cinnamon, and salt. Remove from the heat and allow to cool slightly. 6. Spoon half of the cinnamon swirl on top of the cheesecake filling in the baking pan. Use a knife to cut the cinnamon swirl through the filling several times for a marbled effect. Top with the rest of the cheesecake filling and cinnamon swirl. Cut the cinnamon swirl through the cheesecake filling again several times. 7. Place a trivet in the bottom of the Instant Pot and pour in the water. Use a foil sling to lower the baking pan onto the trivet. Cover the cheesecake with 3 large sheets of paper towel to ensure that condensation doesn't leak onto it. Tuck in the sides of the sling. 8. Lock the lid. Select the Manual mode and set the cooking time for 26 minutes at High Pressure. 9. When the timer beeps, use a natural pressure release for 10 minutes. Carefully remove the lid. 10. Use the foil sling to lift the pan out of the Instant Pot. 11. Let the cheesecake cool, then place in the refrigerator for 4 hours to chill and set completely before slicing and serving.

Pine Nut Mousse

Prep time: 5 minutes | Cook time: 35 minutes | Serves 8

- 1 tablespoon butter
- 1¼ cups pine nuts
- 1¼ cups full-fat heavy cream
- 2 large eggs

- 1 teaspoon vanilla extract
- 1 cup Swerve, reserve 1 tablespoon
- 1 cup water
- 1 cup full-fat heavy whipping cream

1. Butter the bottom and the side of a pie pan and set aside. 2. In a food processor, blend the pine nuts and heavy cream. Add the eggs, vanilla extract and Swerve and pulse a few times to incorporate. 3. Pour the batter into the pan and loosely cover with aluminum foil. Pour the water in the Instant Pot and place the trivet inside. Place the pan on top of the trivet. 4. Close the lid. Select Manual mode and set the timer for 35 minutes on High pressure. 5. In a small mixing bowl, whisk the heavy whipping cream and 1 tablespoon of Swerve until a soft peak forms. 6. When timer beeps, use a natural pressure release for 15 minutes, then release any remaining pressure and open the lid. 7. Serve immediately with whipped cream on top.

Crustless Creamy Berry Cheesecake

Prep time: 10 minutes | Cook time: 40 minutes | Serves 12

- 16 ounces (454 g) cream cheese, softened
- 1 cup powdered erythritol
- ¼ cup sour cream
- 2 teaspoons vanilla extract
- 2 eggs
- 2 cups water
- ¼ cup blackberries and strawberries, for topping

1. In large bowl, beat cream cheese and erythritol until smooth. Add sour cream, vanilla, and eggs and gently fold until combined. 2. Pour batter into 7-inch springform pan. Gently shake or tap pan on counter to remove air bubbles and level batter. Cover top of pan with tinfoil. Pour water into Instant Pot and place steam rack in pot. 3. Carefully lower pan into pot. Press the Cake button and press the Adjust button to set heat to More. Set time for 40 minutes. When timer beeps, allow a full natural release. Using sling, carefully lift pan from Instant Pot and allow to cool completely before refrigerating. 4. Place strawberries and blackberries on top of cheesecake and serve.

Lemon-Ricotta Cheesecake

Prep time: 10 minutes | Cook time: 30 minutes | Serves 6

- Unsalted butter or vegetable oil, for greasing the pan
- 8 ounces (227 g) cream cheese, at room temperature
- ¼ cup plus 1 teaspoon Swerve, plus more as needed
- ⅓ cup full-fat or part-skim ricotta cheese, at room temperature
- Zest of 1 lemon
- Juice of 1 lemon
- ½ teaspoon lemon extract
- 2 eggs, at room temperature
- 2 tablespoons sour cream

1. Grease a 6-inch springform pan extremely well. I find this easiest to do with a silicone basting brush so I can get into all the nooks and crannies. Alternatively, line the sides of the pan with parchment paper. 2. In the bowl of a stand mixer, beat the cream cheese, ¼ cup of Swerve, the ricotta, lemon zest, lemon juice, and lemon extract on high speed until you get a smooth mixture with no lumps. 3. Taste to ensure the sweetness is to your liking and adjust if needed. 4. Add the eggs, reduce the speed to low and gently blend until the eggs are just incorporated. Overbeating at this stage will result in a cracked crust. 5. Pour the mixture into the prepared pan and cover with aluminum foil or a silicone lid. 6. Pour 2 cups of water into the inner cooking pot of the Instant Pot, then place a trivet in the pot. Place the covered pan on the trivet. 7. Lock the lid into place. Select Manual and adjust the pressure to High. Cook for 30 minutes. When the cooking is complete, let the pressure release naturally. Unlock the lid. 8. Carefully remove the pan from the pot,

and remove the foil. 9. In a small bowl, mix together the sour cream and remaining 1 teaspoon of Swerve and spread this over the top of the warm cake. 10. Refrigerate the cheesecake for 6 to 8 hours. Do not be in a hurry! The cheesecake needs every bit of this time to be its best.

Lemon and Ricotta Torte

Prep time: 15 minutes | Cook time: 35 minutes | Serves 12

- Cooking spray

Torte:

- 1⅓ cups Swerve
- ½ cup (1 stick) unsalted butter, softened
- 2 teaspoons lemon or vanilla extract
- 5 large eggs, separated
- 2½ cups blanched almond flour
- 1¼ (10-ounce / 284-g) cups whole-milk ricotta cheese
- ¼ cup lemon juice
- 1 cup cold water

Lemon Glaze:

- ½ cup (1 stick) unsalted butter
- ¼ cup Swerve
- 2 tablespoons lemon juice
- 2 ounces (57 g) cream cheese (¼ cup)
- Grated lemon zest and lemon slices, for garnish

1. Line a baking pan with parchment paper and spray with cooking spray. Set aside. 2. Make the torte: In the bowl of a stand mixer, place the Swerve, butter, and extract and blend for 8 to 10 minutes until well combined. Scrape down the sides of the bowl as needed. 3. Add the egg yolks and continue to blend until fully combined. Add the almond flour and mix until smooth, then stir in the ricotta and lemon juice. 4. Whisk the egg whites in a separate medium bowl until stiff peaks form. Add the whites to the batter and stir well. Pour the batter into the prepared pan and smooth the top. 5. Place a trivet in the bottom of your Instant Pot and pour in the water. Use a foil sling to lower the baking pan onto the trivet. Tuck in the sides of the sling. 6. Seal the lid, press Pressure Cook or Manual, and set the timer for 30 minutes. Once finished, let the pressure release naturally. 7. Lock the lid. Select the Manual mode and set the cooking time for 30 minutes at High Pressure. 8. When the timer beeps, perform a natural pressure release for 10 minutes. Carefully remove the lid. 9. Use the foil sling to lift the pan out of the Instant Pot. Place the torte in the fridge for 40 minutes to chill before glazing. 10. Meanwhile, make the glaze: Place the butter in a large pan over high heat and cook for about 5 minutes until brown, stirring occasionally. Remove from the heat. While stirring the browned butter, add the Swerve. 11. Carefully add the lemon juice and cream cheese to the butter mixture. Allow the glaze to cool for a few minutes, or until it starts to thicken. 12. Transfer the chilled torte to a serving plate. Pour the glaze over the torte and return it to the fridge to chill for an additional 30 minutes. 13. Scatter the lemon zest on top of the torte and arrange the lemon slices on the plate around the torte. 14. Serve.

Daikon and Almond Cake

Prep time: 10 minutes | Cook time: 45 minutes | Serves 12

- 5 eggs, beaten
- ½ cup heavy cream
- 1 cup almond flour
- 1 daikon, diced
- 1 teaspoon ground cinnamon
- 2 tablespoon erythritol
- 1 tablespoon butter, melted
- 1 cup water

1. In the mixing bowl, mix up eggs, heavy cream, almond flour, ground cinnamon, and erythritol. 2. When the mixture is smooth, add daikon and stir it carefully with the help of the spatula. 3. Pour the mixture in the cake pan. 4. Then pour water and insert the trivet in the instant pot. 5. Place the cake in the instant pot. 6. Set the lid in place. Select the Manual mode and set the cooking time for 45 minutes on High Pressure. When the timer goes off, do a quick pressure release. Carefully open the lid. 7. Serve immediately.

Caramelized Pumpkin Cheesecake

Prep time: 15 minutes | Cook time: 45 minutes | Serves 8

Crust:
- 1½ cups almond flour
- 4 tablespoons butter, melted
- 1 tablespoon Swerve
- 1 tablespoon granulated

Filling:
- 16 ounces (454 g) cream cheese, softened
- ½ cup granulated erythritol
- 2 eggs
- ¼ cup pumpkin purée

- erythritol
- ½ teaspoon ground cinnamon
- Cooking spray

- 3 tablespoons Swerve
- 1 teaspoon vanilla extract
- ¼ teaspoon pumpkin pie spice
- 1½ cups water

1. To make the crust: In a medium bowl, combine the almond flour, butter, Swerve, erythritol, and cinnamon. Use a fork to press it all together. 2. Spray the pan with cooking spray and line the bottom with parchment paper. 3. Press the crust evenly into the pan. Work the crust up the sides of the pan, about halfway from the top, and make sure there are no bare spots on the bottom. 4. Place the crust in the freezer for 20 minutes while you make the filling. 5. To make the filling: In a large bowl using a hand mixer on medium speed, combine the cream cheese and erythritol. Beat until the cream cheese is light and fluffy, 2 to 3 minutes. 6. Add the eggs, pumpkin purée, Swerve, vanilla, and pumpkin pie spice. Beat until well combined. 7. Remove the crust from the freezer and pour in the filling. Cover the pan with aluminum foil and place it on the trivet. 8.

Add the water to the pot and carefully lower the trivet into the pot. 9. Set the lid in place. Select the Manual mode and set the cooking time for 45 minutes on High Pressure. When the timer goes off, do a quick pressure release. Carefully open the lid. 10. Remove the trivet and cheesecake from the pot. Remove the foil from the pan. The center of the cheesecake should still be slightly jiggly. 11. Let the cheesecake cool for 30 minutes on the counter before placing it in the refrigerator to set. Leave the cheesecake in the refrigerator for at least 6 hours before removing the sides and serving.

Almond Butter Keto Fat Bombs

Prep time: 3 minutes | Cook time: 3 minutes | Serves 6

- ¼ cup coconut oil
- ¼ cup no-sugar-added almond butter
- 2 tablespoons cacao powder
- ¼ cup powdered erythritol

1. Press the Sauté button and add coconut oil to Instant Pot. Let coconut oil melt completely and press the Cancel button. Stir in remaining ingredients. Mixture will be liquid. 2. Pour into 6 silicone molds and place into freezer for 30 minutes until set. Store in fridge.

Hearty Crème Brûlée

Prep time: 5 minutes | Cook time: 30 minutes | Serves 4

- 5 egg yolks
- 5 tablespoons powdered erythritol
- 1½ cups heavy cream
- 2 teaspoons vanilla extract
- 2 cups water

1. In a small bowl, use a fork to break up the egg yolks. Stir in the erythritol. 2. Pour the cream into a small saucepan over medium-low heat and let it warm up for 3 to 4 minutes. Remove the saucepan from the heat. 3. Temper the egg yolks by slowly adding a small spoonful of the warm cream, keep whisking. Do this three times to make sure the egg yolks are fully tempered. 4. Slowly add the tempered eggs to the cream, whisking the whole time. Add the vanilla and whisk again. 5. Pour the cream mixture into the ramekins. Each ramekin should have ½ cup liquid. Cover each with aluminum foil. 6. Place the trivet inside the Instant Pot. Add the water. Carefully place the ramekins on top of the trivet. 7. Close the lid. Select Manual mode and set cooking time for 11 minutes on High Pressure. 8. When timer beeps, use a natural release for 15 minutes, then release any remaining pressure. Open the lid. 9. Carefully remove a ramekin from the pot. Remove the foil and check for doneness. The custard should be mostly set with a slightly jiggly center. 10. Place all the ramekins in the fridge for 2 hours to chill and set. Serve chilled.

Deconstructed Tiramisu

- 1 cup heavy cream (or full-fat coconut milk for dairy-free)
- 2 large egg yolks
- 2 tablespoons brewed decaf espresso or strong brewed coffee
- 2 tablespoons Swerve, or more to taste
- 1 teaspoon rum extract
- 1 teaspoon unsweetened cocoa powder, or more to taste
- Pinch of fine sea salt
- 1 cup cold water
- 4 teaspoons Swerve, for topping

1. Heat the cream in a pan over medium-high heat until hot, about 2 minutes. 2. Place the egg yolks, coffee, sweetener, rum extract, cocoa powder, and salt in a blender and blend until smooth. 3. While the blender is running, slowly pour in the hot cream. Taste and adjust the sweetness to your liking. Add more cocoa powder, if desired. 4. Scoop the mixture into four ramekins with a spatula. Cover the ramekins with aluminum foil. 5. Place a trivet in the bottom of the Instant Pot and pour in the water. Place the ramekins on the trivet. 6. Lock the lid. Select the Manual mode and set the cooking time for 7 minutes at High Pressure. 7. When the timer beeps, use a quick pressure release. Carefully remove the lid. 8. Keep the ramekins covered with the foil and place in the refrigerator for about 2 hours until completely chilled. 9. Sprinkle 1 teaspoon of Swerve on top of each tiramisu. Use the oven broiler to melt the sweetener. 10. Put in the fridge to chill the topping, about 20 minutes. 11. Serve.

Vanilla Crème Brûlée

- 1 cup heavy cream (or full-fat coconut milk for dairy-free)
- 2 large egg yolks
- 2 tablespoons Swerve, or more to taste
- Seeds scraped from ½ vanilla bean (about 8 inches long), or 1 teaspoon vanilla extract
- 1 cup cold water
- 4 teaspoons Swerve, for topping

1. Heat the cream in a pan over medium-high heat until hot, about 2 minutes. 2. Place the egg yolks, Swerve, and vanilla seeds in a blender and blend until smooth. 3. While the blender is running,

slowly pour in the hot cream. Taste and adjust the sweetness to your liking. 4. Scoop the mixture into four ramekins with a spatula. Cover the ramekins with aluminum foil. 5. Add the water to the Instant Pot and insert a trivet. Place the ramekins on the trivet. 6. Lock the lid. Select the Manual mode and set the cooking time for 7 minutes at High Pressure. 7. When the timer beeps, perform a quick pressure release. Carefully remove the lid. 8. Keep the ramekins covered with the foil and place in the refrigerator for about 2 hours until completely chilled. 9. Sprinkle 1 teaspoon of Swerve on top of each crème brûlée. Use the oven broiler to melt the sweetener. 10. Allow the topping to cool in the fridge for 5 minutes before serving.

Glazed Pumpkin Bundt Cake

Cake:
- 3 cups blanched almond flour
- 1 teaspoon baking soda
- ½ teaspoon fine sea salt
- 2 teaspoons ground cinnamon
- 1 teaspoon ground nutmeg
- 1 teaspoon ginger powder

- ¼ teaspoon ground cloves
- 6 large eggs
- 2 cups pumpkin purée
- 1 cup Swerve
- ¼ cup (½ stick) unsalted butter (or coconut oil for dairy-free), softened

Glaze:
- 1 cup (2 sticks) unsalted butter (or coconut oil for
- dairy-free), melted
- ½ cup Swerve

1. In a large bowl, stir together the almond flour, baking soda, salt, and spices. In another large bowl, add the eggs, pumpkin, sweetener, and butter and stir until smooth. Pour the wet ingredients into the dry ingredients and stir well. 2. Grease a 6-cup Bundt pan. Pour the batter into the prepared pan and cover with a paper towel and then with aluminum foil. 3. Place a trivet in the bottom of the Instant Pot and pour in 2 cups of cold water. Place the Bundt pan on the trivet. 4. Lock the lid. Select the Manual mode and set the cooking time for 35 minutes at High Pressure. 5. When the timer beeps, use a natural pressure release for 10 minutes. Carefully remove the lid. 6. Let the cake cool in the pot for 10 minutes before removing. 7. While the cake is cooling, make the glaze: In a small bowl, mix the butter and sweetener together. Spoon the glaze over the warm cake. 8. Allow to cool for 5 minutes before slicing and serving.

Appendix1: Instant Pot Cooking Timetable

Dried Beans, Legumes and Lentils

Dried Beans and Legume	Dry (Minutes)	Soaked (Minutes)
Soy beans	25 – 30	20 – 25
Scarlet runner	20 – 25	10 – 15
Pinto beans	25 – 30	20 – 25
Peas	15 – 20	10 – 15
Navy beans	25 – 30	20 – 25
Lima beans	20 – 25	10 – 15
Lentils, split, yellow (moong dal)	15 – 18	N/A
Lentils, split, red	15 – 18	N/A
Lentils, mini, green (brown)	15 – 20	N/A
Lentils, French green	15 – 20	N/A
Kidney white beans	35 – 40	20 – 25
Kidney red beans	25 – 30	20 – 25
Great Northern beans	25 – 30	20 – 25
Pigeon peas	20 – 25	15 – 20
Chickpeas (garbanzo bean chickpeas)	35 – 40	20 – 25
Cannellini beans	35 – 40	20 – 25
Black-eyed peas	20 – 25	10 – 15
Black beans	20 – 25	10 – 15

Fish and Seafood

Fish and Seafood	Fresh (minutes)	Frozen (minutes)
Shrimp or Prawn	1 to 2	2 to 3
Seafood soup or stock	6 to 7	7 to 9
Mussels	2 to 3	4 to 6
Lobster	3 to 4	4 to 6
Fish, whole (snapper, trout, etc.)	5 to 6	7 to 10
Fish steak	3 to 4	4 to 6
Fish fillet	2 to 3	3 to 4
Crab	3 to 4	5 to 6

Fruits

Fruits	Fresh (in Minutes)	Dried (in Minutes)
Raisins	N/A	4 to 5
Prunes	2 to 3	4 to 5
Pears, whole	3 to 4	4 to 6
Pears, slices or halves	2 to 3	4 to 5
Peaches	2 to 3	4 to 5
Apricots, whole or halves	2 to 3	3 to 4
Apples, whole	3 to 4	4 to 6
Apples, in slices or pieces	2 to 3	3 to 4

Meat

Meat and Cuts	Cooking Time (minutes)	Meat and Cuts	Cooking Time (minutes)
Veal, roast	35 to 45	Duck, with bones, cut up	10 to 12
Veal, chops	5 to 8	Cornish Hen, whole	10 to 15
Turkey, drumsticks (leg)	15 to 20	Chicken, whole	20 to 25
Turkey, breast, whole, with bones	25 to 30	Chicken, legs, drumsticks, or thighs	10 to 15
Turkey, breast, boneless	15 to 20	Chicken, with bones, cut up	10 to 15
Quail, whole	8 to 10	Chicken, breasts	8 to 10
Pork, ribs	20 to 25	Beef, stew	15 to 20
Pork, loin roast	55 to 60	Beef, shanks	25 to 30
Pork, butt roast	45 to 50	Beef, ribs	25 to 30
Pheasant	20 to 25	Beef, steak, pot roast, round, rump, brisket or blade, small chunks, chuck,	25 to 30
Lamb, stew meat	10 to 15		
Lamb, leg	35 to 45	Beef, pot roast, steak, rump, round, chuck, blade or brisket, large	35 to 40
Lamb, cubes,	10 to 15		
Ham slice	9 to 12	Beef, ox-tail	40 to 50
Ham picnic shoulder	25 to 30	Beef, meatball	10 to 15
Duck, whole	25 to 30	Beef, dressed	20 to 25

Vegetables (fresh/frozen)

Vegetable	Fresh (minutes)	Frozen (minutes)	Vegetable	Fresh (minutes)	Frozen (minutes)
Zucchini, slices or chunks	2 to 3	3 to 4	Mixed vegetables	2 to 3	3 to 4
Yam, whole, small	10 to 12	12 to 14	Leeks	2 to 4	3 to 5
Yam, whole, large	12 to 15	15 to 19	Greens (collards, beet greens, spinach,	3 to 6	4 to 7
Yam, in cubes	7 to 9	9 to 11	kale, turnip greens, swiss chard) chopped		
Turnip, chunks	2 to 4	4 to 6	Green beans, whole	2 to 3	3 to 4
Tomatoes, whole	3 to 5	5 to 7	Escarole, chopped	1 to 2	2 to 3
Tomatoes, in quarters	2 to 3	4 to 5	Endive	1 to 2	2 to 3
Sweet potato, whole, small	10 to 12	12 to 14	Eggplant, chunks or slices	2 to 3	3 to 4
Sweet potato, whole, large	12 to 15	15 to 19	Corn, on the cob	3 to 4	4 to 5
Sweet potato, in cubes	7 to 9	9 to 11	Corn, kernels	1 to 2	2 to 3
Sweet pepper, slices or chunks	1 to 3	2 to 4	Collard	4 to 5	5 to 6
Squash, butternut, slices or chunks	8 to 10	10 to 12	Celery, chunks	2 to 3	3 to 4
Squash, acorn, slices or chunks	6 to 7	8 to 9	Cauliflower flowerets	2 to 3	3 to 4
Spinach	1 to 2	3 to 4	Carrots, whole or chunked	2 to 3	3 to 4
Rutabaga, slices	3 to 5	4 to 6	Carrots, sliced or shredded	1 to 2	2 to 3
Rutabaga, chunks	4 to 6	6 to 8	Cabbage, red, purple or green, wedges	3 to 4	4 to 5
Pumpkin, small slices or chunks	4 to 5	6 to 7	Cabbage, red, purple or green, shredded	2 to 3	3 to 4
Pumpkin, large slices or chunks	8 to 10	10 to 14	Brussel sprouts, whole	3 to 4	4 to 5
Potatoes, whole, large	12 to 15	15 to 19	Broccoli, stalks	3 to 4	4 to 5
Potatoes, whole, baby	10 to 12	12 to 14	Broccoli, flowerets	2 to 3	3 to 4
Potatoes, in cubes	7 to 9	9 to 11	Beets, small roots, whole	11 to 13	13 to 15
Peas, in the pod	1 to 2	2 to 3	Beets, large roots, whole	20 to 25	25 to 30
Peas, green	1 to 2	2 to 3	Beans, green/yellow or wax,	1 to 2	2 to 3
Parsnips, sliced	1 to 2	2 to 3	whole, trim ends and strings		
Parsnips, chunks	2 to 4	4 to 6	Asparagus, whole or cut	1 to 2	2 to 3
Onions, sliced	2 to 3	3 to 4	Artichoke, whole, trimmed without leaves	9 to 11	11 to 13
Okra	2 to 3	3 to 4	Artichoke, hearts	4 to 5	5 to 6

Rice and Grains

Rice & Grain	Water Quantity (Grain: Water ratios)	Cooking Time (in Minutes)	Rice & Grain	Water Quantity (Grain: Water ratios)	Cooking Time (in Minutes)
Wheat berries	1:3	25 to 30	Oats, steel-cut	1:1	10
Spelt berries	1:3	15 to 20	Oats, quick cooking	1:1	6
Sorghum	1:3	20 to 25	Millet	1:1	10 to 12
Rice, wild	1:3	25 to 30	Kamut, whole	1:3	10 to 12
Rice, white	1:1.5	8	Couscous	1:2	5 to 8
Rice, Jasmine	1:1	4 to 10	Corn, dried, half	1:3	25 to 30
Rice, Brown	1:1.3	22 to 28	Congee, thin	1:6 ~ 1:7	15 to 20
Rice, Basmati	1:1.5	4 to 8	Congee, thick	1:4 ~ 1:5	15 to 20
Quinoa, quick cooking	1:2	8	Barley, pot	1:3 ~ 1:4	25 to 30
Porridge, thin	1:6 ~ 1:7	15 to 20	Barley, pearl	1:4	25 to 30

Appendix 2: Measurement Conversion Chart

VOLUME EQUIVALENTS(DRY)

US STANDARD	METRIC (APPROXIMATE)
1/8 teaspoon	0.5 mL
1/4 teaspoon	1 mL
1/2 teaspoon	2 mL
3/4 teaspoon	4 mL
1 teaspoon	5 mL
1 tablespoon	15 mL
1/4 cup	59 mL
1/2 cup	118 mL
3/4 cup	177 mL
1 cup	235 mL
2 cups	475 mL
3 cups	700 mL
4 cups	1 L

VOLUME EQUIVALENTS(LIQUID)

US STANDARD	US STANDARD (OUNCES)	METRIC (APPROXIMATE)
2 tablespoons	1 fl.oz.	30 mL
1/4 cup	2 fl.oz.	60 mL
1/2 cup	4 fl.oz.	120 mL
1 cup	8 fl.oz.	240 mL
1 1/2 cup	12 fl.oz.	355 mL
2 cups or 1 pint	16 fl.oz.	475 mL
4 cups or 1 quart	32 fl.oz.	1 L
1 gallon	128 fl.oz.	4 L

TEMPERATURES EQUIVALENTS

FAHRENHEIT(F)	CELSIUS(C) (APPROXIMATE)
225 °F	107 °C
250 °F	120 °C
275 °F	135 °C
300 °F	150 °C
325 °F	160 °C
350 °F	180 °C
375 °F	190 °C
400 °F	205 °C
425 °F	220 °C
450 °F	235 °C
475 °F	245 °C
500 °F	260 °C

WEIGHT EQUIVALENTS

US STANDARD	METRIC (APPROXIMATE)
1 ounce	28 g
2 ounces	57 g
5 ounces	142 g
10 ounces	284 g
15 ounces	425 g
16 ounces (1 pound)	455 g
1.5 pounds	680 g
2 pounds	907 g

Appendix 3: Recipes Index